Collaborative Learning Techniques

Collaborative Learning Techniques

A Handbook for College Faculty

**Elizabeth F. Barkley,
K. Patricia Cross, and
Claire Howell Major**

 JOSSEY-BASS
A Wiley Imprint
www.josseybass.com

Library of Congress Cataloging-in-Publication Data
Barkley, Elizabeth F.
  Collaborative learning techniques : a handbook for college faculty / Elizabeth F. Barkley, K. Patricia Cross, Claire Howell Major.— 1st ed.
    p. cm.
  Includes bibliographical references and index.
  ISBN 0-7879-5518-3 (alk. paper)
  1. Team learning approach in education—Handbooks, manuals, etc. 2. College teaching—Handbooks, manuals, etc. I. Cross, K. Patricia (Kathryn Patricia), 1926- II. Major, Claire Howell. III. Title.
  LB1032.B318 2004
  378.1′2—dc22

                                                                    2004015337

Printed in the United States of America

FIRST EDITION

PB Printing   10 9 8 7 6

The Jossey-Bass Higher and Adult Education Series

Contents

Preface

THE TWENTY-FIRST CENTURY poses a paradox for higher education. At a time when students and parents consider a college education a necessity and getting into a "good" college is more important and more competitive than ever before, legislators, accrediting agencies, the American public, and educators themselves are raising questions about what students are learning in college—and they are asking for evidence.

Widespread concern has spawned more research, more publications, more legislation, and more exhortation for improvement focused on teaching and learning than at any other time in history. The major questions driving this attention involve how to improve the quality of student learning, how to improve the effectiveness of teaching, and how to do both affordably and efficiently. While opinions differ on how much progress we have made in this quest thus far, there is virtually unanimous agreement on the enduring need for improvement.

Collaborative learning continues to attract interest because it addresses several major concerns related to improving student learning. First, the predominant conclusion from a half-century of research is that teachers cannot simply transfer knowledge to students. Students must build their own minds through a process of assimilating information into their own understandings. Meaningful and lasting learning occurs through personal, active engagement. The advantages of collaborative learning for actively engaging students are clear when compared with more traditional methods—such as lecture and large-group discussions—in which only a few students typically can, or do, participate.

Second, many employers consider willingness and readiness to engage in productive teamwork a requirement for success. For some companies and professions, it is a prerequisite for employment. Collaborative learning offers students opportunities to learn valuable interpersonal and teamwork skills and dispositions by participating in task-oriented learning groups; thus, even beyond enhancing the learning of content or subject matter, collaborative groups develop important skills that prepare students for careers.

Third, our increasingly diverse society requires engaged citizens who can appreciate and benefit from different perspectives. At the same time, most local, national, and global challenges require long-term, collective responses. Learning to listen carefully, think critically, participate constructively, and collaborate productively to solve common problems are vital components of an education for citizenship in the twenty-first century.

Finally, colleges and universities want to provide greater opportunities for a wider variety of students to develop as lifelong learners. In traditional lectures, students generally are treated as a single, passive, aggregated entity. Collaborative learning engages students of all backgrounds personally and actively, calling individuals to contribute knowledge and perspectives to the education developed from their unique lives as well as academic and vocational experiences.

Background and Audience

It is in this context that we came to this work, a collaborative endeavor in itself. We share some characteristics: we are educators seeking to make higher education better, we are researchers seeking evidence about how to accomplish that, and we are teachers with a vested interest in improving practice. We came to this project with the following questions about collaborative learning:

- How will collaborative learning improve learning? What is the pedagogical rationale for collaborative learning?

- What is the evidence that collaborative learning promotes and improves learning? And how convincing is that evidence?

- Which students are most likely to benefit from collaborative learning? And for which learning tasks is it most appropriate?

- How can discipline-oriented college teachers organize effective learning groups in their classrooms? How are groups formed and learning tasks structured?

- What are some imaginative and creative strategies and techniques for challenging students? How can teachers adapt Collaborative Learning Techniques (CoLTs) to their courses and teaching goals?

In this handbook, we address these questions, and many others as well. After several years spent preparing this book, we considered the evidence for collaborative learning sufficiently compelling to add a new question: *Given the evidence demonstrating that most students learn more, and more deeply, when teachers employ collaborative methods effectively, why don't more teachers use collaborative learning?* We believe the answer may lie in the following reasons: Many teachers are unaware of the evidence about the benefits of collaborative learning, and many teachers do not know how to implement group learning activities effectively. The primary purpose of this handbook, therefore, is to provide college and university teachers—regardless of prior knowledge and experience with instructional design or pedagogy—a resource for implementing collaborative work successfully.

A second purpose of this handbook is to encourage faculty to experiment with collaborative learning methods in well-informed and reflective ways. It is no more possible to learn to teach effectively by reading alone than it is to learn to practice medicine by only studying books. Both are part art and part technique. Both take practice. For that practice to be most effective, however, it should be well informed and reflective. Informed teaching requires making instructional decisions based on the collected wisdom from scholarship and practice. Reflective teaching implies assessing and documenting its efficacy. Without this, it is difficult to know whether even well-informed innovations actually make a positive difference in student learning, or enough difference to justify the effort invested. To that end, we have included advice on assessment techniques that can help document and determine the effectiveness of collaborative learning activities.

This handbook is written for the use of college and university teachers, current and aspiring. We hope it will be read and used in collaborative ways, and not just by individual teachers. We hope that this handbook will be useful to faculty developers, instructional designers, department chairs, and other academic administrators interested in promoting teaching and improving learning. The use of this book by teaching circles, seminars, departments, and other groups of teachers can provide participants with opportunities to try out collaborative learning techniques on themselves before employing them in the classroom. Furthermore, these groups of teachers can discuss and get each other's perspectives on their experiences using collaborative learning.

How to Use This Book Effectively

This handbook is divided into three parts, in which we attempt to address the *Why, How,* and *What* questions of collaborative learning. Part One: Introduction is a brief but comprehensive review of the literature and research on collaborative learning. It addresses the question, *Why use collaborative learning?* It explains the epistemological underpinnings that differentiate cooperative and collaborative learning, summarizes current learning theory, presents the pedagogical rationale for collaboration, and synthesizes the research regarding the effectiveness of collaborative learning.

Part Two: Implementing Collaborative Learning offers the benefit of the experience of many teachers who have used collaborative learning in their classrooms, across many types of colleges and disciplines. It addresses the issue of how to use collaborative learning effectively in the classroom, offering practical advice on how to form groups, how to structure the learning task, how to anticipate and solve problems, and how to ensure individual accountability through assessment and grading.

Part Three: Collaborative Learning Techniques (CoLTs) contains detailed descriptions of thirty techniques for creating effective group work assignments. It offers answers to the question, *What can I do, in a practical way, to engage students actively in collaborative learning?* Organized into five categories based on task, the CoLTs are simple and flexible tools that can be adapted to fit a wide variety of disciplines, instructional goals, and learning contexts.

We are deeply indebted to many colleagues, past and present. The literature of collaborative learning is huge, and the number of practitioners quietly using collaborative learning in their classrooms is even larger. Researchers, practitioners, workshop facilitators, even students have been generous in sharing their knowledge with us—contributing and reviewing CoLTs, revising techniques, critiquing chapters, and talking with us about their experiences and experiments in collaborative learning. Very little in this handbook is new. Our contribution is to pull together the vast resources that exist in collaborative learning and cast the results in a format accessible to discipline-oriented faculty. Since the format of *Classroom Assessment Techniques* (Angelo & Cross, 1993) proved enormously popular with college teachers, we have adapted that practical format here.

Collaborative Learning Techniques is not a book that must be read in a linear fashion. Readers may start at the point that is most useful and appealing and read the rest of the text out of order. Thus, experts at collaborative learning may want to skip directly to Part Three to find new techniques. Those familiar with the theory and research regarding collaborative learning but have little classroom experience with it may benefit from starting with Part Two. The majority of teachers, however, will find it most useful to begin with Part One.

The Authors

Elizabeth F. Barkley is professor of music at Foothill College, Los Altos Hills, California. She has been named California's Higher Education Professor of the Year by the Carnegie Foundation for the Advancement of Teaching (1998), formally recognized by the California state legislature for her contributions to undergraduate education (1999), selected as her district's "Innovator of the Year" in conjunction with the National League for Innovation (1999), presented with the Hayward Award for Educational Excellence (1999), and honored by the Center for Diversity in Teaching and Learning in Higher Education (1999). Additionally, her *Musics of Multicultural America* course was selected as "Best Online Course" by the California Virtual Campus (2001).

Barkley's interests include online education and the scholarship of teaching and learning. She was named a 1999–2000 Carnegie Scholar by the Carnegie Foundation in conjunction with the Pew Charitable Trusts. Her electronic course portfolio *From Bach to Tupac: An Analysis of a Curricular Transformation* is housed on the Carnegie Foundation's Knowledge Media Laboratory. She is also a contributing author to the AAHE publication, *Electronic Portfolios: Emerging Practices in Student, Faculty, and Institutional Learning* (2001).

Barkley holds an M.A. from University of California, Riverside, and a Ph.D. from University of California, Berkeley. She is the author of several music textbooks, including *Crossroads: Popular Music in America* (2002).

K. Patricia Cross is professor of higher education, emerita, at the University of California, Berkeley. In a career spanning forty years in higher education, she has served as Dean of Students at Cornell, Distinguished Research Scientist at Educational Testing Service, professor of higher education and chair of the Department of Administration, Planning, and

Social Policy at the Harvard Graduate School of Education, and David Pierpont Gardner Professor of Higher Education at Berkeley. Author of eight books, including *Beyond the Open Door* (1971), *Accent on Learning* (1976), *Adults as Learners* (1981), *Classroom Assessment Techniques* (with Tom Angelo, 1993), and *Classroom Research* (with Mimi Steadman, 1996), her interest is primarily in the improvement of teaching and learning in higher education.

Cross has been recognized for her scholarship by election to the National Academy of Education, receipt of the E. F. Lindquist Award from the American Educational Research Association, the Sidney Suslow Award from the Association for Institutional Research, and the Howard Bowen Distinguished Career Award from the Association for the Study of Higher Education.

Elected chair of the Board of the American Association of Higher Education twice (1975 and 1989), she has received many awards for her leadership in education, most recently the 2004 PBS/O'Banion Prize for "inspiring significant change in teaching and learning." She has been awarded fifteen honorary degrees and is listed in *Who's Who in America, International Who's Who of Women,* and *Who's Who in American Education.*

Cross received her bachelor's degree in mathematics from Illinois State University and master's and Ph.D. degrees in social psychology from the University of Illinois.

Claire Howell Major is associate professor of higher education administration in the College of Education at the University of Alabama. Prior to her current position, Major served at Samford University as director of Problem-Based Learning, a grant funded project supported by the Pew Charitable Trusts. She also taught English in several two-year and four-year institutions in the Southeast.

Major's research centers on teaching and learning in higher education, focusing largely on innovative instructional methods. She has published numerous articles and has presented her research nationally and internationally. She has worked with faculty at institutions around the country to promote teaching excellence. And she has firsthand experiences using active and collaborative methods for teaching diverse groups of students.

Major holds a bachelor's and master's degree in English from the University of South Alabama and the University of Alabama at Birmingham, respectively, and a Ph.D. in higher education from the University of Georgia.

Part One

Introduction

Chapter 1

The Case for Collaborative Learning

MAKING THE CASE FOR collaborative learning seems almost too easy. More research on learning in small groups exists than on any other instructional method, including lecturing (Johnson, Johnson, & Smith, 1991; Slavin, 1989–90). While most of this is credible and positive, it is dominated by research and investigation in K–12, and higher education is coming late to the scene.

Exploding research on cognition and the brain confirms so much of what we have learned about the effectiveness of peer interaction in promoting active learning that college teachers need not fear that experimenting with collaborative learning in their classrooms will plunge them into uncharted territory. Unlike much research in higher education that is often reported in unrelated studies, scholars studying collaborative learning have mapped the terrain and conducted helpful meta-analyses that synthesize findings across topics and institutions.

The purpose of this introduction to the extensive literature on interactive group learning is to glean from experience and research information that is useful to college teachers in deciding whether collaborative learning will be effective in accomplishing their teaching goals. Specifically, this introduction addresses the following questions:

- What do we mean by *collaborative learning?*
- What is the difference between collaborative learning and cooperative learning?
- What are the defining characteristics of effective learning groups?
- What is the pedagogical rationale for collaborative learning?
- What is the evidence that collaborative learning promotes and improves learning?

- Which students gain the most from collaborative learning?
- Is everyone happy with collaborative learning?

Thus, Part One of this handbook provides an overview of the theoretical and research bases for collaborative learning.

What Do We Mean by *Collaborative Learning?*

To *collaborate* is to work with another or others. In practice, collaborative learning has come to mean students working in pairs or small groups to achieve shared learning goals. It is learning through group work rather than learning by working alone. There are other terms for this kind of activity, such as *cooperative learning, team learning, group learning,* or *peer-assisted learning.* In this handbook, however, we use the phrase *collaborative learning* to refer to learning activities expressly designed for and carried out through pairs or small interactive groups. While we believe that a flexible definition of collaborative learning is best, there are some features that we see as essential.

The first feature of collaborative learning is intentional design. All too often, teachers simply tell students to get into groups and work. In collaborative learning, however, faculty members structure intentional learning activities for students. They may do this by selecting from a range of pre-structured activities, such as those we have included in Part Three of this text, or they may do this by creating their own structures. Whether using existing or new structures, the focus is on *intentional* structure.

In addition to intentional design, co-laboring is an important feature of collaborative learning. The meaning of the Latin-based term *collaborate* shines through as clearly today as in antiquity: to co-labor. All participants in the group must engage actively in working together toward the stated objectives. If one group member completes a group task while the others simply watch, then it is not collaborative learning. Whether all group members receive the same task, or whether members complete different tasks that together comprise a single, large project, all students must contribute more or less equally. Equitable engagement is still insufficient, however.

The third feature of collaborative learning is that meaningful learning takes place. As students work together on a collaborative assignment, they must increase their knowledge or deepen their understanding of course curriculum. The task assigned to the group must be structured to accomplish the learning objectives of the course. Shifting responsibility to students, and having the classroom vibrate with lively, energetic small-group work is attractive, but it is educationally meaningless if students are not achieving intended instructional goals, goals shared by the teacher and students. Collaborative learning, then, is two or more students laboring together and sharing the workload equitably as they progress toward intended learning outcomes.

What Is the Difference Between Cooperative and Collaborative Learning?

Although to most educators—and indeed to the lexicographers who compile dictionaries—the terms *collaborative* and *cooperative* have similar meanings, there is considerable debate and discussion as to whether they mean the same thing when applied to group learning. Some authors use the terms *cooperative* and *collaborative* interchangeably to mean students working interdependently on a common learning task. Others, however, insist on a clear epistemological distinction (Bruffee, 1995). Advocates for distinguishing between the two suggest that cooperative learning differs from collaborative learning in that, in cooperative learning, the use of groups supports an instructional system that maintains the traditional lines of classroom knowledge and authority (Flannery, 1994). To other authors, cooperative learning is simply a subcategory of collaborative learning (Cuseo, 1992). Still others hold that the most "sensible approach" is to view collaborative and cooperative learning as positioned on a continuum from most structured (cooperative) to least structured (collaborative) (Millis & Cottell, 1998). Since those who insist on a sharp distinction between cooperative and collaborative learning do so for epistemological reasons, it may help to clarify the nature of the argument.

Cooperative Learning

The most straightforward definition of cooperative learning is "the instructional use of small groups so that students work together to maximize their own and each others' learning" (Smith, 1996, p. 71). Cooperative learning arose primarily as an alternative to what was perceived as the overemphasis on competition in traditional education. Cooperative learning, as the name implies, requires students to work together on a common task, sharing information and supporting one another. In cooperative learning, the teacher retains the traditional dual role of subject matter expert and authority in the classroom. The teacher designs and assigns group learning tasks, manages time and resources, and monitors students' learning, checking to see that students are on task and that the group process is working well (Cranton, 1996; Smith, 1996).

Most research and most discussion of group learning assumes a traditional view of the nature of knowledge, namely that there is a "correct" answer or at least a "best solution," and that different students will have knowledge about different aspects of the task. There is also the assumption that the teacher is an expert in the subject matter, knows the correct answers, and that ultimately the group should arrive at "the best" or "most logical" or "correct" conclusion. Most teachers using interactive student learning in their classrooms and writing about their experiences are talking about cooperative learning. Knowingly or not, they are capitalizing on the research findings that students who establish social relationships with faculty and other students in the community are more actively involved in learning, report greater personal and academic growth, and are better satisfied with their education than are students who are more isolated (Astin, 1993; Light, 2001; Pascarella & Terenzini, 1991).

Collaborative Learning

Collaborative learning is based on different epistemological assumptions, and it has its home in social constructivism. Matthews captures the essence of the philosophical underpinnings of collaborative learning: "Collaborative learning occurs when students and faculty work together to create knowledge. . . . It is a pedagogy that has at its center the assumption that people make meaning together and that the process enriches and enlarges them" (Matthews, 1996, p. 101).

Rather than assuming that knowledge exists somewhere in reality "out there," and that it is waiting to be discovered by human endeavors, collaborative learning, in its tightest definition, assumes that knowledge is socially produced by consensus among knowledgeable peers. Knowledge is "something people construct by talking together and reaching agreement" (Bruffee, 1993, p. 3). Bruffee, the most ardent advocate of collaborative learning, wants to avoid having students become dependent on the teacher as the authority on either subject matter content or group process. Thus, in his definition of collaborative learning, it is not up to the teacher to monitor group learning, but rather the teacher's responsibility is to become a member, along with students, of a community in search of knowledge.

Collaborative Versus Cooperative Learning

In an article for *Change* magazine, subtitled, "Cooperative Learning *versus* Collaborative Learning" (Bruffee, 1995, emphasis added), Bruffee contends, "Describing cooperative and collaborative learning as complementary understates some important differences between the two. Some of what collaborative learning pedagogy recommends that teachers do tends in fact to undercut some of what cooperative learning might hope to accomplish, and vice versa" (p. 16).

The essence of his position is that, whereas the goal of cooperative learning is to work together in harmony and mutual support to find the solution, the goal of collaborative learning is to develop autonomous, articulate, thinking people, even if at times such a goal encourages dissent and competition that seems to undercut the ideals of cooperative learning.[1] While cooperative education may be appropriate for children, he says, collaborative learning is more appropriate for college students.

Bruffee has made something of a brand name of collaborative learning in higher education circles. He intends the role of the teacher to be less the traditional expert in the classroom and more the peer of students. Knowledge at the college level, he says, is "likely to address questions with dubious or ambiguous answers, answers that require well-developed judgment to arrive at, judgment that learning to answer such questions tends, in turn, to develop. . . . The authority of knowledge taught in colleges and universities should always be subject to doubt" (p. 15).

As a practical matter in planning and operating college classroom learning groups, most teachers will not be much concerned with the philosophical and semantic distinctions between cooperative and collaborative learning, but will use the level of authority and control that feels comfortable for them and that accomplishes their goals. If there is a trend in clarifying the nomenclature of interactive group learning, however, it seems to be in the direction of using the term *collaborative learning* in higher education and *cooperative learning* in K–12 education.

In this handbook, we have labeled our techniques *CoLTs, Co* standing for either "Cooperative" or "Collaborative" and *LT* standing for "Learning Techniques," because the techniques described come from the literature of both cooperative and collaborative learning. Inventing a new term would free us from the baggage accumulated by the advocates of the postmodern version of collaborative learning, but it would also add to the jargon of education. Instead, we follow the growing practice of using the term *collaborative learning* to refer to interactive learning groups in higher education, from structured to unstructured. It is important to be aware, however, that massive confusion reigns in the literature of higher education over terminology. Some authors writing today in higher education use the term *cooperative learning,* and where this is the case, we will use their terminology when discussing their work.

What Are the Defining Characteristics of Effective Learning Groups?

Learning groups exist in many sizes and forms and are created for a wide variety of purposes. Some learning groups are ad hoc, in-class arrangements of convenience that last only a few minutes. For example, in *CoLT 1: Think-Pair-Share,* the instructor asks students to turn to a nearby neighbor to discuss briefly a point made in the lecture. Other teachers may use *CoLT 3: Buzz Groups,* consisting of four to six students grouped for ten to fifteen minutes. This CoLT gives students an opportunity to explore other learners' reactions to course-related questions. There are also more intentionally structured groupings, often organized around specific assignments, such as *CoLT 15: Case Studies* or *CoLT 18: Group Investigation.* In these activities, students may work together for days or weeks until the assignment is completed.

Sometimes groups work together on a course-long project. Membership can remain the same or change depending on the learning goals. There are also long-term "learning communities" that may last a semester or an academic year. Learning communities typically involve integration of curricula, team teaching, and other institutional changes designed to give students a feeling of belonging to a "community" of learners (Gabelnick, MacGregor, Matthews, & Smith, 1990; Matthews, Smith, MacGregor, & Gabelnick, 1997; Tinto, Love, & Russo, 1994).

Groups may be identified with particular teaching methods—such as the case-study method or problem-based learning—in which the purpose is to accomplish specified cognitive goals such as critical thinking and problem solving. There are groups based on an epistemology, such as Bruffee's purist definition of collaborative learning. When interacting, these groups purposely implement social constructivist learning theory, a theory contending that knowledge is socially constructed by consensus among knowledgeable peers (Bruffee, 1995; Vygotsky, 1978).

Johnson and colleagues (Johnson et al., 1991) distinguish types of groups on the basis of duration and purpose. *Formal* learning groups last from one class period to several weeks, whatever it takes to complete a specific task or assignment. The purpose is to use the group to accomplish shared goals, to capitalize on different talents and knowledge of the group, and to maximize the learning of everyone in the group. *Informal* groups are temporary groups that last for only one discussion or one class period. Their major purpose is to ensure active learning. They might be used, for example, to break up a lecture with peer exchanges that require students to organize, explain, and otherwise cognitively process their learning. *Base* groups are long-term groups with a stable membership, more like learning communities. Their main purpose is to provide support and encouragement and to help students feel connected to a community of learners.

In the extensive literature on cooperative learning in K–12, there are dozens of "brand-name" types of cooperative learning groups, each endowed by its creator with particular structural elements that are thought (or demonstrated through research) to enhance learning. Slavin (1996), for example, describes in some detail five methods that have been developed and extensively researched. Although there are distinctive differences in the purposes and philosophies guiding the formulation and operation of groups for learning, it is nevertheless true that all groups share two fundamental purposes: to engage students actively in their own learning and to do so in a supportive and challenging social context.

There is substantial agreement in the literature on what interactive group learning is, as well as what it is not. Karl Smith captures nicely some common misunderstandings about the nature of cooperative/collaborative learning.[2]

> *Many faculty who believe they are using cooperative learning are in fact missing its essence. There is a crucial difference between simply putting students in groups to learn and structuring cooperation among students. Cooperation is not having students sit side by side at the same table to talk with one another as they do their individual assignments. Cooperation is not assigning a report to a group of students, on which one student does all the work and the others put their names. Cooperation is not having students do a task individually and then having the ones who finish first help the slower students. Cooperation is much more than being physically near other students, discussing material with other students, or sharing material among students, although each of these is important in cooperative learning* (Smith, 1996, p. 74).

In contrast to what cooperative learning is *not*, Smith (1996, pp. 74–76) identifies what it *is* by listing five elements that he considers essential for successful cooperative learning groups (see also Johnson, Johnson, & Smith, 1998, pp. 21–23).

1. *Positive interdependence:* The success of individuals is linked to the success of the group; individuals succeed to the extent that the group succeeds. Thus students are motivated to help one another accomplish group goals.

2. *Promotive interaction:* Students are expected to actively help and support one another. Members share resources and support and encourage each other's efforts to learn.

3. *Individual and group accountability:* The group is held accountable for achieving its goals. Each member is accountable for contributing his or her share of the work; students are assessed individually.

4. *Development of teamwork skills:* Students are required to learn academic subject matter (task work) and also to learn the interpersonal and small-group skills required to function as part of a group (teamwork). Teamwork skills should be taught "just as purposefully and precisely as academic skills" (p. 75).

5. *Group processing:* Students should learn to evaluate their group productivity. They need to describe what member actions are helpful and unhelpful, and to make decisions about what to continue or change.

Virtually all collaborative learning methods emphasize the importance of *promotive interaction* and *individual accountability.* Students must not only learn to work together, but they must also be held responsible for their teammates' learning as well as their own. Slavin, in particular, has been insistent that successful groups must endorse individual accountability and team rewards. "It is not enough," he says, "to simply tell students to work together; they must have a reason to take one another's achievement seriously" (Slavin, 1996, p. 21).

Collaborative learning, then, is a structured learning activity that addresses major concerns related to improving student learning. It involves students actively, thereby putting into practice the predominant conclusion from a half-century of research on cognitive development. It prepares students for careers by providing them with opportunities to learn the teamwork skills valued by employers. It helps students appreciate multiple perspectives and develop skills to collaboratively address the common problems facing a diverse society. And it engages all students by valuing the perspective each student can contribute from his or her personal academic and life experience. That said, collaborative learning is not an educational panacea. Collaborative learning is an appropriate method for achieving some learning goals and tasks, but not for others. In most cases, we see collaborative learning not as a replacement for lecture, discussion, or other traditional methods, but rather as a useful complement.

What Is the Pedagogical Rationale for Collaborative Learning?

The closing decades of the twentieth century were exceptionally rich in producing a better understanding of the learning process. Critical to our understanding of that process is the basic tenet of modern cognitive theory: learners must be *actively engaged* in learning. Neurologists and cognitive scientists agree that people quite literally "build" their own minds throughout life by actively constructing the mental structures that connect and organize isolated bits of information. Much as we would like to think that we as teachers can "tell" students what we have learned and thus transfer it into their heads efficiently and accurately, the evidence is clear that we cannot "transfer" our knowledge ready-made into student minds. Instead, students must do the work of learning by actively making connections and organizing learning into meaningful concepts.

The Importance of Making Connections

There is growing evidence that learning is about making connections— whether the mental connections are established by firing synapses in the brain, the "ah ha" experience of seeing the connection between two formerly isolated concepts, or the satisfaction of seeing the connection between an academic abstraction and a "hands-on" concrete application. The important concept is that learners must actively make the connections in their own brains and minds that produce learning for them (Cross, 1999).

Neurological Connections

Stunning new research on the brain by neuroscientists is adding a new dimension to our knowledge about learning, and it is reinforcing rather than changing the tentative conclusions from cognitive science. Neuroscientists have developed a rich imagery about how the brain works. Children do not come into the world with a brain that is hard-wired like a computer. Rather, throughout life, they "grow" their own brains by constantly making connections in the circuitry of the brain through experience and learning. Research is showing that the circuitry of the brain is wired by neurons that spin out axons. These axons connect with many targets to form the transmission lines that carry electrical impulses. At the end of each "wire" is a bulb-and-button unit called a *synapse.* When an electrical signal reaches the button-like ending, a chemical message crosses the gap in the synapse to connect with the receiving cell. Scientists believe that at birth a baby's brain contains 100 billion neurons. Sensory stimulation strengthens connections. Alternatively, "through a process that resembles Darwinian competition, the brain eliminates connections or synapses that are seldom or never used" (Nash, 1997, p. 50). "Use it or lose it" appears to be quite true when applied to the "brain work" of learning. Researchers find that children who are deprived of sensory stimulation develop brains that are 20–30 percent smaller than normal for their age. Although much remains to be learned about the neurological growth of the brain, new insights into the physical development of the brain closely parallel what we are learning about the mental processes of learning.

Cognitive Connections

The parallels between the neurological brain and the working mind envisioned by cognitive scientists are quite remarkable. Modern cognitive science postulates a structure of the mind known as the *schema*—or in plural form, *schemata*, since the brain develops many schemata for different topics. A schema is a cognitive structure that consists of facts, ideas, and associations organized into a meaningful system of relationships. People have schemata for events, places, procedures, and people, for instance. A person's schema for a place, such as a college, might include concepts such as location, reputation, the characteristics of the student population, style of campus architecture, even the location of campus parking lots. Thus, the schema is an organized collection of bits of information that together build the concept of the college for each individual. When someone mentions the college, we "know" what he or she means, but the image brought to mind may be somewhat different for each individual.

What students can learn depends, to a larger extent than previously assumed, on what they already know. It is easier to learn something when we already have some background than it is to learn something completely new and unfamiliar. For example, advanced courses in a subject are often easier to teach and to learn than introductory courses. Cognitive theory would explain that paradox by observing that if the schema is very sparse with respect to a particular subject, connections are hard to find and make, whereas if the schema already has a dense network of vocabulary, terms, and concepts, it is easier to make the connections that constitute learning.

This fundamental assumption about the role of prior knowledge in learning was tested in a classic experiment that compared novice and expert chess players' ability to memorize the layout of chess pieces (de Groot, 1966). Chess players of different skill levels were shown the game pieces on a chessboard for a few seconds and then asked to recall the position of the pieces. The novice players were able to place only five or six pieces correctly, but the experts could recreate nearly the whole board. However, when these players were shown the pieces placed randomly on the board (rather than positions from a real game), novices and experts performed about the same. The conclusion from this rather simple experiment is that the superior performance of experienced chess players in recalling chess positions was not due to higher IQs or to better memories, but rather to a schema for chess that enabled experienced players to associate the patterns shown with those already in memory. The point is that what one knows about a given subject has a substantial impact on the learning process. When teachers complain that students "can't read," they refer not only to the lack of reading skills, but also to the density of the schema for a particular subject matter.

Much of traditional instruction is based on the old images of the mind as an empty vessel, in which the teacher opens the heads of students and pours in new information that adds to their knowledge. Thus we speak erroneously of students knowing "more" as we add to their storehouse of information. Paulo Freire (1970) refers to the "banking model" of education, in which the teacher deposits information that students store to withdraw later. The new cognitive science rejects the notion that real learning occurs when new information simply rests on top of the existing cognitive structure. Alfred North Whitehead (1929) captured the wisdom of active learning in these words: "Beware of inert ideas—ideas that are merely received into the mind without being utilized, or tested, or thrown into fresh combinations."

Some researchers refer to "deep" and "surface" learning to distinguish between learning that makes the connections that lead to deeper *understanding* versus *information,* which rests lightly on the surface, inert and unassimilated (Ramsden, 1992). A finer distinction was made by Säljö, who asked adult learners what they understood by "learning" (Säljö, 1979, cited in Ramsden, 1992, pp. 26–27). Säljö categorized their answers in a hierarchical pattern, observing that each higher conception implied all that preceded it:

1. Learning is acquiring information or "knowing a lot."

2. Learning is memorizing or "storing" information.

3. Learning is acquiring facts and skills that can be used.

4. Learning is making sense or "making meaning" of the various parts of information.

5. Learning involves comprehending or understanding the world by reinterpreting knowledge.

We find, in the literature of learning, all of these conceptions of learning—and to some extent, none—are completely inappropriate. But Berkeley researchers Lyman and Varian note that worldwide information production increased by 30 percent *each year* between 1999 and 2002. "All of a sudden," says Lyman, "almost every aspect of life around the world is being recorded and stored in some information format" (Lyman & Varian, 2003). The computer is so far superior to the human brain in storing and retrieving information that most instruction and learning at the college level is addressing Säljö's definitions 3, 4, and 5.

Social Connections

Vygotsky invented the awkward term "zone of proximal development" (ZPD) to indicate "the distance between the actual developmental level as determined by independent problem solving and the level of potential development as determined through problem solving under adult guidance or in collaboration with more capable peers" (Vygotsky, 1978, p. 86). The theory, applied to cooperative learning, is that students come to the group with diverse backgrounds, but enough overlap to form a common base for communication. Exposing all students to concepts and understandings that are within their ability to grasp, but not yet part of their personal understanding, enables each to learn from other students those concepts that are just beyond their current level of development. Thus, theoretically at least, academically poor students would stand to learn more from better-prepared students than vice versa. Some would claim that the better students are wasting their time, explaining things that they already know. However, ample evidence suggests that peer tutors gain a great deal from formulating and explaining their ideas to others.

What Is the Evidence That Collaborative Learning Promotes and Improves Learning?

To answer this question, we look at the research on peer influence, college environments, collaborative learning in the classroom, and student satisfaction.

Research on Peer Influence

Research support for the impact of peers on student learning is extensive, and it comes from broad-scale studies of college environments as well as from studies directed more specifically to the effects of collaborative learning in the classroom. To date, there is an impressive amount of research, and it comes from highly credible sources.

In 1969, Feldman and Newcomb synthesized the findings of more than 1,500 studies in their now-classic book, *The Impact of College on Students.* In 1991, Pascarella and Terenzini set for themselves the ambitious task of updating the research that had accumulated since Feldman and Newcomb. In a nearly 1,000-page treatise entitled, *How College Affects Students*, they reviewed more than 2,500 publications, concluding basically that "students not only make statistically significant gains in factual knowledge and in a range of general cognitive and intellectual skills, they also change on a broad array of values, attitudinal, psycho-social, and moral dimensions" (p. 557). A large part of this documented change, Pascarella and Terenzini conclude, is determined by the extent to which students interact with faculty members and student peers in and out of the classroom (p. 620).

The demonstrated effect of the social impact of college has stimulated sophisticated theory building on student development as well as further research on learning in the classroom, including the effect of cooperative and collaborative learning. Colleges, under the gun to hold themselves accountable for student learning and to present evidence of such,[3] are collecting their own data about student engagement with the people and activities of the college via such well-known instruments as the National Survey of Student Engagement (NSSE) and the Community College Survey of Student Engagement (CCSSE) (Community College Leadership Program, 2003; Kuh, 2000). The current high interest in student engagement derives in part from cognitive research on the importance of active or engaged learning in the classroom, but it also springs from a long history of interest in the impact of college environments on student attitudes, values, persistence, satisfaction, and motivation for learning (Astin, 1968; Chickering, 1969; Jacob, 1957).

Research on College Environments

Alexander Astin's large-scale statistical studies across hundreds of colleges and thousands of students, using twenty-two measures of student learning outcomes, concluded that two factors had a special potency in academic achievement, personal development, and student satisfaction with college: interactions with fellow students and interactions with faculty members. Astin concluded, "Research has consistently shown that cooperative-learning approaches produce outcomes that are superior to those obtained through traditional competitive approaches, and it may well be that our findings concerning the power of the peer group offer a possible explanation: Cooperative learning may be more potent than traditional methods of pedagogy because it motivates students to become more active and more involved participants in the learning process" (1993, p. 427).

Richard Light, using a different approach to the study of student learning in college, studied one college intensively. He and his colleagues interviewed 570 Harvard undergraduates to see what learning experiences they valued most in their college years. He concluded, "All the specific findings point to, and illustrate one main idea. It is that students who get the most out of college, who grow the most academically, and who are happiest, *organize their time to include interpersonal activities with faculty members, or with fellow students built around substantive, academic work*" (Light, 1992, p. 6, emphasis in the original).

The grand synthesis of research on learning in college is widely known as the *Seven Principles for Good Practice in Undergraduate Education.* The principles "rest on 50 years of research on the way teachers teach and students learn, how students work and play with one another, and how students and faculty talk to each other" (Chickering & Gamson, 1987). The first three principles are

1. Good practice encourages student–faculty contact.

2. Good practice encourages cooperation among students.

3. Good practice encourages active learning.

These three principles apply to both the college environment and the classroom, and they are the backbone of collaborative learning.

Research on Collaborative Learning in the Classroom

Light's (1992) conclusion from the Harvard studies on the productivity of interactions built around substantive academic work is especially important to classroom teachers, and it is vital to our discussion of collaborative learning in college classrooms. While broad studies of the impact of college on students offer evidence that learning in a social context makes positive contributions to a student's college education, the claims for collaborative learning go further. In particular, there is high interest in two important outcomes: (1) What group learning contributes to content mastery, critical thinking, problem solving, and other cognitive attributes, and (2) what group learning contributes to the development of interpersonal skills and other noncognitive factors that are valued in careers and citizenship.

Teachers over the generations have searched for the "best" method of teaching, and there has been considerable research comparing various teaching methods. Psychologists at the University of Michigan reviewed more than five hundred research studies pertaining to teaching and learning in college classrooms. When asked what is the most effective teaching method, McKeachie and his colleagues answered that it depends on the goal, the student, the content, and the teacher—but the next best answer is, "Students teaching other students" (McKeachie, Pintrich, Lin, & Smith, 1986, p. 63).

Collaborative learning, capitalizing on the value of peer interaction, has produced a huge amount of research comparing collaborative learning with other teaching/learning methods as well as attempting to identify the most effective models of cooperative/collaborative learning. As of November 2003, there were 6,887 items listed in ERIC under the descriptor "cooperative learning," and 3,537 of these were published journal articles. While many of these relate to the extensive interest in cooperative learning in

K–12, more than 1,979 of the items on cooperative learning were indexed to higher education. In addition, there were 909 published journal articles on "collaborative learning," 432 of these specifically keyed to collaborative learning in higher education (accessed November 12, 2003). With such an extensive body of literature, it is helpful to have available a large number of syntheses and meta-analyses taking on the task of synthesizing the research on cooperative/collaborative learning.

Virtually all of the compilers and synthesizers of research findings regarding group learning come to largely positive conclusions (Cuseo, 1992; Johnson et al., 1991; Johnson, Johnson, & Stanne, 2000; Millis & Cottell, 1998; Natasi & Clements, 1991; Slavin, 1990; Springer, Stanne, & Donovan, 1998). Natasi and Clements reflect the nature and tone of much of the research, concluding, "Cognitive-academic and social-emotional benefits have been reported for students from early elementary through college level, from diverse ethnic and cultural backgrounds, and having a wide range of ability levels. . . . Furthermore, cooperative learning has been used effectively across a wide range of content areas, including mathematics, reading, language arts, social studies and science" (1991, p. 111, quoted in Millis & Cottell, 1998, pp. 8–9).

There are, by this time, literally dozens of different models of cooperative/collaborative learning groups. Data are presented in exhausting detail by Slavin (1989–90, 1990, 1996) and the Johnson brothers (Johnson & Johnson, 1994; Johnson et al., 1991; Johnson, Maruyama, Johnson, Nelson, & Skon, 1981), who have been the most prodigious compilers and reviewers of research on cooperative learning groups in K–12. (The term *cooperative learning* is used in reporting research results from K–12 because that is the term and conditions used by the researchers.)

Johnson and his colleagues at the University of Minnesota have concentrated largely on comparing learning outcomes from three types of learning structures: cooperative, competitive, and individualistic. *Cooperative learning* involves "promotive interaction," in which students encourage the achievement of other members of the group while also working on their own achievement in order to accomplish group goals. *Competitive structures* are found in environments in which students focus on "increasing their own achievement and on preventing any classmate from achieving higher than they do." And *individualistic structures* are more like mastery learning in which no interaction exists; "students focus only on improving their own achievement and ignore as irrelevant the efforts of others" (Johnson et al., 1991, p. 31).

In extensive meta-analyses across hundreds of studies, cooperative arrangements were found superior to either competitive or individualistic structures on a variety of outcome measures, generally showing higher achievement, higher-level reasoning, more frequent generation of new ideas and solutions, and greater transfer of what is learned in one situation to another. The Johnson team concluded, "Cooperative learning is indicated whenever the goals of learning are highly important, mastery and retention are important, the task is complex or conceptual, problem solving is desired, divergent thinking or creativity is desired, quality of performance is expected, and higher level reasoning strategies and critical thinking are needed" (1991, p. 40). Given that conclusion, it is hard to think of any educational situation in higher education in which cooperative learning would *not* be recommended by the Johnson team.

Robert Slavin at Johns Hopkins University also reported highly positive results (1989–90, 1990, 1996). Slavin's particular research interest is in comparing the outcomes from various models of cooperative learning as well as comparing cooperative learning groups with traditional control groups. He located ninety studies that met his rigorous criteria for research design. His analysis of these studies is set forth in extensive tables (Slavin, 1996) and in more detail than is appropriate to report here, but Slavin, like the Johnson team, concluded that achievement under cooperative learning structures was significantly positive. The size of the effect differed depending on the particular type of cooperative learning structure. Slavin's most important conclusion is that "cooperative learning has its greatest effects on student learning when groups are recognized or rewarded based on the individual learning of their members" (Slavin, 1996, p. 52). Students must have an incentive, he says, to help each other put forth maximum effort. "If a group member wants her group to be successful," reasons Slavin, "she must teach her group mates (and learn the material herself). If she simply tells her group mates the answers, they will fail the quiz that they must take individually" (p. 53). Slavin's conclusion, after extensive review of research on cooperative learning in K–12, is that "cooperative learning methods can be an effective means of increasing student achievement, but only if they incorporate group goals and individual accountability" (Slavin, 1990, p. 32).

Research on group learning in higher education is more limited, but recently Springer, Stanne, and Donovan (1999) conducted an impressive meta-analysis of the effects of small-group learning on student achievement, persistence, and attitudes in classes in undergraduate science, mathematics, engineering, and technology (SMET). Their work directs research attention to assessing student learning under the conditions of live classroom settings. They located 383 reports related to small-group learning in postsecondary SMET from 1980 or later. Thirty-nine of the studies met their exacting requirements for providing adequate research data on achievement, persistence, and/or attitudes. In condensed form, their major conclusions are as follows:

- SMET students who learned in small groups demonstrated greater achievement than students in traditional instruction (d = .51, which is roughly equivalent to moving a student from the 50th to the 70th percentile on a standardized test).

- The effects of small-group learning on achievement were significantly greater when measured on instructor-made exams or grades than on standardized instruments.

- Student persistence was significantly higher in small-group learning classes than in traditional classes (d = .46, which is enough to reduce attrition from SMET classes by 22 percent).

- The findings were equally positive for women and men, SMET majors and non-majors, first-year and other students, and for underrepresented minorities (African Americans and Latinas/Latinos).

- Small-group learning leads to more favorable attitudes toward learning of the material.

- Out-of-class meetings (typically study sessions) have greater effects on achievement than in-class collaboration, but in-class collaborations have more favorable effects on student attitudes than out-of-class meetings.

In a succinct summary of their meta-analysis, the researchers offer this conclusion: "Students who learn in small groups generally demonstrate greater academic achievement, express more favorable attitudes toward learning, and persist through SMET courses or programs to a greater extent than their more traditionally taught counterparts. The reported effects are relatively large in research on educational innovation and have a great deal of practical significance" (Springer et al., 1999, p. 42).

Research on Student Satisfaction

The evidence is strong and quite consistent across a broad array of educational research studies that students who study under various forms of peer interaction, including class discussion (versus lecture), have more positive attitudes toward the subject matter, increased motivation to learn more about the subject, and are better satisfied with their experience than students who have less opportunity to interact with fellow students and teachers (Johnson et al., 1991; Light, 1992; Springer, Stanne & Donovan, 1998). The data also indicate that students working in learning groups like the instructor better and perceive the instructor as more supportive and accepting academically and personally (Fiechtner & Davis, 1992; Johnson et al., 1991).

Cabrera (1998) found, in a study of more than two thousand students completing their second year of study at twenty-three campuses, that participation in cooperative learning groups was positively related to perceived gains in personal development, appreciation for fine arts, analytical skills, and understanding of science and technology as measured by the College Student Experiences Questionnaire (CSEQ). Fiechtner and Davis (1992) sought student reactions to cooperative learning experiences in upper-division classes at two universities. Asking students to rate the effectiveness of their group experiences on an eighteen-item survey, they found, in four different administrations of the survey, that 74–81 percent of the students rated their cooperative learning experience "significantly" or "somewhat more effective" than traditional college instruction in general academic achievement; 70–82 percent felt that their group experience was superior in promoting higher-level thinking skills; and 75–86 percent claimed it promoted greater interest in the subject matter. A striking 83–90 percent claimed better class morale under conditions of group learning.

Which Students Gain the Most from Collaborative Learning?

Although most studies evaluating the effects of group learning for different kinds of students claim equal benefits for students across a wide range of backgrounds and abilities, some researchers report that underprepared students may benefit more from student-led discussions than better students (Gruber & Weitman, 1962). The explanation offered is that when a group contains sufficient student resources of knowledge and higher-level thinking skills, less skilled students may be helped to restructure and deepen their understanding.

However, there is also ample research and experiential evidence to suggest that in peer tutoring, students *doing* the teaching learn more, especially at a conceptual level, than students receiving the tutoring (Annis, 1983; McKeachie et al., 1986). Teachers who have spent many hours preparing a lecture or designing a learning exercise know firsthand that organizing knowledge to explain it to others is a powerful learning experience. Thus, there should be considerable value to good students in having to organize and articulate their own learning to make it understandable to others. Indeed, Slavin (1996, p. 53) found in his review across hundreds of research studies that "students who give each other elaborated explanations (and, less consistently, those who receive such explanations) are the students who learn the most in cooperative learning."

Taken as a whole, the research appears to substantiate the claim that both underprepared and well-prepared students benefit from group learning, but perhaps for different reasons. Good students may benefit from having to formulate their thoughts and knowledge into concepts understandable to others, while academically poorer students may benefit from the explanations of their peers.

Other categories of students in which there is high interest is any group that has been underrepresented in higher education in the past. Obtaining diversity in student populations is appealing to colleges for pedagogical as well as social reasons. The evidence is strong—for a variety of reasons—that students who might be considered nontraditional college students prefer cooperative group learning and stand to benefit more from it than traditional students. Women, members of underrepresented racial and ethnic groups, adult and re-entry students, commuters, and international students have been identified as students for whom peer and group learning seem especially valued and valuable.

In a study of 2,051 students at twenty-three institutions, Cabrera (1998) found that minority students expressed a greater preference for learning in groups than did majority students, and Treisman (1985) found that the five-year retention rate for African American students majoring in mathematics or science at Berkeley was 65 percent for those who were involved in collaborative learning groups, compared with 41 percent for African American students not involved. In an intensive study of a special program for ethnically diverse calculus students at the University of Wisconsin, Millar (1999) reported positive findings on the effectiveness of learning in groups. The Wisconsin learning groups emphasized three factors: intensive group work, carefully chosen and very difficult problems, and instructors who function as guides. Students learning under these conditions were about twice as likely as other students to receive a B or above in calculus, and they "showed higher levels of confidence in their mathematical ability and greater comfort in performing calculus problems; learned to value multiple and creative ways of problem solving; and developed the interest and ability to acquire a deeper, more conceptual understanding of calculus" (pp. 8–9).

This finding is consistent with the Harvard studies that found that students who persist to degree completion in science tend to work in small, student-centered study groups, whereas students who leave science rarely report working with other students (Light, 1992). These findings may be especially significant for women, who tend to transfer out of the sciences more frequently than men (Tobias, 1990) and who tend to favor the more collaborative learning styles that are associated with "connected knowing"—in other words, gaining access to knowledge through other people (Belenky, Clinchy, Goldberger, & Tarule, 1986).

The simple answer to the question, *Who benefits from group learning situations?* seems to be "Almost everyone." Furthermore, it appears that group work enhances and enriches a goal that many colleges consider paramount for students today: learning from diversity. Cuseo notes, "Cooperative learning has the potential to capitalize on the contemporary wave of student diversity—converting it from a pedagogical liability (which instructors must somehow adapt to or accommodate) into a pedagogical asset—by capitalizing on the multiple, socio-cultural perspectives that can be experienced when students from diverse backgrounds are placed in heterogeneously-formed cooperative learning groups" (1996, p. 24).

Is Everyone Happy with Collaborative Learning?

Research on instructional methods is sometimes criticized for comparing carefully designed experimental methods with average, across-the-board, traditionally taught classes. This is, in a sense, "stacking the cards" in favor of the experimental method. It may be that the reason for the generally positive findings in the published reports of the contributions of group learning to achievement is that the groups studied are usually carefully structured to accomplish student learning. Research on lectures that were carefully planned to raise questions and involve students in actively thinking about what was being said would also show more positive results than across-the-board studies of the efficacy of active lecturing.

To answer the criticism of comparing well-designed collaborative learning methods with average, across-the-board traditional teaching, Wright and colleagues (Wright, Millar, Kosciuk, Penberthy, Williams, & Wampold, 1998) conducted an interesting and powerful comparison of the "best" lecture/discussion classes with the "best" cooperative learning classes in analytical chemistry at the University of Wisconsin. They placed considerable emphasis on careful assessment of the learning that was taking place. In their words, their assessment strategy "emerged from an ad hoc committee of skeptical chemistry faculty who met prior to the 1995 course. They concluded that the only type of assessment data they would find credible would be faculty-conducted oral examinations of all students. It was important that the assessment be done orally in order to probe student understanding and problem-solving ability. It was also important that the assessment involve external faculty who are independent of the course faculty" (p. 987).

Their findings left little doubt that students in the cooperative learning classes "had quantifiably better reasoning and communication skills" than students taught in lecture/discussion classes. Moreover, both student and faculty questionnaires showed "very significant differences in the perception of the students' preparation for future science courses" (p. 989). This study, published in the *Journal of Chemical Education,* is one of the most carefully designed research studies of instructional methods that we found in our search of the research on collaborative learning in higher education.

Issues on Which Research Is Lacking

The aggregated evidence from research studies appears highly positive, but we found student criticism or dissatisfaction with group work strangely lacking in the research reports. The research just did not seem to report on or take cognizance of the student criticisms that every instructor who has tried group work hears from time to time. We found that any criticisms of learning groups were enumerated largely in the work of practitioners. Miller and her colleagues reported their experiences in teaching a biology class: "Some groups literally crackle with excitement and creativity. All members seem to live, breathe, eat, and sleep the current project and are ecstatic with their working arrangements. . . . At the opposite end of the spectrum, there are groups in which one or more members cannot be reached by telephone, do not show up for meetings, break commitments to their group and in the worst case disappear for several weeks with the entire group's work in their possession" (Miller, Trimbur, & Wilkes, 1994, p. 34).

We also found a report of negative as well as positive student reactions on a Web site (http://www.wcer.wisc.edu/nise/CL1/CL/story/middlecc/TSCMA.htm). Cathy Middlecamp asked two hundred students in a chemistry class for non-majors at the University of Wisconsin to give advantages and disadvantages of the group work that she had used from time to time in the class. While she disavows a systematic research approach to the collection of data, her posting on the Web of a sample of student comments regarding cooperative learning groups will ring true to many practitioners. The advantages listed by students consist of those that appear commonly in the literature of cooperative and collaborative learning. They include recognition that different members of the group bring different knowledge and talents to bear, that deeper learning results from the discussion, that students are less hesitant to speak or raise questions in small peer groups than in a large class or with the instructor, and that working in groups is more fun and gives students an opportunity to know their fellow students better. Some students, especially business majors, were also likely to mention the career value of learning to work on teams.

The disadvantages listed by students included recognition that people need to go at different speeds, that some students dominate the group while others are "easy riders" who fail to pull their fair share, that discussion gets off the topic and wastes time, and that some groups "just don't get along." The advantages listed by students appear to represent the outcomes of groups that are productive, well planned, and carefully monitored. The disadvantages represent groups that are dysfunctional for one or more reasons, most of which are probably correctable. The purpose of this handbook is to help faculty capitalize on the advantages and defuse the disadvantages inherent in group work (see "Addressing Problems" in Chapter Five, Facilitating Student Collaboration).

There is almost no research on groups that fail, and more specifically, how that experience impacts the learning of its members. Does collaborative learning carry risks if done poorly? We assume so, but we just don't know what students learn from a poorly run group. The evidence, however, is so strong that collaborative learning has multiple advantages if done well, that it would be folly not to learn how to operate collaborative learning groups productively.

Much to our surprise, we found no attempt to systematically study the impact of collaborative learning on teachers. Does it take more time? Does it sacrifice "coverage" of material? Does it result in greater satisfaction in the profession of teaching? What are the rewards, intrinsic and extrinsic? We just don't know via systematic research study the answers to these questions. There are scattered testimonials to the satisfaction of working closely with colleagues, and a growing band of devotees offer anecdotes on their increased interest in teaching via collaborative learning. Certainly centers established on campuses to improve teaching and learning are increasingly using workshops, faculty mentors, team teaching, and what could be called "collaborative learning for teachers" as the basic formula for their work.

In 1993, TIAA/CREF established the Hesburgh Awards "to acknowledge and reward successful, innovative faculty development programs that enhance undergraduate teaching." A review of 450 Hesburgh finalists between 1993 and 2001 illustrated the impact of collaborative learning for faculty development (Cross, 2001). A predominant feature of these cutting-edge programs was the emphasis on collaborative learning for faculty: faculty members were collaborating across disciplines and generations to share the "wisdom of practice." As faculty find satisfaction and professional growth in collaboration, perhaps they will carry their experiences with their own learning into their classrooms. But the fact remains that there is little research to document advantages and disadvantages to teachers of collaborative learning.

Conclusion

Collaborative learning seems to be a teaching/learning innovation whose time has come. Done well, it puts into practice the major conclusions from modern cognitive learning theory, specifically, that students must be actively engaged in building their own minds. Research to date supports and enriches the theory. There is a large amount of empirical evidence that small groups of peers learning together have advantages for academic achievement, motivation, and satisfaction. As Millis and Cottell (1998, p. 24) conclude, "The good news is that the research consistently shows that structured small-group work that builds on positive interdependence and individual accountability also raises student achievement." There does not seem to be much "bad news" in the research findings. But most of the research reported in the literature is on carefully structured groups, designed to accomplish learning. The critically important qualifications that have emerged from that research are that positive interdependence and individual accountability are factors that make for success.

As more and more faculty in higher education introduce collaborative learning into their classrooms, the accumulation of research and wisdom will grow. But there is already plenty of experience to help classroom teachers avoid the pitfalls and capitalize on the potential of collaborative learning. A major purpose of this handbook is to pull together information from both research and experience to help teachers design creative, challenging, and effective group assignments.

Notes

1. While Bruffee (1995) assumes that cooperative learning does not involve conflict, Johnson and Johnson (1994, p. 67) assert that "within cooperative learning groups, intellectual conflict should be encouraged and nurtured, rather than suppressed or avoided."

2. Karl Smith and the Johnson brothers have spent many years leading the cooperative learning movement in K–12. In turning their attention recently to higher education, they have brought with them the term *cooperative learning*.

3. The *Handbook of Accreditation* of WASC sets forth standards that require "evidence of educational effectiveness, including student learning" (Western Association of Schools and Colleges, 2001, p. 29).

Part Two

Implementing Collaborative Learning

EMBARKING UPON COLLABORATIVE LEARNING should be a reasonable adventure—stimulating, challenging, and requiring thoughtful advanced planning. It is neither a high-risk venture, an abandonment of all things familiar and comfortable about the traditional classroom in favor of total commitment to the unknown, nor something to introduce spontaneously on a slow day to "see what happens" when the responsibility for learning is turned over to students. For collaborative learning to be successful, the instructor must give thoughtful consideration to a host of factors. Thus, the purpose of Part Two: Implementing Collaborative Learning is to collect and synthesize the wisdom from practice and scholarship about *how* to create productive learning environments through the use of collaborative learning groups.

Central to considering how to implement collaborative learning are philosophical positions regarding the role of the college teacher in the classroom, as views of these positions have a major influence on how teachers choose to implement collaborative learning. In general, the role of college teachers has shifted dramatically over the past decade, stimulated in part by the assessment movement, with its assumptions of institutional accountability for student learning, and in part by major advances in our understanding of the learning process. As Part One indicates, research on cognition demonstrates convincingly that learners must actively engage in building their own minds; teachers cannot simply pour knowledge into students' heads and hope that they will assimilate it into the understandings that we call "learning."

Recent advances in knowledge about how students learn, coupled with demands for institutional accountability for student learning, make new demands on teachers. Today's teachers must not only know their subject matter, they must also know how to get students actively involved in working with the concepts of the discipline to make the knowledge their own. Creating a stimulating learning environment in which students challenge and motivate fellow students to get involved in learning is a substantial task, requiring depth of knowledge about the subject and about teaching, and it constitutes part of what we know as the "scholarship of teaching" (Boyer, 1990).

With the growth and increasing popularity of collaborative learning, there are honest differences, forcefully expressed in the literature of collaborative learning, about the appropriate roles for instructors in creating this learning environment. Opinions run the gamut from convictions that instructors should play a minimal role in shaping and directing the work of student learning groups to beliefs that instructors have the responsibility to structure the learning tasks, monitor group progress, and intervene if students get off track.

Kenneth Bruffee, for example, contends that students must be "clearly and unequivocally on their own to govern themselves and pursue the task in the way that they see fit" (Bruffee, 1995, p. 17). He takes his position on the grounds that shifting responsibility for learning from instructor to students "helps students become autonomous, articulate, and socially and intellectually mature, and it helps them learn the substance at issue not as conclusive 'facts' but as the constructed result of a disciplined social process of inquiry." Others encourage more traditional roles for instructors, contending that instructors have the responsibility to make assignments, monitor the group process to assure that all are participating and that the group is staying on task, intervene if students get off track, and evaluate group process and effectiveness (Johnson, Johnson, & Smith, 1998).

The different positions derive from epistemological convictions about the nature of knowledge and learning as described in Part One, but as a practical matter, most instructors probably fall somewhere in the middle or cruise along the continuum, depending on the discipline, course objectives, personal style and comfort of the instructor, student experience, and a host of other variables involved in any given classroom. Some instructors see themselves as "coaches," observing, correcting, and working with students to improve their performance; some prefer the concept of "facilitator," which implies arranging the learning environment to encourage self-directed learning; some use the term "manager," emphasizing a sequential process of setting the conditions and managing the process to produce the desired outcomes. Some prefer the concept of "co-learner," emphasizing the social role of constructing knowledge.[1]

The terminology is more than semantics; it reflects a variety of self-perceptions of the new faculty role in the classroom. On one matter, however, there is virtually universal agreement. The new college teacher is more than a "dispenser of information." If there is any convergence in advice offered in the literature by experienced teachers of group learning, it is toward flexibility coupled with enough structure to assure those two stalwarts of the collaborative learning movement: positive interdependence and individual accountability.

In this handbook, we suggest that the role of the instructor in collaborative learning includes the following responsibilities: orienting students to the goals and purposes of collaborative learning; making decisions about size, duration, and operation of the learning groups; designing and assigning learning tasks; assuring active, constructive participation; and assessing and evaluating learning. Part Two, therefore, is organized into the following chapters:

Chapter Two:	Orienting Students
Chapter Three:	Forming Groups
Chapter Four:	Structuring the Learning Task
Chapter Five:	Facilitating Student Collaboration
Chapter Six:	Grading and Evaluating Collaborative Learning

Note

1. Roles teachers adopt in the classroom are reflections of teaching styles. Several inventories of teaching styles exist, and one of these, Grasha's (1996) Teaching Style Inventory, is available online at the following URL: http://plato.ftr.indstate.edu/fcrcweb_old/tstyles3.html. Grasha has identified five teaching styles, which converge in a cluster and comprise characteristic ways professors design instructional settings. These clusters range on a continuum from Expert/Formal/Authority (a teacher-centered approach in which instructors present information and students receive knowledge) to Delegator/Facilitator/Expert (a student-centered model that involves designing complex tasks that require student initiative, and often group work, to complete). One's preferred teaching style shapes the type and degree of collaborative learning one chooses to implement.

Chapter 2
Orienting Students

IN COLLABORATIVE LEARNING, students, like teachers, have new and different responsibilities from what they may be accustomed to in traditional education. MacGregor (1990, p. 25) defines seven shifts that students have to make, as shown in Exhibit 2.1. These are major changes for students involving new roles and requiring different skills.

Bosworth (1994) contends that we must teach students these skills just as we would teach any other set of skills and proposes a taxonomy of collaborative skills that includes interpersonal skills, group management skills, inquiry skills, conflict resolution skills, and synthesis and presentation skills. In some cases, instructors can model the requisite skills, but the primary method for teaching collaborative learning skills lies in the structuring of the learning task so that the practice of the skill is essential to the accomplishment of the task.

Although best taught within the context of content-based learning tasks, teachers can start orienting students to new roles and helping them develop collaborative learning skills beginning the first day of class. This chapter contains ideas for introducing students to collaborative roles and skills early in the course in three categories: introductions and icebreakers, course policies and procedures, and orientation to collaborative learning.

Introductions and Icebreakers

In the collaborative classroom, the instructor purposefully creates a learning environment in which students interact with each other. This is different from what goes on in many college classrooms, in which students sit alone, spend a significant amount of time passively listening to the "sage on the stage," and are expected not to talk because this distracts attention

---

EXHIBIT 2.1

Comparing Student Roles in the Traditional Versus Collaborative Classroom

Traditional Classroom Students shift from ...	Collaborative Classroom to ...
Listener, observer, and note taker	Active problem solver, contributor, and discussant
Low or moderate expectations of preparation for class	High expectations of preparation for class
Private presence in the classroom with few or no risks	Public presence with many risks
Attendance dictated by personal choice	Attendance dictated by community expectation
Competition with peers	Collaborative work with peers
Responsibilities and self-definition associated with learning independently	Responsibilities and self-definition associated with learning interdependently
Seeing teachers and texts as the sole sources of authority and knowledge	Seeing peers, self, and the community as additional and important sources of authority and knowledge

Source: MacGregor (1990, p. 25)

---

that is supposed to be focused on the instructor. It is important, therefore, to establish up front that in a collaborative classroom students will be interacting. One way to encourage students to interact is to provide class members with an opportunity to get to know each other. Structured activities for introductions and greetings called "icebreakers" are good getting-acquainted techniques. Icebreakers ease the tension and awkwardness of the initial classes, helping students develop feelings of comfort. They also create an expectation of interaction and are therefore useful entrees into meaningful, ongoing collaboration. Even if instructors decide to retain a predominantly lecture-based course, they will find that incorporating some level of icebreakers may reduce student stress and increase their willingness to speak up in whole class discussion.

Social Icebreakers

An instructor who learns students' names shows students that the instructor values them as individuals. Helping students to learn each other's names, and to identify shared interests and experiences as well as intriguing differences, demonstrates that the instructor values students knowing each other as well.

Name Game If possible, arrange desks or chairs into a circle. Have the first student state her name, the second student state his name and the first student's name, the third student state her name and the previous two students' names, and so on. If the class is small, do this as a whole class. If the class is large, consider forming groups of eight to twelve students so that at least subsets of students will learn each other's names. Consider repeating this activity for a few minutes at the beginning of several class sessions, either to reinforce recall of names or to give students in larger classes a chance to learn everyone's names.

Question of the Day Form pairs or small groups, use *CoLT 1: Think-Pair-Share, CoLT 2: Buzz Groups,* or *CoLT 5: Three-Step Interview,* and ask students to answer a simple question such as, *What was one of the best movies you've seen and why? If you could be someone famous, who would you be and why? If you could have lunch with any person, living or dead, who would it be and why?*

Scavenger Hunt Create and distribute a list of characteristics or skills students may have (for example, speaks a second language, plays a musical instrument, has a part-time job, and so forth). Ask students to try to find students who have that characteristic and write their names next to that characteristic on the list.

Interviews Create and distribute a handout with a few questions such as, *What is your name? Your academic major? How long have you been a student here? Why are you taking this class? Do you know what you plan to do when you finish school?* and so forth. Form pairs and ask students to alternate "interviewing" each other. Consider expanding this activity by implementing *CoLT 5: Three-Step Interview.*

While social icebreakers can be fun for many students, some students may be uncomfortable sharing personal information with each other or feel that the activity seems too "touchy-feely." Don't ask questions or solicit information that is too personal; as an alternative, consider using collaborative activities that introduce course content.

Course Introductions

Collaborative activities can be used to introduce students to the content of the course, thus helping students get to know each other as they also learn the subject matter. These activities can help students identify useful prior knowledge as well as clarify learning gaps. Students may feel reassured knowing that others are at a similar starting place, and they may be able to identify exceptional knowledge or abilities of future group members. Using course content also underscores the academic rather than social purposes of collaborative learning activities. The following techniques are useful for this purpose.

Common-Sense Inventory Use a variation of *CoLT 21: Team Matrix* and assemble an inventory of 5–15 interesting true or false statements related to the discipline or course. Ask students to form pairs or small groups and mark statements as True or False. In a follow-up whole-class discussion, project a blank matrix on an overhead and ask groups to report out and explain their decisions, recording responses by placing tally marks in the T/F columns. After discussion of each statement or at the end of the activity, either give the "correct" responses or leave them as "cliffhangers," telling students they will learn the answers as the course unfolds (Nilson, 2003).

Problem Posting Use *CoLT 1: Think-Pair-Share* or *CoLT 2: Round Robin* and ask students to identify problems (or topics, questions, issues, information, and so forth) that they think the course should address. As students report out in a follow-up whole-class discussion, use their responses to reinforce or clarify course goals and content. Consider augmenting planned course content to include modules or activities on student-generated ideas if their suggestions seem appropriate (McKeachie, 1994).

Course Concept Mapping Use *CoLT 23: Word Webs* and ask students to map out a concept that is central to the course, such as, *How do we learn about the past?* (for history) or *What is art?* (for art appreciation). In a follow-up whole-class discussion, ask team spokespersons to show and explain the ideas and associations in their group's web, and use these reports as the basis for explaining the purpose or organization of the course.

Activities that focus on learning rather than subject matter are also useful ways to orient students to the course.

Future Employer Use *CoLT 2: Round Robin* or *CoLT 3: Buzz Groups* and ask students to generate a list of skills they believe a future employer (either generic or for a representative career in the discipline) will be looking for. Common responses include "mastery of the subject area," "ability to work in teams," "written and oral communication skills," "problem-solving ability," and "ability to learn on my own." Use this as the basis for a discussion of the learning objectives and goals for the course (Miller, Groccia, & Wilkes, 1996).

Goal Ranking and Matching Use *CoLT 1: Think-Pair-Share* and ask students to jot down three to five of their learning goals for the course and to rank them by importance to their lives, from 1 (most important) to 5 (least important). Explain that a goal such as "to complete a requirement" or "I want to do well in this course" is a general goal shared by many students, and that you are asking them to focus on a goal that is specific and individual to them. Ask students to share their responses with their partner, looking for ways their responses compare or contrast. Ask pairs to report out and write their responses on the board. Alternately, collect the responses, and let students know when you will discuss the tallied results. After collecting the information, look for patterns and organize data into groups with common ideas and tally how many students have similar goals. In providing feedback to students, discuss areas of common ground and areas where the goals don't coincide. If willing, adjust the course goals to accommodate the students' goals; if not, explain why not (Angelo & Cross, 1993, pp. 290–294).

It may also be constructive—perhaps somewhat later in the term after students have built up trust—to assign collaborative activities that help students focus more directly on the ways they learn.

Self-Assessment of Ways of Learning Select a theoretical framework for learning (such as Meyers-Briggs Type Indicator or the Firo-B) to help students identify their general learning styles. When students have selected or been identified as possessing a specific learning style profile, organize students into small groups with the same or similar styles. Use *CoLT 20: Group Grid* and ask students to identify the pros and cons of their particular learning style, or the advantages and disadvantages of collaborative learning for their particular styles. Alternately, use *CoLT 3: Buzz Groups* and ask students to respond to questions such as, *How would someone who fits in Learning Style X approach this particular task?* (Angelo & Cross, 1993, pp. 295–298).

Focused Autobiographical Sketches Ask students each to write a one- or two-page autobiographical sketch focused on a successful (or unsuccessful) past learning experience that is relevant to learning in the current course. This provides information about the students' self-concepts and self-awareness as learners within a specific field (Angelo & Cross, 1993, pp. 281–284). Pair students to share and discuss responses before submitting essays. Or consider implementing *CoLT 24: Dialogue Journals,* asking that these essays be the first entries into journals that individuals will maintain and exchange with peers throughout the semester.

Course Policies and Procedures

Developing shared understandings of course policies and procedures is important for class cohesiveness. Following are ideas for collaborative activities that can help students learn important course information and establish group norms.

Syllabus Review

Course information is typically provided to students in the syllabus, but reading over a syllabus can be boring for students and for faculty alike. Using collaborative activities to engage students in learning course information is important for several reasons. First, the syllabus is often the initial point of contact and connection between and among all of the class participants, and thus it helps set the tone for the remainder of the course. Second, it is the teacher's opportunity to describe beliefs about educational purposes and identify how instructional methods (especially collaborative learning activities) help accomplish those purposes. Third, it can outline the new roles and responsibilities of both the instructor and the students, thus clarifying expectations and reducing the potential of future problems with individuals or groups.

Basic Syllabus Review Activity Form groups of four to six students, identify a recorder, and use *CoLT 2: Round Robin* to ask students to generate a list of questions about the course. Pass out the syllabus, and ask students to read the syllabus to determine which of their questions have been answered and which have not. Ask them to note any information the syllabus provided about the course about which they had not thought to ask. Close with a whole-class discussion on the syllabus based on their unanswered questions and their discoveries about the course.

- *Variation 1:* Pass out the syllabus first, use *CoLT 3: Buzz Groups,* and ask students to read together and generate questions about the syllabus. Initiate class discussion of the syllabus by starting with these student-generated questions. This variation has the advantage of providing structure and focus to the first-day discussion.

- *Variation 2:* Create a quiz with common questions regarding the course, such as, *How do I get an A? What is the first deadline? What is the make-up policy?* and distribute these questions to small groups along with the syllabus. Have student groups work together to find the answers to the questions in the syllabus (Millis & Cottell, 1998).

The course syllabus contains elements essential for students to understand, such as academic honesty policies and safety practices. Therefore, if the collaborative activity does not cover topics such as these, make sure to cover them when addressing the full group at some point during the class session. (See Exhibit 2.2 for policies and procedures related to collaborative learning to consider including in the syllabus.)

EXHIBIT 2.2

Break-Out 1

Including Collaborative Learning Policies and Procedures in the Syllabus or Orientation

Course syllabi typically include general course policies such as those regarding attendance, grading, and academic honesty. Classroom procedures (such as attendance monitoring) may be included in the syllabus, or may be covered in the first-day orientation. Consider incorporating one or more of the following elements either into the syllabus or orientation to help manage collaborative learning.

Collaborative Learning Policy	A statement that summarizes why, how, and in what ways collaborative learning will be a part of the course as well as plans for assessing and grading group work; this statement can help to make plans and expectations clear to students.
"Three Before Me" Statement	Students often expect instructors to jump in and provide them with the answers. When choosing to implement an extensively collaborative class in which students will work as independently as possible, establish guidelines in advance. For example, Kagan (1992) asks students to consult three resources before asking him for a response.
Classroom Set-Up Teams	With extensive use of small groups, the classroom needs to be set up accordingly. Consider conserving time by assigning students to teams that are responsible for setting up the room as soon as they get to class (Cohen, 1986).
Entry/Exit Ticket	Taking attendance can be time consuming, and in courses in which students do considerable group work, it can delay or interrupt group interaction. Consider as an alternative having students complete and turn in tickets as they walk in the door for each class session. These Entry Tickets consist of slips of paper on which students write their names as well as questions, comments, and topics that they would like to cover, problems regarding group work, or other course-related information or questions. If desired, these tickets can be used later to record attendance on a roster. It is also important to respond to student remarks to show students that their comments are important. Similar to the Entry Ticket, students can turn in Exit Tickets instead, submitting the slips of paper with their questions and comments at the end of class rather than at the beginning (Bender, Kendall, Larson, & Wilkes, 1994).
Signal to Stop Group Work	Before starting group work, prearrange a signal that lets students know that it is time to turn their attention to you. The signal should be something that students will easily recognize even if they are actively involved in group work, such as flashing the lights or ringing a desktop bell. When they see or hear this signal, students should respond by stopping the conversation and making eye contact with you (Millis & Cottell, 1998). By establishing the signal the first time groups meet, students will likely observe it for the entire term.
Student Folders/Folios	Student groups may keep a folder of their work that contains attendance sheets, assignments, and group feedback forms. Instructors can spot-check the folders to make sure that groups are completing the assigned work. Passing out folders and explaining their use early in the semester establishes their importance, and random checking throughout the terms ensures their continued use.

Establishing Group Work Ground Rules

If you plan to use collaborative activities extensively throughout the course, establishing group ground rules early in the course can be a productive use of time and help improve group functioning. Although instructors can develop these rules, involving students in determining group work policies allows them to assume ownership and responsibility for observing and enforcing them.

Group Ground Rules Form groups, and ask one person in each group to serve as recorder. Use a combination of *CoLT 2: Round Robin* and *CoLT 20: Group Grid*, asking students to take turns answering the following questions: *What behaviors do you think will be most helpful for groups? What behaviors will be least productive in groups?* The recorder writes student responses in the appropriate "Helpful" or "Not Helpful" column of the grid. Using their completed grids, groups may either develop a list of ground rules for group behavior, or they may report out in a whole-class discussion and create a general list of ground rules. Consider developing a completed grid in advance to ensure that all productive and counterproductive behaviors have been identified in the full discussion.

Alternately, provide teams a list of several ground rules, and ask students to discuss and select a number of them from the list that they think are the most important. Or use an adaptation of *CoLT 5: Three-Step Interview* and solicit a small number of volunteers to interview groups of six to eight students. Ask the interviewers to report their findings to the class, and use their reports as the basis for a whole-class discussion to develop general group ground rules (Silberman, 1996).

If students develop their own group rules, it may be important to ensure that these rules are realistic and appropriate.

Group Learning Contract

Once ground rules are set, it may be useful to have students sign a *Group Learning Contract.* Either the teacher or the students draw up and both sign a formal agreement that outlines policies, procedures, and penalties regarding group work. The contract serves as a formal record and adds emphasis and legitimacy to the group ground rules. If the students draw up the contract, consider having them submit the contract for review to allow suggestions for revision where appropriate before the final signing. Since it is likely that students will not know how to draw up a contract, it may help to have a sample form, like the one in Exhibit 2.3, for them to use (Knowles, 1986).

EXHIBIT 2.3

Sample Group Learning Contract

For the next several class periods, I will be participating in a group to learn:

_____

_____

_____

I am committed to participating effectively in this group learning activity and will strive to do the following. *Students supply their agreed-upon ground rules, such as:*

    ___Come to class regularly and on time

    ___Come prepared and ready to share in my group

    ___Listen actively to what others have to contribute

    ___Be supportive of the efforts and initiatives of others

If I do not follow the above rules, I will do the following to compensate. *Students supply their own ideas or penalties, such as:*

    ___If I miss a class, I agree to ask a group member ahead of time to take notes for me. If it is an unintended absence, I will get the notes from a group member and make up any group work I missed.

    ___If I am unable to prepare for a group assignment, I will make up for and do an additional proportional share of the work on the next assignment.

    ___If I notice or if someone points out that I am not listening, I will stop what I am doing and immediately give my full attention to whomever is speaking.

    ___If someone notices that I am too critical or am otherwise unsupportive, I will make efforts to watch my words and interactions in the future.

Signed_____Date_____

Consider including other items of information such as names of group members, required tasks, evaluation criteria, and so forth.

Orienting Students to Collaborative Learning

Students will most likely be coming to class with a range of experiences and attitudes regarding group work. Many teachers have been incorporating collaborative learning in their classes, and therefore several students will be primed and ready to participate effectively in group work. In fact, these students might feel disoriented in a traditional lecture course. To reinforce positive views of collaborative learning and to redirect students who may have negative feelings about collaborative work, consider activities to orient students to the value of collaborative learning.

Collaborative Learning Pro and Con Grid Use *CoLT 20: Group Grid,* and ask students to complete a grid in which they identify the advantages and disadvantages of collaborative learning. Consider adding a column next to the "Con" column, and after students have completed identifying the pros and cons, ask them to review the problems in the "Con" column to see whether they can identify a solution. For example, if students have stated that some individuals do most of the work while others get away with minimal work, groups might offer a suggestion for ensuring equity and individual accountability. In a follow-up whole-class discussion, make sure to address the "cons." Reassure students with negative attitudes that their concerns have been heard and implement strategies for eliminating or ameliorating that "con" upfront.

Individual Versus Group Knowledge Quiz Use a variant of *CoLT 12: Test-Taking Teams,* and give students a quiz that contains introductory questions regarding course content. Questions should be challenging, but ones for which it is conceivable that students could answer from prior knowledge. For example, in a history course, a question might be, *Who were the presidents in office during the following critical events?* Or in geography, *Draw a map of the world.* Give students time to take the quiz individually, and then ask them to retake it as a group to demonstrate that their collective knowledge is superior to the knowledge possessed by an individual.

Group Résumé Use a variation of *CoLT 20: Group Grid,* with the left column containing group members' names and the remaining columns including relevant student skills and background, such as in Exhibit 2.4. This activity allows students to interact and get to know each other better as they discover the talents and skills of other group members. It also helps students to see the benefit of collaborative work as they learn to value what their peers have to offer.

- *Variation 1:* Ask students to name their groups, preferably with a name that is relevant to the class (for example, a business class might have groups form an entertainment consulting company called Show Biz).
- *Variation 2:* Give student groups a specific purpose that relates to the class. For example, if student groups will complete a service-learning component with a local business, have the groups put together the résumé to send as a means of introduction to those who will serve as their supervisors.
- *Variation 3:* Use the Group Résumé as the first component of a comprehensive portfolio that will evolve and include products or artifacts that groups generate during the class (Silberman, 1996, pp. 38–39).

EXHIBIT 2.4

Sample Group Résumé

Student Name	Educational Background and Academic Major	General Knowledge of Course Content	Specialized Knowledge (Web Page Construction, Presentation Software, Graphic Software ...)	Skills (Writing, Presenting, Drawing, Acting, Facilitating ...)
Student 1				
Student 2				
Student 3				
Student 4				
Student 5				

Course Commercial/Infomercial Students work in teams to develop a commercial advertising the importance of collaborative learning that they present or act out to the class. Alternately, have teams create a brochure, newspaper advertisement, or other written form of advertisement. As students "sell" collaborative learning to others, they increase their understanding of the value of it to themselves. After teams have presented their commercials, hold a whole-class discussion on the benefits—as well as the challenges—of collaborative learning (Silberman, 1996, p. 41).

In addition to the activities just mentioned, there are a host of general team-building games and activities that help develop positive group dynamics or demonstrate that groups are more likely to make better decisions than individuals. Activities such as *Tag-Team Tic Tac Toe* (Zakon, 2002), *Winter Survival* (Johnson & Johnson, 1975), and *Lost on the Moon* (Per Bang, 2001) show students the benefits of collaboration and illustrate the detriments of competition. Additional resources for group games are available and may be located using a Web search with keywords such as "team building" or "group games." When planning extensive collaborative work or anticipating significant resistance to collaborative work, consider including one of these kinds of activities as part of the orientation strategy.

EXHIBIT 2.5

Break-Out 2

Orienting Students to Collaborative Learning in the Online Classroom

Faculty who teach online classes report that one of their greatest challenges is implementing successful and appropriate collaborative activities. Throughout this handbook, we provide advice and suggestions for incorporating group work into online courses. The following are ideas for adapting or supplementing the strategies described in the rest of this section to fit the needs of online classes.

Introductions and Icebreakers	If the class is reasonably small, create a Threaded Discussion titled "Introductions" and ask students to write and post an introduction according to a structured framework. For example, ask students specifically to give their names, academic majors, experience with technology or online classes, and so forth, or consider one of the prompts suggested in the icebreakers in this chapter. For classes with large enrollment, consider forming Base Groups of eight to twelve students and assigning each group an initial name (for example, Group A). Create for each Base Group a separate forum in which they can interact throughout the semester. Ask students to introduce themselves to other members of their Base Group as their first activity. Consider asking them to choose a Group Name based on the information that they learn about each other in the introductions.
Course Policies and Procedures	Create a Threaded Discussion titled "Syllabus Review" and initiate the discussion with a prompt such as *After reading the syllabus, what questions do you still have about the course?* or *Is there anything about the course that surprises you, that is different from what you had expected?* Ask students to respond both to the prompt and to a reply posted by at least one other student.
	In a similar manner, create a Threaded Discussion for the whole class or for Base Groups titled "Group Ground Rules" and ask students to use the forum to generate rules and penalties.
	It is useful to develop a required "Syllabus Quiz" in order to ensure that online students take the time to read the syllabus carefully. This can also provide a record to show that students were aware of the deadlines, grading procedures, academic honesty policy, and so forth should they attempt to use "ignorance" as an excuse later in the course.
Orienting to Collaborative Learning	Some students select online courses because they wish to work independently, or their time constraints and schedules do not permit them to commit to specific dates or times for interaction. Be sensitive to their needs and consider minimizing demands for synchronous activities, and instead take advantage of the benefits of asynchronous activities.
	If group participation will be graded, establish and communicate to students the criteria (quantity? quality?) by which their participation will be evaluated.
	Consider creating a Threaded Discussion in which students share their perceptions of the advantages and disadvantages for collaborative work both in general and in online classes specifically.

Conclusion

Collaborative learning requires students to assume new roles and develop skills that are different from those they are accustomed to using in traditional classrooms. Although learning these roles and skills is best achieved on an ongoing basis in content-focused learning tasks, it is helpful to introduce students to the shift in expectations early in the class. In this chapter, we offered ideas for activities to help orient students to varying degrees of collaboration. If teachers choose a predominantly lecture-and discussion-based delivery, incorporating a few activities such as an icebreaker and a collaborative *Syllabus Review* can help students feel comfortable with each other and significantly improve their willingness to speak up in whole-class discussion. If, on the other hand, instructors plan to implement a considerable amount of group work, they may wish to add more comprehensive activities such as *Establishing Group Rules* or *Group Résumé.* Setting aside sufficient time for students to get to know each other, to build trust, to develop a sense of class community, and to establish group rules can ensure that the course gets off to a positive start by helping orient students to effective collaborative learning.

Chapter 3

Forming Groups

OUTSIDE THE ACADEMIC WORLD, groups are a basic social structure. They form and reform in a variety of ways for multiple purposes: individuals gather together in social situations, coordinate to accomplish job-related tasks, or join committees because of a shared civic interest. While groups on campus also form easily and for a variety of purposes, forming groups within the classroom can be a complicated and unnatural process. Yet for collaborative learning to be successful, it is important to form effective groups. This section provides advice about group formation in three topic areas: group types, group size, and group membership.

Group Types

Collaborative learning groups vary in type according to the goal, the activity, and the length of time students will work together. Groups can be formal, informal, or base (Johnson, Johnson, & Smith, 1991). *Informal groups are* formed quickly, randomly, and to work together for a brief period of time. They are created to respond to a question, brainstorm ideas, or participate in some other endeavor that serves as a break out to a longer class activity. Many of the CoLTs in Part Three, such as *CoLT 1: Think-Pair-Share* and *CoLT 25: Round Table,* are intended for informal groups. These groups may be formed frequently and have new members each class.

Formal groups are formed to work together to achieve a more complex goal such as writing a report or developing a presentation. These groups work together until that task is accomplished, which generally takes several class sessions or even weeks. CoLTs such as *CoLT 6: Critical Debate* or *CoLT 18: Group Investigation* are examples of techniques that work best in formal groups.

Base groups stay together for the entire term or even the academic year. Base groups are intended to form a community of learners who work on a variety of tasks. Because of the long-term nature of these groups, their purpose is to achieve an overarching course goal and to offer members support and encouragement (Johnson et al., 1991). Within a course, base groups might be formed either to accomplish a term-length project—such as *CoLT 24: Dialogue Journals*—or they may be formed and then assigned a series of learning tasks that incorporate a sequence of CoLTs. For example, each base group might first participate in *CoLT 2: Round Robin* to generate ideas for a semester-long research project. They might sort the ideas and identify themes in *CoLT 19: Affinity Grouping*, conduct and write up their research in *CoLT 28: Collaborative Process Writing*, and then share their findings in *CoLT 30: Paper Seminar.*

Thus, the type of group you decide to use—informal, formal, or base–depends upon the task and the time it will take to complete the assignment.

Group Size

For effective collaborative work, group size usually ranges from two to six students. While size may be dictated by any number of factors and preferences, Bean (1996, p. 160) gives a cogent rationale for settling on five as the most effective size for formal and informal classroom groups. He observes that six will work almost as well, but that larger groups dilute the experience; groups of four tend to divide into pairs; and groups of three split into a pair and an outsider. Of course, many times pairs work best, especially in quick exchanges such as an interrupted lecture where minimal disruption is desired. Bean suggests that base groups work well when they are smaller—three seems optimal. Smith (1996, p. 77) prefers to keep groups small (two or three), especially in the beginning, in order to maximize involvement. Smaller groups can also schedule meetings more easily. Group size may also be dictated by the physical facilities. For example, groups of two or three might be the only practical arrangement for large-enrollment classes or science or computer laboratory assignments.

The size of the group thus depends on the type of group, the nature of the assignment, the duration of the task, and to some extent the physical setting. Generally, collaborative learning advocates suggest that the group be small enough so that students can participate fully and build confidence in one another, yet large enough to have sufficient diversity and the necessary resources to accomplish the learning task.

Group Membership

There are many ways to constitute groups: membership can be random, student selected, or teacher determined; membership can be based on interests, abilities, attitudes, or a host of other characteristics; and groups can be heterogeneous or homogeneous. Broadly speaking, research supports heterogeneous grouping because working with diverse students exposes individuals to people with different ideas, backgrounds, and experiences. This is a major educational value of collaborative learning. There is also some evidence that diverse groups are more productive and better suited for multidimensional tasks (Aronson, Blaney, Stephan, Sikes, & Snapp, 1978; Cranton, 1998; Johnson et al., 1991; Sharan & Sharan, 1992).

There are, however, some disadvantages in heterogeneous groups. Students can be uncomfortable with the diversity of opinion and the possible tension that results from disagreement. Distributing minority or female students among groups in order to achieve heterogeneity can isolate them, putting them into the position of being the sole representative of their group. This can be detrimental to their academic success because they can become marginalized, placed in stereotypical roles, and not permitted to flourish (Felder, Felder, Mauney, Hamrin, & Dietz, 1995; Rosser, 1997; Sandler, Silverberg, & Hall, 1996). Finally, when academic achievement is used to create a heterogeneous group, there may be insufficient opportunities for low achievers to show leadership (if a high achiever dominates) and not enough contact between high achievers (who may miss academic stimulation).

Homogeneous grouping offers advantages for some kinds of learning activities. For example, students who share common characteristics may feel sufficiently at ease with each other to discuss or explore highly sensitive or personal issues (Brookfield & Preskill, 1999). Homogeneous groups may also master most efficiently highly structured skill-building tasks, since students can communicate with each other starting from a similar level of knowledge. Homogeneous groups may be good for language learning or other specific content mastery in which group reinforcement of similar knowledge or skills is important (Cooper, Prescott, Cook, Smith, Mueck, & Cuseo, 1990; Johnson & Johnson, 1984). Additionally, students tend to prefer working with students similar to themselves, and hence satisfaction with collaborative learning often increases when groups are homogeneous. The greatest disadvantage to homogeneous groups is that students do not experience the rich interactions and exchange that can occur working with a diverse group of peers.

How groups are constituted depends on the goals of the course and the learning tasks that are assigned. In the absence of any clear rationale for assigning group membership, instructors may simply opt for random assignment or choose to mix groups throughout the term such that sometimes groups are homogeneous and other times they are heterogeneous.

Selecting Group Members

There are basically three methods for assigning group membership: random, student selection, and instructor determined.

Random

Instructors can form groups quickly and efficiently using a variety of random selection techniques. Random selection is ideal for most informal groups organized for short-term assignments, and it is also useful for breaking up longer-term formal or base groups to create variety. Students perceive this selection process as "fair," and although random selection does not guarantee heterogeneity, if used often, random grouping gives students opportunities to work with most or all of their classmates. Several techniques can help randomly form groups (McKeachie, 1994; Millis & Cottell, 1998; Silberman, 1996):

Free-Form Walk among the students and form groups as you go, simply pointing and saying, "You five are a group," "You four are a group," and so forth. If you point to students sitting next to each other, this method will tend to form homogeneous groups.

Odd-Even Walk up classroom aisles saying "Odd," "Even," "Odd," "Even" for each row, and then ask students in the "odd" row to turn around to talk to students in the "even" row behind, forming themselves into groups of four to six.

Count Off Ask students to count off in class. The first student starts with saying "One," the second "Two," and so on, counting up to the number of groups one wishes to have and then starting the cycle again. All of the "ones" form a group, all of the "twos" form a group, and so forth. This method tends to break up cliques of students sitting together.

Numbered Slips of Paper Distribute numbers written on slips of paper or have students select a number out of a hat or other container. This works well for large classes in which the number of students in the class could cause confusion in a count-off procedure.

Playing Cards Give a playing card to each student, distributing four cards of each kind (for example, four aces, four kings, four queens). Students find the other students with the same card rank to form groups of four. If you wish to form groups of five, add cards taken from another deck. If the class does not divide evenly, the one to three remaining students receive a wildcard (the joker) and they may choose a group to join, but no more than one student with a wildcard may join any one group.

Created Cards Make your own cards. Write on each card A-1 (for Group A, Member 1), A-2, B-1, B-2, and so forth, or use different discipline-based team names, colored dots, or decorative stickers to identify teams.

Line Up and Divide Ask students to line up in order of their birthdays (or in alphabetical order of their first or last names, or by height, and so forth). Break the line to form groups with the number of students needed for an activity.

Jigsaw Match-Ups Find a number of pictures or graphics, tear or cut each into pieces, and ask students to find others with matching pieces. This works well in geography, art, landscape design, or other courses where visual images are important.

Text Match-Ups Use a line from a poem or other text and have students find students with other lines from the same poem or text. This works particularly well in a course where recognition of language, literature, or other text passages is important.

Student Selection

Allowing students to choose their partners or group members can be a fast, efficient group-forming technique. Students may feel more comfortable and be more motivated to work together if they are permitted to choose their own group members (Brookfield & Preskill, 1999). However, student choice tends to create groups based on friendships, thus leaving some students feeling like outsiders and risking that students will stray off task. Student choice also tends to reinforce homogeneity and may fail to expose students to a rich diversity of ideas, values, and perspectives (Fiechtner & Davis, 1992). Unless there is some specific reason for allowing students to choose their own groups, it is probably better to assign students to groups. Following are techniques in which students select group members.

Free-Form Have students form groups with minimal instructions. You may wish to set an approximate number of students to work in each group. Ensure that every student is able to find a group.

Group Leader Choice Assign student leaders, and then ask leaders to select group members. Consider giving them criteria, such as asking them to choose students who have the most complementary skills to theirs, or who would provide the most diversity, or whom team leaders have not worked with before.

Team Hiring Set up a team hiring method (Hughes, 1996, cited in Millis & Cottell, 1998). Identify students who will function as "employers." These students are responsible for identifying the characteristics that will contribute best to the success of their team. Depending upon the assignment, these characteristics might include content knowledge, a specific group work skill (such as facilitation, research, or presentation skills), or certain demographic characteristics. Other students draw up résumés that identify their qualifications in terms of these characteristics. Team leaders are given equal amounts of "money" and a hiring budget to submit bids for the members they desire. After tabulating the bids, the instructor forms teams. This will work well in a class where "hiring" is related to the subject matter, such as in business or personnel management.

Instructor Determined

For formal or base groups, instructors often determine membership in groups. Organization can be based on student interests or student characteristics. Interest grouping is useful for motivating students and for assigning students to roles based upon a particular viewpoint, such as in *CoLT 10: Role Play* or *CoLT 6: Critical Debates.* The disadvantages of interest grouping are that it may reinforce homogeneity and students may not be comfortable having their views on certain topics aired publicly.

Selecting membership based on student characteristics is known as *stratification.* In stratified groups, instructors organize student characteristics (such as demographics or level of academic achievement) into similar "layers" and then use this information to create groups. Although this approach is generally used to create heterogeneous groups (with groups formed by choosing individuals from different strata), the same data can be used to create homogeneous groups. The following techniques are useful for sorting groups by interest or characteristics (Cooper, Prescott, Cook, Smith, Mueck, & Cuseo, 1990; Fiechtner & Davis, 1992; Millis & Cottell, 1998; Nurrenbern, 1995; Silberman, 1996).

Show of Hands Have students raise their hands to respond to a series of questions and assign groups based on responses.

Student Sign-Up Choose topics for students to investigate, write these on a sign-up sheet or post these on several signs around the room, and ask students to sign up for their preferences. Predetermine the number of slots available for each group, and allow students to sign up on a first-come, first-served basis, or leave the number of slots open and organize into groups after everyone has indicated their preference.

Single-Statement Likert Scale Rating Prepare a statement that encapsulates an important or controversial issue in the field on which attitudes and opinions will vary. Ask students to select from a five-point Likert scale the number that best describes their positions (1 = strongly agree to 5 = strongly disagree). Form groups based on the numbers they chose. For homogeneous groups, ask students to form groups of four with students who selected the same number. For heterogeneous groups, ask students to form groups with a 1, 2, 3, and 4 in each group.

Corners Designate a type of characteristic or a specific "interest" for each of the four corners of the room. For example, the corners might represent clusters of academic majors or answers to a multiple-choice question (such as "The greatest value of college life comes from (a) academic subjects studied; (b) social skills acquired; (c) networks formed with peers and professors; (d) the opportunity to interact with people of differing backgrounds, cultures and views") (Millis & Cottell, 1998, pp. 83–84). For homogeneous groups, assign students within each corner to the same group; for heterogeneous groups, assign one student from each corner to the same group.

Essay Ask students each to write an essay on a controversial statement or question, and form groups based on qualitative analysis of their comments.

Data Sheet Develop a data sheet that can be distributed with the syllabus to elicit demographic characteristics, skills, or academic information such as expertise in technology, academic major, the number of courses taken in the major, job-related experience, and so forth. Use this information to form either homogeneous or heterogeneous groups. Consider asking for telephone number, e-mail address, schedule of availability, and so forth to provide groups with information to facilitate communication. Allow students to check whether they are willing to have this information shared with other students.

Course-Based Test Scores Use pretest or recent test scores to form groups based on levels of knowledge.

Learning Style Select a personality or learning style inventory (such as Meyers-Briggs Type Indicator or the Firo-B) and form groups based on learning style profiles.

Discipline-Related Products Form groups based on an example of discipline-related achievement, such as a writing sample or a painting.

College-Based Achievement Ranking If the information is available, use past grades, standardized exams, or entrance examinations to list students by ranking and form groups based on demonstrated academic achievement.

The choice of selection method can be varied throughout the term, depending upon the learning activity. For example, random techniques work best for quick formation of informal groups, instructor-determined techniques work better for formal and base groups. Alternately, elements of different selection techniques can be combined, such as allowing students to identify three classmates with whom they would like to work, and then making an effort to assign one identified classmate to the requesting student's team.

Changing Group Members

Questions often arise over whether to change group membership frequently (in order to give students a chance to work with more people) or rarely (to give groups a chance to form strong working relationships). Most experienced teachers who use group work come down on the side of keeping groups intact for as long as possible. Even when groups appear to be deteriorating, as they sometimes do, Miller and colleagues argue that "teachers must have faith that in time they will pull out of their tailspin. Intervening immediately to shuffle the groups can set them back, lose hard-won experience, and force them to start all over again" (Miller, Trimbur, & Wilkes, 1994, p. 40). Groups take time to mature, and some of the most valuable learning experiences come from learning to work through difficult disagreements.

Assigning Roles to Group Members

Many instructors choose to assign (or allow students to select) specific group roles. A specific role gives each student a purpose for participating within the group and ensures that various aspects of a learning task are addressed. It also encourages interdependence among group members and thus helps improve group processes. Commonly used roles (such as

EXHIBIT 3.1

Break-Out 3
Forming Groups within Various Classroom Settings

Some types of classrooms are more conducive to group work than others, but faculty can include collaborative activities in any kind of classroom. The following are suggestions for achieving collaborative work in specific types of classrooms (adapted from Silberman, 1996, pp. 10–16).

Fixed Seat Auditorium or Lecture Hall	Students seated next to each other on the same level can form pairs or trios. Although pairs can turn around in their seats for a limited period of time to work with a pair behind them, activities may best be limited to short brainstorming or brief discussions. Since groups are unable to work together for long periods in uncomfortable conditions, more complex collaborative assignments should be done outside of scheduled class time.
Laboratories	Laboratories most often contain workstations where groups of students can work together. Depending upon the kind of laboratory, groups of different sizes can form and re-form throughout the class session. For example, in a computer laboratory, pairs might work best for an assignment, but for brief periods another pair could gather and look over their shoulders, forming a quad.
Moveable Desks	Students can form pairs or small groups. Because students do not have a single shared workspace, writing together or manipulating pieces of paper (such as in a graphic organizer CoLT) may be challenging.
Moveable Tables	The flexibility offered by this type of setting makes it ideal for a variety of group activities. In addition to pairs and pair-cluster arrangements, larger student teams can work together at a table. The tables can be pulled together to create one large conference table. The tables and chairs may also be arranged in a U-shape. Almost any kind of collaborative activity can be accomplished in this type of classroom.
Seminar	Organize the class into two or three teams; one team can work at the middle of the table, and the remaining teams can take different corners or ends of the table.
Large Classroom with Break-Out Space or Rooms	Students can come together for a large session and then spread out for teamwork. This classroom allows for groups to work independently on projects without disturbing other groups and is ideal for medium or long-term groups.
Online Class	Factors such as the level of student (lower division or graduate seminar?) and the size of the class (12 or 120?) influence how to form groups in online classes. In small classes with stable enrollment, it may work best to assign partners or triads early in the semester to work together throughout the term. In large classes with unstable enrollment and participation, it may work best to form larger groups of eight to twelve. Regardless of group size, identify groups (for example, Group A, Group B), assign membership, and provide groups with their own "space" to discuss their work (such as a Threaded Discussion Forum). Depending upon the nature of the assignment, consider providing only group members access to their group's discussion area. Consider creating these forums as adjuncts to a whole-class discussion area.

facilitator or recorder) quickly communicate the expected function and can get groups working fast and efficiently. Millis and Cottell (1998, pp. 54–55) define six common role assignments, shown in Exhibit 3.2, that work well in college level collaborative learning groups.

There are also other kinds of roles, such as roles that emerge out of a specific learning task. For example, in *CoLT 15: Case Study*, students might be asked to assume a role and view the case from the perspective of a chief executive officer, chief financial officer, board member, or stockholder. In *CoLT 17: Analytic Teams*, students might be asked to assume roles that focus on the analytic process, such as proponent, critic, summarizer, or example giver.

Not every group member needs to be assigned a role for every task. For example, a straightforward task such as an informal group generating a list using *CoLT 2: Round Robin* might require only one student to assume a recorder role. For long-term formal or base groups, rotating assigned roles gives all students opportunities to practice various social, communication, and leadership skills, and discourages domination by one person. Millis and Cottell summarize Miller's (1996) rationale for rotating role

---

EXHIBIT 3.2

Six Common Group Roles

Facilitator	Moderates all team discussions, keeping the group on task for each assignment and ensuring that everybody assumes their share of the work. Facilitators strive to make sure that all group members have the opportunity to learn, to participate, and to earn the respect of the other group members.
Recorder	Records any assigned team activities. Recorders take notes summarizing discussion, keep all necessary records (including data sheets such as attendance and homework check-offs), and complete worksheets or written assignments for submission to the instructor.
Reporter	Serves as group spokesperson and orally summarizes the group's activities or conclusions. Reporters also assist the recorder with the preparation of reports and worksheets.
Timekeeper	Keeps the group aware of time constraints, works with the facilitator to keep the group on task, and can also assume the role of any missing group member. The timekeeper is also responsible for any set-up and for ensuring that the team's work area is in good condition when the session ends.
Folder Monitor	If the instructor has created group work folders, the monitor picks up the team folder, distributes all material other than data sheets, and returns all papers, assignments, or notes to team members. Folder monitors ensure that all relevant class materials are in the folder at the end of the class session.
Wildcard	Assumes the role of any missing member or fills in however they are needed.

assignments, observing that students often "opt for tasks that come easily" and "circumvent tasks that challenge them. Assigning rotating roles in a group, a practice perceived as equitable, allows all students to be stretched by a variety of tasks" (Millis & Cottell, 1998, p. 54).

Millis and Cottell (1998) also offer suggestions for identifying role assignments at the same time groups are formed.

Using "Count Off" to Assign Roles If using the count-off method for group formation, then all "ones" are assigned the same role.

Playing Cards If using Playing Cards in which the rank of the card has determined the group, then the suit of the card determines the role. The joker card becomes the wildcard role assignment.

Conclusion

Teachers make various decisions as they form groups. They must choose the type (informal, formal, or base), the size (generally two to six students), and determine whether they want group membership to be homogeneous or heterogeneous. They must then choose a method for selecting group members (random, student, or instructor determined) and decide which roles, if any, they wish to assign. The issues that attend these choices are important. While we want students to learn course concepts, we also want them to develop collaborative skills. While we want students to be motivated and comfortable, we also want to challenge thinking and promote diversity. While we want students to forge long-lasting relationships and give them sufficient time to cohere as groups, we also want them to meet new people. Thus many factors influence how teachers form groups.

Chapter 4

Structuring the Learning Task

CENTRAL TO IMPLEMENTING COLLABORATIVE learning effectively is constructing the learning task itself. Although students are charged with taking responsibility for their own learning in collaborative learning, the responsibility for defining and structuring the learning task lies with the instructor. Miller and her colleagues warn that "a common mistake of teachers in first adopting an active learning strategy is to relinquish structure along with control, and the common result is for students to feel frustrated and disoriented" (Miller, Groccia, & Wilkes, 1996, p. 17). There is a difference between structure and control. In traditional lecture/discussion classes, the teacher retains control of the procedures minute by minute, determining what is discussed, when, and by whom. In collaborative learning, the teacher structures the learning situation so that students can take control of the learning process. The question is not *whether* to structure the learning situation, but *how.*

The two most critical elements in constructing the collaborative learning situation are (1) designing an appropriate learning task, and (2) structuring procedures to engage students actively in performing that task. If the learning task is not suitable, or if it is not clearly understood by students, activities will lag, attention will wander, and frustration will abound. Unless procedures are planned in advance, students will flounder, waste time, and fail to benefit from interaction with their fellow students.

The CoLTs described in Part Three assist instructors in these two important duties. The *procedures* of the CoLTs are carefully spelled out in detail. Most of the CoLTs come from the literature and have survived the test of time by teachers using and modifying them for use in their own classrooms. Examples of *learning tasks* are given for each CoLT in several disciplines, providing teachers with a model to serve as a starting point. But because good learning tasks are so essential, we provide additional practical advice on structuring them in this chapter. Advice is organized in three areas: an overview of the general elements to keep in mind when structuring the task, specific suggestions for designing task prompts, and ideas for integrating tasks into a broader course framework.

General Considerations When Structuring the Task

There are several general considerations to keep in mind when structuring the task in collaborative learning (adapted from Davis, 1993, pp. 147–154). First, make sure that the assignment is relevant and integral to achieving course objectives so that it does not feel like "busy work." Second, take care to match the task to students' skills and abilities. For example, don't assign a complex *CoLT 6: Critical Debate* if students have low-level speaking, analysis, investigation, and presentation skills.

Third, design the task to promote interdependence, so that each member is responsible to and dependent upon the others to succeed. One way to help achieve this is to make the task sufficiently complex so that it provides opportunities for broad participation and perhaps even requires students to divide up the labor in order to complete the task. Try as well to structure the task so that each member can contribute equally and the labor can be divided fairly.

Fourth, try to ensure individual accountability. Individuals need to know that they must do their share of the work. This can be accomplished by implementing a grading structure that assesses and evaluates individual student performance as well as group performance. Individual accountability can also be promoted by giving impromptu quizzes, calling on individuals to present their group's progress, or providing students with a mechanism to deal with uncooperative or "easy rider" students. See Chapter Six, Grading and Evaluating Collaborative Learning for additional ideas to ensure accountability.

Finally, plan for each phase of the collaborative activity, from how to form groups to how group work will be evaluated. (See the introduction to Part Three, Collaborative Learning Techniques, for specific elements in each phase.) The CoLTs in Part Three also help teachers in this regard, as each technique offers advice on the size and type of groups, explains any special preparation required, gives step-by-step procedures, estimates the approximate time the task will take, and often provides suggestions for closing activities and assessment. Still, the creative work of designing the "prompt" that actually starts the collaborative group work is course-specific and is the responsibility of the teacher.

Designing the Learning Task Prompt

What is it that we want students to learn? Most learning tasks start with a question to be addressed or a problem to be solved. Modern research in cognition is confirming John Dewey's basic premise that significant learning starts with the learner's active engagement with a problem. The "problems" that are presented vary by discipline, of course, but Bean (1996, p. 152) advises that generally speaking, learning tasks should be open-ended, requiring critical thinking with supporting evidence or arguments. Tasks should promote controversy, result in some type of group product, and be directed toward a learning goal of the course.

Exhibit 4.1 provides a number of question or problem "stems" for structuring the task prompt. The prompt stems in Exhibit 4.1 provide ideas that can be adapted to a variety of learning activities. An application question such as *How does ____ apply to ____?* could be used to prompt a *CoLT 3: Buzz Group* discussion, or it could be used as one of the study guide questions that students prepare for in *CoLT 12: Test-Taking Teams,* or it might be used as one of several suggestions for students to use in *CoLT 26: Dyadic Essays.*

Incorporating collaborative work into other class activities may help deepen student learning. For example, *CoLT 1: Think-Pair-Share* is an effective strategy for breaking up a lecture and increasing student participation in discussion. *CoLT 7: Note-Taking Pairs* is a technique in which partners cross-check notes for missing information and inaccuracies, thus helping students create a superior, combined set of notes. Courses organized around service learning or problem-based learning are examples of this approach. In a course that emphasizes service learning, *CoLT 24: Dialogue Journals* helps students share observations and reflect upon their own as well as others' experiences. In courses organized around problem-based learning, *CoLT 13: Think-Aloud Pair Problem Solving (TAPPS)* and *CoLT 16: Structured Problem Solving* offer procedures for students to practice and improve problem-solving skills together.

Creating Tasks That Connect to Broader Course Design

Fink (2003) observes wryly that in his experience, professors put together courses using one of two main approaches. The first approach is to create a list of eight to twelve topics–drawn either from the teacher's own understanding of the subject or from the table of contents of a good textbook—and then develop a series of lectures to go with it. He notes, "With the addition of a midterm exam or two plus a final, the course is ready to go." This approach is fast and efficient, but Fink argues it focuses on the organization

EXHIBIT 4.1

Sample Task Prompts

Question Type	Purpose	Example
Exploratory	Probe facts and basic knowledge	What research evidence supports ____?
Challenge	Examine assumptions, conclusions, and interpretations	How else might we account for ____?
Relational	Ask for comparison of themes, ideas, or issues	How does ____compare to ____?
Diagnostic	Probe motives or causes	Why did ____?
Action	Call for a conclusion or action	In response to ____, what should ____ do?
Cause and effect	Ask for causal relationships between ideas, actions, or events	If ____occurred, what would happen?
Extension	Expand the discussion	What are additional ways that ____?
Hypothetical	Pose a change in the facts or issues	Suppose ____ had been the case, would the outcome have been the same?
Priority	Seek to identify the most important issue	From all that we have discussed, what is the most important____?
Summary	Elicit syntheses	What themes or lessons have emerged from ____?
Problem	Challenge students to find solutions to real or hypothetical situations	What if? (To be motivating, students should be able to make some progress on finding a solution, and there should be more than one solution.)
Interpretation	Help students to uncover the underlying meaning of things	From whose viewpoint or perspective are we seeing, hearing, reading? What does this mean? or, What may have been intended by ...?
Application	Probe for relationships and ask students to connect theory to practice	How does this apply to that? or, Knowing this, how would you ...?
Evaluative	Require students to assess and make judgments	Which of these are better? Why does it matter? and, So what?
Critical	Require students to examine the validity of statements, arguments, and conclusions and to analyze their thinking and challenge their own assumptions	How do we know? and, What's the evidence and how reliable is the evidence?

Source: Davis, 1993, pp. 83–84; McKeachie, 1999, pp. 51–52

of information, paying little or no attention to how that information will be learned. Furthermore, it emphasizes coverage of information, which tends to support superficial learning that is quickly forgotten. Fink prefers a second, alternative approach that he describes as "learner centered." A learner-centered approach requires teachers to determine what would constitute high-quality learning in a given situation and then design "that quality into the course and into the learning experience" (p. 61).

In practice, most teachers probably blend elements of both approaches when they organize their courses. But his distinction between a content-coverage and a learning-centered approach is useful. While incorporating collaborative activities into a content-coverage approach may help deepen student learning, it is possible that the activities will feel as though they are simply "add-ons." Collaborative learning tasks will most likely be more compelling and effective if they are integrated into a course that has been designed to be learner centered.

There are several models for creating a learner-centered course, but most incorporate the common elements of (1) determining the learning goals and objectives, (2) identifying activities that help students achieve the objectives, and (3) creating formative assessment strategies to ascertain how well students are achieving the objectives in order to make adjustments. Following are two models that structure collaborative learning tasks so that they reflect a learner-centered approach. The first uses Bloom's Taxonomy of Educational Objectives (1956), and the second uses Angelo and Cross's Teaching Goals Inventory and Classroom Assessment Techniques (1993).

Bloom's Taxonomy of Educational Objectives

Curriculum frameworks and individual teachers often refer to Bloom's taxonomy for guidance on creating learning activities and assessment strategies that address multiple levels of learning. Bloom's taxonomy was created by a group of educational psychologists to classify levels of behavior important in learning. It includes three overlapping domains: cognitive, affective, and psychomotor. The cognitive taxonomy is referred to most frequently and consists of six levels of learning, including knowledge, comprehension, application, analysis, synthesis, and evaluation. Although some individuals and organizations in higher education are suggesting new taxonomies (and we look at two examples of alternative taxonomies in the Appendix), the general familiarity with Bloom's taxonomy makes it a useful starting point.

Using the taxonomy as a guiding framework for designing a learner-centered course might involve (1) identifying the most important educational objectives (for example, beginning courses may need to concentrate on developing students' knowledge and comprehension, while advanced courses can shift emphasis to synthesis and evaluation), (2) crafting learning activities that focus on the corresponding level of learning, and (3) creating evaluation strategies that assess learning at the appropriate level.

Arguably, the most effective courses tend to reflect the entire taxonomy in the goals, activities, and assessment. Even in beginning courses, students should be synthesizing and evaluating, just as in advanced courses, students should be acquiring new knowledge. Also, attempting to include the entire span of thinking and learning levels addresses student diversity. As Davis points out, "If assignments and exams include easier and harder questions, every student will have a chance to experience success as well as challenge" (1993, p. 197). One of the primary benefits of collaborative learning is that each activity can achieve multiple objectives. For ease of illustration, however, suggestions for CoLTs with examples of tasks that focus on learning at single levels of Bloom's cognitive hierarchy follow.

Knowledge

Knowledge involves remembering previously learned material such as definitions, principles, and formulas. Task prompts typically contain words such as *define, recall, recognize, remember, who, what, where, how,* and *when.*

CoLT 2: Round Robin To ensure students are actively listening during lecture, form small groups and ask students to generate a list as they recall important pieces of information from a recent lecture. For example, after a lecture on the determination of national income in an economics course, ask students to *List and define as many concepts regarding the determination of national income as you can recall from today's lecture.* Students in each group speak, moving from one student to the next, so that each student has an opportunity to contribute.

CoLT 7: Note-Taking Pairs Ask students to pool information from their individual notes on lectures, reading assignments, or other learning activities. For example, after reading and taking notes on an article about Chinese immigration to the United States, form pairs and ask students to work together to create an improved, partner version of their notes.

CoLT 20: Group Grid Form groups and provide students with pieces of information that they place in the blank cells of a grid. For example, sort this list of authors, genres, time frames, and quotes into the appropriate rows or columns of this grid.

Comprehension

Comprehension involves understanding the meaning of remembered material, usually demonstrated by restating or citing examples. Typical words used for assignments include *describe, compare, contrast, rephrase, put in your own words,* and *explain the main idea.*

CoLT 1: Think-Pair-Share After lecturing on a topic, present a prompt such as *Explain the main idea behind _____. How does what I just talked about (or demonstrated) compare with _____? Summarize in your own words_____.* Ask students to think individually for a few minutes, and then pair up with a classmate to discuss and compare their responses in pairs before sharing with the entire class.

CoLT 21: Team Matrix Form pairs or small groups and ask students to discriminate between similar concepts by noticing and marking on a chart the presence or absence of important, defining features. For example, *To demonstrate your understanding of the differences between Modernism and Postmodernism, put a checkmark in the column indicating which of the two is most clearly defined by the following list of features.*

CoLT 24: Dialogue Journals For a longer-term project, ask students to record their thoughts in a journal that they exchange with peers for comments and questions. Occasionally ask students to respond to specific, comprehension-based prompts. For example, *In your journal tonight, write five examples of similes, five examples of analogies, and five examples of metaphors.*

Application

Application involves using information in a new context to solve a problem, answer a question, or perform a task. Prompts include words such as *apply, classify, use, choose, write an example,* and *solve.*

CoLT 3: Buzz Groups Form small groups and ask students to discuss questions such as, *What are additional examples of _____? How could _____ be used to _____? How does _____ apply to your life outside of school?*

CoLT 10: Role Play Create a scenario and ask students to act out or assume identities that require them to apply their knowledge, skills, or understanding as they speak and act from a different, assigned perspective. For example, in a business sales class, pair students and ask one to be the salesperson and the other the potential client as they apply a structured sales technique.

CoLT 13: Think-Aloud Pair Problem Solving (TAPPS) Form student pairs and ask students to take turns solving problems aloud to try out their reasoning as their partners listen. For example, in a music fundamentals class, distribute a handout containing a variety of different intervals and ask students to take turns identifying the quantity and quality for each interval.

Analysis

Analysis involves thinking critically and in depth; breaking a concept into its parts and explaining the interrelationships; distinguishing relevant from extraneous material. Task prompts include words such as *identify motives/causes, draw conclusions, determine evidence, support, analyze,* and *why does this happen?*

CoLT 6: Critical Debates Form teams and ask students to analyze an issue in preparation for a debate. For example, in a biology class, ask students to consider the statement, *Individuals should be allowed to sell one of their kidneys to a wealthy person in need of a kidney.* Ask students to develop arguments and determine evidence that support the side of the issue that is in opposition to their personal views.

CoLT 8: Learning Cell Ask students to develop questions about a reading assignment or other learning activity. Provide them with sample analysis question stems, such as, *Explain why (or how) _____. What are the strengths and weaknesses, pros and cons, costs and benefits, and so forth of _____? Why is _____ happening? How does _____affect _____? Why is _____important? What do you think causes _____ and why?* Form pairs and have the students answer the questions their partners created.

CoLT 23: Word Webs Ask students to analyze a course-related concept such as *clinical depression* or *networking technology* by generating a list of related ideas and then organizing them in a graphic, identifying relationships by drawing lines or arrows to represent the connections.

Synthesis Skills

These skills involve putting parts together to form a new whole; solving a problem requiring creativity or originality. Task prompts include words such as *predict, produce, write, design, develop, synthesize, construct, how can we improve, what would happen if, can you devise, how can we solve.*

CoLT 17: Analytic Teams Form teams and ask individuals to perform component tasks of an analysis of a reading assignment, video, or presentation. For example, in an introductory science course, assign tasks such as summarizer, supporter, and critic to individuals in small groups and then ask them to read an article that attempts to nullify evolutionary theory. Ask students to integrate their perspectives into a composite essay.

CoLT 18: Group Investigation Have student teams plan, conduct, and report on an in-depth project, such as *Investigate the origin and development of Black American English.*

CoLT 29: Team Anthologies Have student teams compile and annotate an anthology of course-related materials. For example, in a course on education, ask students to *Create an annotated anthology of articles that address home schooling.*

Evaluation

Evaluation involves using a set of criteria to arrive at a reasoned judgment of the value of something. Key words include *evaluate, assess,* and *appraise.*

CoLT 5: Three-Step Interview Have student pairs take turns interviewing each other, asking questions that require a student to assess the value of competing claims, and then make a judgment as to the best. For example, *Which of these recorded performances of Bach's Prelude and Fugue in C Minor do you find most historically accurate, and why?*

CoLT 11: Jigsaw Form small groups and ask students to develop knowledge about a given topic and formulate the most effective ways of teaching it to others. For example, in a survey of international business course, ask groups to *Develop their best strategies for teaching fellow students about the trade opportunities in different Third World and developing nations.*

CoLT 30: Paper Seminar Assign individual students to write an original paper and then present it to a small group for evaluative feedback and discussion.

Created by cognitive psychologists, Bloom's taxonomy organizes learning into a hierarchy of levels that can be used as a framework to guide design of learning objectives, activities, and assessment. Angelo and Cross (1993) developed a different framework that emerged out of the higher education assessment movement.

Angelo and Cross's Teaching Goals Inventory (TGI) and Classroom Assessment Techniques (CATs)

Angelo and Cross (1993) observe that "learning can and often does take place without the benefit of teaching—and sometimes even in spite of it—but there is no such thing as effective teaching in the absence of learning. Teaching without learning is just talking" (p. 3). But how do teachers know how well students are learning? *Classroom Assessment Techniques* provides advice and procedures to help teachers become effective assessors of student learning in order to improve their teaching.

Identifying goals is an important starting point for assessing student learning. Rather than viewing goals as terminal destinations, however, Angelo and Cross see goals as "reference points that we use to measure our progress and to determine whether we are headed in the right direction. Without clear goals, we cannot readily assess the effectiveness of our efforts or realize when we are off course, how far off we are, and how to get back on the right track" (p. 13). Thus, in addition to endpoints, they suggest establishing goals to serve as guideposts for formative assessment of student learning. Clarifying one's goals can guide decisions on the learning tasks and assist teachers in assessing whether or not students are learning what teachers are trying to teach.

In an effort to help teachers identify, clarify, and rank teaching goals, Angelo and Cross began constructing the self-scorable Teaching Goals Inventory (TGI) in 1986. Field tested and repeatedly revised from 1987 through 1990, they settled on the current version. This inventory is available in the book (Angelo & Cross, 1993, pp. 393–397) and online at http://www.uiowa.edu/~centeach/tgi/index.html.

The TGI consists of a series of fifty-two teaching goal statements such as, "Develop analytic skills," "Improve writing skills," "Develop an informed historical perspective," "Develop leadership skills," and "Cultivate a sense of responsibility for one's own behavior."

In completing the TGI, teachers rate the importance of each goal from 1 (not applicable) to 5 (essential). The inventory organizes these fifty-two goals into six clusters:

1. Higher-Order Thinking Skills

2. Basic Academic Success Skills

3. Discipline-Specific Knowledge and Skills

4. Liberal Arts and Academic Values

5. Work and Career Preparation

6. Personal Development

Teachers can see how many goals they rated as essential and compute cluster scores. The advantage of the TGI is that individual teachers have distinctive profiles that emerge out of some combination of individually determined ranking of fifty-two instructional goals. The uniqueness of each individual profile is noted in the variation the authors observed while field testing the TGI:

> In the first administration of the Teaching Goals Inventory (TGI) in 1988, we found that every one of the forty-eight instructional goals included in the TGI received the full range of responses. For example, a goal that some teachers rated "essential" was rated "irrelevant" by some of their colleagues at the same institution (Cross and Fideler, 1988). When we administered a revised version of the TGI in 1990, the same pattern of responses emerged in response to the fifty-two goals on that inventory. Individual faculty members do not think in the aggregate, of course, and their goals are often quite different one from the other. Even two instructors of the same sex and age group, teaching in the same department at the same college, may legitimately have different instructional goals for the same course. (Angelo & Cross, 1993, p. 27)

The TGI helps teachers identify broad goals, but instructors still need to personalize and contextualize the goal for a specific course. To guide this step, Angelo and Cross suggest instructors use *CAT 13: One Sentence Summary* and answer the question, *Who does what to/for whom, when, where, how, and why?* and then cobble the answers into one summary sentence (p. 41).

Using Collaborative Learning Techniques to Implement This Model

Angelo and Cross provide an example of a second-semester calculus teacher who might identify Cluster I Goal 3 (to help students develop effective problem-solving skills) as essential. A summary sentence that translates this general teaching goal into a course-specific goal would be,

Who: I (the calculus teacher)
Does what: want to develop my students' skill at figuring out which questions to ask next
To/for whom: (my students)
When: when they don't know how to solve a problem
Where: in their homework assignments
How: by teaching them a variety of techniques for getting "unstuck"
Why: so that they can become more effective, independent problem solvers. (p. 43)

This course-specific goal becomes the basis from which to craft related, focused assessable questions. Three examples of assessable questions derived from this goal include:

1. *How accurately can my students now determine when, where, and why they have gotten "stuck" when they cannot solve a given problem?*

2. *What kinds of questions do my students ask themselves when they feel stuck?*

3. *What techniques do they use now to get "unstuck" when they don't know how to solve a particular problem? (p. 43)*

An assessment project that might help answer these questions would include the specific assessment technique *CAT 21: Documented Problem Solutions* (pp. 222–225). This CAT prompts students to keep track of—and briefly explain in writing—the steps they take in solving a problem. When the teacher reviews these detailed protocols, he or she can gain valuable insights into students' problem-solving skills. For example, using this CAT as a diagnostic pretest, the calculus teacher might prepare three or four problems of increasing difficulty and give students the problem set along with instructions to indicate when and where, and explain why they have become stuck when they cannot solve one of the problems. Depending upon the information and patterns the professor finds as he or she reviews the students' work, the professor might implement one or more of the following CoLTs:

CoLT 9: Fishbowl Review the *CAT 21* student responses and look for particularly good explanations of problem-solving reasoning. Ask these students to model their strategies to other students through a fishbowl arrangement in which they form an inner circle, and ask the observing students to form an outer circle. If there are several students with good understanding of the problem-solving techniques, form several "small" fishbowls.

CoLT 11: Jigsaw Jigsaw takes advantage of the observation that one of the best ways to learn something is to have to teach it. Divide students into small groups (ignoring individual student ability, as demonstrated in the *CAT 21* responses) with each group assigned to a specific type of problem. Ask students to work to formulate effective ways of teaching problem-solving strategies for that kind of problem to another group of students. When students have had sufficient time to master their type of problem and determine ways to help others learn how to solve it, student groups are reformed into "jigsaw" groups that contain an "expert" in each type of problem, who is responsible for teaching techniques for solving their type of problem to their group.

CoLT 13: Think-Aloud Pair Problem Solving (TAPPS) Review the students' explanation of their problem-solving steps and identify the type of problem most students got stuck on, paying particular attention to a specific step that seemed most troublesome. Then form student pairs and give students a series of similar problems. Ask students to alternate roles of "problem solver" and "listener," switching with each problem. The problem solver "thinks aloud," talking through the steps of solving a problem while the partner listens. The listener follows the steps, attempts to understand the reasoning behind the steps, and offers suggestions if the problem solver makes a misstep.

Additional Course Design Models

For readers interested in exploring how collaborative activities might be structured within other learner-centered curricular frameworks, we provide two additional models in the Appendix. The first model is drawn from Wiggins and McTighe's *Understanding by Design* (1998). This model uses a "backward design" approach to create a course that emphasizes teaching for deep, enduring understanding. To help identify whether students have achieved enduring understanding, Wiggins and McTighe created a taxonomy that consists of six facets of learning: explanation, interpretation, application, perspective, empathy, and self-knowledge. Backward design proposes that teachers identify what in their course is worthy of deep understanding, determine what would constitute evidence that students have developed deep understanding, and then create the appropriate learning activities.

The second model is Fink's "integrated design" to create "significant learning experiences" described in *Creating Significant Learning Experiences* (2003). To guide teachers in designing significant learning experiences, Fink constructed a taxonomy that, like Wiggins and McTighe's, is relational and interactive rather than hierarchical. It consists of foundational knowledge, application, integration, human dimension, caring, and learning how to learn. His integrated design combines this taxonomy with a teaching strategy, active learning, and formative, educative assessment. Both models are described more fully along with examples incorporating collaborative learning techniques in the Appendix.

Conclusion

Structuring the learning task requires that instructors know what benefits they expect to be derived from student participation in learning groups, what specific learning goals they wish to accomplish, and how to define and launch the probes that start the learning. Faculty will incorporate collaborative learning on a continuum: some will continue to use a primary teaching strategy such as lecture/discussion, employing CoLTs simply to break up the time or vary the activities. Others will organize their entire course around collaboration and will want to find multiple ways to incorporate collaborative activities. Wherever teachers are on this continuum, designing and structuring the learning task is central to implementing collaborative learning effectively. The two critical aspects in this construction are designing an appropriate task and structuring procedures to engage students actively in performing the task. This chapter provided ideas for accomplishing both aspects of task design.

Chapter 5

Facilitating Student Collaboration

AFTER LEARNING TASKS HAVE been designed and assigned, the instructor's task is to help groups work effectively. This chapter, therefore, focuses on facilitating student collaboration. It includes advice on introducing the collaborative activity, observing and interacting with groups, addressing problems, choosing reporting out techniques, and helping groups achieve closure.

Introducing the Activity

The manner in which teachers introduce the task sets the tone for the activity. Following are some suggestions for introducing the activity so that students understand the task clearly (Johnson, Johnson, & Smith, 1998; University of Waterloo, 2000):

- *Explain the activity.* Providing students with a basic overview helps students see "the big picture."

- *Clarify the objectives.* Telling students the purpose of the activity offers an opportunity to relate the task to larger class goals and prior knowledge or to suggest new concepts that will be addressed, thus helping students see the benefit of the activity.

- *Outline the procedures.* Describing exactly what students are going to do in a step-by-step format minimizes or eliminates confusion during the activity itself. Procedures may be presented orally, written on the whiteboard, distributed as a handout, or outlined (perhaps with a flow chart or sequential diagram) on an overhead transparency or presentation software slide. Providing written procedures is helpful to all students, but it is particularly helpful to some kinds of learners, such as hearing-impaired or ESL students. Written procedures are essential if the activity is complex, long-term, or if the groups will leave the room to work.

- *Present examples if needed.* Providing a concrete example that illustrates the process or shows a model final product can help students get a clearer idea of what they need to do.

- *Remind groups of the rules for group interaction.* Reviewing or establishing ground rules helps prevent future problems. Particularly if groups will work together for a long period of time, review policies and procedures for working with each other, mentioning, for example, aspects such as mutual respect, active listening, the signal that will be used to indicate a shift from group work to whole-class work, and techniques for group decision making. See Chapter Two, Orienting Students, for suggestions on how to involve students in developing rules.

- *Set time limits.* Establishing a time limit helps students pace themselves. If the estimate is on the low side, students may work quickly and efficiently, and the time limit can always be extended if needed. On the other hand, if the estimate is on the high side, some students may take time to be more reflective. If many groups finish more quickly than you had anticipated, shorten the time. Be prepared for groups to finish at different times, however, and have in mind extension activities such as additional questions (perhaps for bonus points) that keep groups occupied until all groups finish.

- *Provide the prompt.* Most often, prompts will come in the form of questions or problems, but they may also include short topics or statements for exploration or debate. (See Chapter Four, Structuring the Learning Task.) It may be appropriate to include the prompt with the procedures.

- *Query the students for understanding, and let students ask questions.* Asking students whether they have questions before they begin the activity will provide an opportunity to clarify any aspects of the activity that may still be confusing.

Observing and Interacting with Groups

Observing student groups can help teachers acquire information about group interaction, identify problems, and determine if students are achieving learning goals. As teachers observe, they might notice, for example, whether students are staying on task, whether one student is dominating, or whether tensions are brewing. Observation provides information about when things are going well; it also creates opportunities to redirect students or to probe them with questions to promote deeper learning. Knowing such information can help teachers organize groups or modify tasks for future collaborative activities.

Observation should be as unobtrusive as possible so that it does not interfere with natural group processes: circulate among the groups, but don't hover. In collaborative learning, we want students to assume responsibility. If the teacher is nearby, students tend to seek direction. Furthermore, faculty presence can have unintended consequences, such as stifling group discussion. It may be appropriate to leave the room for a *short* time so that students have the opportunity to share uncertainties and disagreements without having the faculty member present (Jaques, 2000).

While most often students should work on their own, there are times when they will want and need teacher interaction. When teachers do interact with the students, the interaction should be supportive rather than directive. In supportive interaction, the instructor and the students are mutually responsible for the learning that occurs in the classroom. Johnson and Johnson (1984) and Silberman (1996, pp. 24–26) suggest several strategies that instructors can employ that help provide supportive rather than directive supervision.

- *Be available to clarify instruction, review procedures, and answer questions about the assignment.* Students may believe they understand the assignments and instructions, but upon meeting with other group members, find that they have different interpretations about what they should do. The instructor should be able to clarify these points for students early on so that they do not spend time struggling with the wrong assignment.

- *Paraphrase or ask a question to clarify what a student has said.* Students sometimes state ideas in a way that other students may not immediately get. If group members look puzzled by a student's comments, ask a question that can help the student restate the point and clarify it for the group. Or paraphrase what the student has contributed. This can be reinforcing for the student, demonstrating that his or her idea has been transmitted and understood and helping make it clearer for other students.

- *Compliment the student on an interesting or insightful comment.* Students need reinforcement, and complimenting a student can be a powerful motivator.

- *Elaborate on a student's statement or suggest a new perspective.* Stopping to share with the group a new perspective on an idea can help the group delve into deeper levels of thinking about a topic.

- *Energize by using humor or by asking for additional contributions.* This can be particularly helpful when students are struggling with complex material and have become frustrated. It can help students put things into perspective, and make class fun.

- *Disagree with a student comment, but be gentle.* Instructors are sometimes hesitant to correct students for fear of stifling their creativity and causing students to be more reluctant to speak the next time, but if you overhear misinformation, it is important to correct it. If done gently and tactfully, students will appreciate that they got the correct response. It is also important for them to recognize that there is a difference of opinion or another side to the issue. Pointed questions are also a good way to redirect the conversation.

- *Mediate between students.* If students are having trouble working together, try to let them work it out, but if the conflict is escalating and the discussion is becoming heated, intervene to prevent a permanent breach. A statement like, "These are both very good points," or "You can see why there is so much controversy about this issue," or "Both sides have very good arguments" can help ease tensions.

- *Pull together ideas by pointing out relationships.* Students do not have the same familiarity with the course concepts that instructors do. If groups are struggling with making connections between ideas and information, remind them how the task they're performing relates to something they studied previously or to something current in the news.

- *Summarize the group's major views.* Ascertain the group's major views in order to note the connections between group ideas and prepare for moving to a full-class discussion. This will also validate the work that students have been doing, and it can help them mentally review the major points of discussion.

It may also be useful to share these strategies with group leaders so that they have guidelines for interacting effectively with team members.

Addressing Problems

Much of the responsibility for facilitating group work lies with the group members themselves. Although collaborative learning activities can run smoothly and without incident, the instructor should be prepared to address problems. General interventions include not taking individual student behavior personally, getting to know students at a personal level, ignoring mild behaviors, forming groups to maximize personality strengths and minimize weaknesses, varying group size, discussing extreme problems in private or suggesting students seek professional assistance, and as a last effort, regrouping (Johnson & Johnson, 1987; Silberman, 1996).

Next we identify specific strategies for addressing some common group work problems. The information comes from a variety of sources

(Culbertson, 2000–2001; Johnson & Johnson, 1987; McKeachie, 2002; Millis & Cottell, 1998; Silberman, 1996; University of Waterloo, 2000), our own experiences, and the experiences of faculty with whom we have worked throughout the years. Many of the problems arise when groups are not self-facilitating. Even so, it is important to remember not to jump in too hastily to try to solve problems, particularly since the problem may just be a normal stage of group development. Tuckman's (1965) classic article on the stages of group work suggests that groups go through five stages of development. In the *Forming* stage, group members get to know one another and shape mutual expectations. In the *Storming* stage, learners test out their

---

EXHIBIT 5.1

Break-Out 4

Group Decision-Making Techniques

Groups must sometimes make important decisions, but because many students have had little training in reaching a group decision, arriving at a decision can be challenging. Explaining to groups some common approaches to decision making can improve the process (University of Waterloo, 2000).

Authority	The group generates ideas and holds open discussions, but one person such as the group leader makes the final decision. This method is a quick decision-making technique, but it does not maximize the strengths of the individuals in the group, and the group may not be motivated to implement a decision made by one person.
Majority	After a period of discussion, the group holds a vote on the issue at hand, and the majority wins. This method has the advantage of relying on the democratic process, but the majority often overwhelms minority views and may have the effect of encouraging factionalism.
Negative Minority	The group holds a vote for the most unpopular idea, eliminates it, and votes again until only one idea is left. This method has the advantage of being democratic and can build consensus when there are many ideas and few voters. However it is time consuming, and some group members may feel resentful if their ideas prove unpopular.
Consensus	The group discusses and negotiates a discussion until everyone affected by it understands and supports the decision. This technique has the advantage of allowing all members to feel that they have had an opportunity to express themselves and to influence the decision. Group members will be likely to support a decision made by consensus. However, it may be difficult to reach a consensus, and the method can be extremely time consuming.
Using Criteria	Participants explore, identify, and agree on criteria for a successful solution, and then they evaluate alternatives against these criteria. This method has the advantage of giving an objective measure of the quality of a solution; however, it can be difficult to come up with appropriate criteria.
Compromise	Rather than making a single decision that excludes other decisions, groups create a compromise decision, perhaps combining multiple solutions into one. In this way, groups avoid either/or decisions, but implementation may take longer because more than one idea is being considered.

relationships with one another and struggle with individual members' level of commitment. When they proceed to *Norming,* students clarify group norms, members' roles, and relationships among people. As they engage in the *Performing* stage, the work takes place. Finally, in the *Adjourning* phase, the group's work is done and people part from each other. Although no group will follow these steps exactly, awareness of these stages may help you recognize where students are in the group development process so that you avoid subverting natural group progression.

Inequitable Participation

Unequal participation is a challenging problem in the collaborative classroom. Some students want to dominate, monopolizing conversations and taking over the group project. Other students say little or nothing, come unprepared, and contribute little to the activity. The strategies for addressing either over- or under-participation are similar.

Use techniques like *CoLT 1: Think-Pair-Share* or *CoLT 19: Affinity Grouping* that build into the activity quiet reflection time so that domineering students must be quiet and receding students get a chance to prepare their comments. Or use activities like *CoLT 4: Talking Chips* or *CoLT 2: Round Robin* that structure participation so that everyone contributes more or less equally. Consider assigning a role that requires students to perform in appropriate ways. For example, assign the domineering student largely "silent" task roles such as recorder, timekeeper, or end-of-activity summarizer; assign the quiet student a task that requires speaking, such as spokesperson, facilitator, or group leader.

Consider talking with the student privately. Explain to the over-participating student that while you are pleased that he or she has much to contribute and is so engaged, other members of the group should have time to express their views as well. When talking to the under-participating student, try to determine the cause of his or her reticence, as this will help to identify solutions. If the reason is shyness or minimal English language skills, consider forming pairs or smaller groups to increase the student's comfort level. Use one or more icebreakers to help students build trust (see Chapter Two, Orienting Students). Provide online discussion opportunities so that these students can think about and write out their comments before posting. If the reason is selfishness or laziness, make sure the activity has built in ways to ensure individual accountability and that there are clear consequences for lack of participation (see Chapter 6, Grading and Evaluating Collaborative Learning). Finally, reform groups often so that no one suffers an excessively domineering or under-participating student for long.

Student Resistance to Group Work

Student resistance to collaborative work may manifest in several ways: undermining the group work, complaining about it, or demonstrating anger or hostility to group members. Find out the reason for the resistance. For example, if resistance is due to previous bad experiences with group work, ask students to identify problems and then suggest solutions. Involve students in establishing Group Ground Rules and incorporate these into a Learning Contract. Make sure that you have built into the task interdependence and individual accountability and that the rewards (and penalties) are clear. Make every effort to craft good tasks and implement appropriate structure so that the potential pitfalls of collaborative work are minimized or eliminated. Consider taking time to do a more extensive orientation to the benefits of collaborative learning (such as involving students in a game that demonstrates the value of group cooperation over individual competition, or emphasizing, for example, the importance of collaborative skills for future employment). See Chapter Two, Orienting Students, for additional ideas.

Students with poorly developed interpersonal skills may be quite vocal that they learn better alone than in a group. Often these students are good students, but they may become belligerent when assigned to groups. This student may feel like he or she has "learned the game" in the traditional class and doesn't want to learn a new game. To encourage such a student to participate, use an activity that requires all to participate, such as *CoLT 17: Analytic Teams* or *CoLT 30: Paper Seminar*. Structure the reward system in your course (that is, grades) to value the group work.

Off-Task Behavior

The behavior of two or more students together, particularly when it involves some sort of social relationship, can be detrimental to collaborative learning. These relationships may result in students chatting, arguing, joking around, or engaging in other off-task behavior. To minimize this, consider assigning groups so that best friends, worst enemies, and couples don't work together, or reassign often so that they don't work together for long. Set a hard-to-reach time limit to discourage off-task behavior. If students do not seem to be making timely progress on a large task, divide the task into smaller tasks, and ask for reports on these subtasks throughout the class period. Physically move closer to the students—sometimes the physical presence of the teacher can deter off-task behavior. Speak with students individually and together, reminding them of how this behavior would be viewed in a work environment. Confront students, giving students a chance to explain their behavior; there may be a good reason, even if it is not immediately apparent. Praise groups publicly that are performing well together, pointing out effective behaviors.

Groups That Don't Get Along

At times, some members of a group just can't (or won't) get along. The result is that the entire group begins to engage collectively in negative behavior and fails to progress in the learning task. First, give students time to work it out on their own, because jumping in too soon prevents them from learning or practicing valuable problem-solving skills. If students are unable to solve the problems, consider speaking with the group as a whole (or take individual students aside) and ask them to identify and articulate why they are not getting along. Once the problem has been identified, work with them (or have them work with another group) to identify a solution. As a last resort, reorganize groups.

Several or No Students Want to Assume Leadership

Having several students who want to be group leaders is not an uncommon occurrence; however, if they engage in a power struggle and no one is willing to compromise, the group can suffer. Explain to students that being an effective leader means being able to share leadership and help others succeed. Acknowledge that it is also important to be a good follower. Alternately, a group may struggle because no one seems willing to stand up and take responsibility. Without someone working to energize the group and move it forward toward a common goal, the group can flounder. Consider assigning additional points for leadership roles. Or suggest that students flip a coin or draw straws to determine who will assume the leadership role. In either case, consider assigning and rotating roles (facilitator, recorder, spokesperson, and so forth) so that everyone participates in different ways.

Different Ability Levels

Howard Gardner's (1983) work on multiple intelligences confirms teachers' longtime observations that students come to the classroom with different skills and abilities. According to Gardner, for example, students may be linguistically intelligent, logistically-mathematically intelligent, spatially intelligent, bodily-kinesthetically intelligent, musically intelligent, interpersonally intelligent, intrapersonally intelligent, or naturalistically intelligent. Gardner suggests that in higher education we tend to place value primarily on the first two types of intelligence. The collaborative classroom creates opportunities as well as challenges for multiple intelligences, as students are placed into situations in which they must work with students who have different gifts than theirs.

This can become problematic when, for example, a high-achieving student by standard academic measures does not feel adequately challenged by the group. To help this kind of student maximize his or her role in the group, select a role suitable for someone with strong academic skills, such as explaining how answers are derived, observing and analyzing data, and integrating materials. Use some of the Reciprocal Teaching CoLTs such as *CoLT 9: Fishbowl* or *CoLT 11: Jigsaw* to give these students an opportunity to help others learn. Try matching the student with other academically high-achieving students and assign them more demanding tasks. Consider partnering the student with someone who has dissimilar skills or assigning a task that requires different skills to present him or her with new challenges.

Some students will have low-level skills or physical or learning disabilities. These students may simply require more time to process information, so consider using activities such as *CoLT 1: Think-Pair-Share* that allow for processing time. Also consider forming smaller groups. This type of student may have trouble keeping up with the rapid-fire exchange that can happen in larger groups and may work better in small groups that allow more one-to-one conversation. Consider using Reciprocal Teaching CoLTs so that another student can assume a tutoring role with them. Finally, use different kinds of activities. The Graphic Organization CoLTs or techniques such as *CoLT 10: Role Play* may help these students demonstrate their best skills.

Groups That Work at Different Rates

It is a given that groups will work at different speeds. To address different work rates, consider setting a time limit and making it public, as having a time frame will help students monitor their progress. Assign someone in the group the role of taskmaster/timekeeper. This individual can help the group pace itself. Plan a "sponge" or extension activity for students who complete the task early. An extension activity can discourage groups from rushing through an activity and doing it superficially. But avoid "punishing" groups who finish early simply because they are efficient and capable. Consider assigning bonus points to reward their good work.

Attendance Issues

Attendance issues are a major source of contention among working groups. If a student is absent excessively, follow up and determine why, as this will guide your response. For example, if illness is the reason, work with the student to determine whether he or she can continue in the course. Or consider encouraging alternative communication methods such as e-mail or conference calls. If the student is struggling and discouraged, you may wish to invite former students to come to class to share their experiences and strategies for success. The best general solution is to set attendance and participation policies at the beginning and then enforce them. If an attendance policy is included in Group Ground Rules or a Group Learning Contract (see Chapter Two, Orienting Students), you will have penalties in place. Reform groups if necessary so that a group does not suffer because of a member's chronic absences.

Cheating

Academic dishonesty is receiving increased attention in higher education, and there are many suggestions in the literature and on the Internet for how to address it. In terms of collaborative learning, it is important that both teachers and students understand that there is a difference between "cheating" and "collaborating." Make sure that the distinction is explained and understood, perhaps including this when you orient students to collaborative learning (see Chapter Two, Orienting Students).

In some ways, collaborative activities can help discourage cheating. For example, McKeachie (2002, pp. 172–173) observes that when students are required to write a paper, they seem to face three alternatives: (1) copy a paper from the Web, a friend, or a fraternity or sorority file; (2) find a book in the library that covers the material and copy it with varying degrees of paraphrasing; or (3) (*what teachers actually hope happens*) review relevant resources, analyze and integrate information, and write a paper that reveals understanding and original thinking. McKeachie notes that in his experience, students often cheat because they feel trapped with no other way out. Either because of lack of planning or self-perception of lack of ability or background, they have arrived at the due date feeling that it is impossible to write a paper that will achieve a satisfactory grade. Their only solution is to find an already written paper. He also points out that cheating sometimes results from student frustration and desperation, and may be even a way of "getting back at an unreasonable, hostile teacher" (p. 98).

A thoughtfully constructed collaborative task using a technique such as *CoLT 18: Group Investigation* can (1) relieve the pressure on a single student and emphasize instead students supporting each other and capitalizing on the special talents of the group members; (2) make the task manageable because the assignment is broken up into chunks with interim due dates that help teams structure the investigation process and learn from each step; (3) make it difficult to find an available product (paper, presentation, and so forth) that adequately addresses the assignment, and (4) help foster personal relationships with other students, so that students realize others care and that they will not get away with cheating because they are not anonymous members of a crowd. Still, groups may use several strategies that qualify as cheating. They may use group work from previous years. They may share work between and among groups without instructor permission. They may fail to properly acknowledge sources or authorities used in developing a group product.

McKeachie's general strategies for preventing cheating apply to both individual and collaborative work. First, reduce the pressure by providing a number of opportunities for students to demonstrate achievement so that their entire grade isn't dependent upon a single activity. Second, address academic honesty in the syllabus, so that students know what constitutes cheating. Third, create interesting assignments that make reasonable demands on students. Fourth, develop group norms that encourage academic honesty. For example, use a discussion CoLT (such as *CoLT 2: Round Robin* or *CoLT 3: Buzz Groups*) to have students talk about why cheating is bad and to develop their own policy in their Group Ground Rules or Learning Contract (see Chapter 2, Orienting Students). Fifth, if groups are not doing well, talk to them and try to help them find ways to improve so that they don't feel compelled to resort to cheating (McKeachie, 2002, pp. 98–99).

Beyond this, consider changing assignment prompts from year to year or from group to group. Outline the constraints of the assignments, making explicit how students may and may not collaborate. Ensure individual accountability by having students turn in individual work along with the group product. If different groups should not work together outside of class, give students time to work on the assignment in class, make sure groups are physically separated, and monitor their projects. Consider making the assignment a friendly competition between groups. Finally, have groups document their work, perhaps using a Classroom Assessment Technique such as *Documented Problem Solutions* (CAT 21, Angelo & Cross, 1993, pp. 222–225).

Reporting Out Techniques

Group reporting is a valuable closing stage for collaborative activities. First, providing opportunities for groups to share their learning can enhance the learning of all students in the class. Second, as students articulate their experiences and outcomes, they begin to own knowledge in new and different ways. Third, reporting can help students reinforce ideas as they hear from others who have come to similar findings or conclusions. Fourth, hearing recurring themes provides students with the sense that they are on the right track. Fifth, reporting out can reveal omissions, helping both the teacher and students identify—and fill—learning gaps. The following activities are useful reporting out techniques (Davis, 1993; Johnson, Johnson, & Smith, 1998; Millis & Cottell, 1998; Tiberius, 1995).

Stand Up and Share A selected representative from each group shares ideas from the group. After the first round, the representatives share only new ideas and information.

Symposium, Colloquium, Panel, Seminar Students make a series of brief presentations to the class, followed by discussion in which panel participants receive questions from the audience.

Simulated Business Meeting Students present as if they are making a presentation at a business meeting to a board. These presentations may involve multimedia, such as presentation software, Web sites, and so forth. Consider having groups present to an audience of external experts or volunteers. Using professionals from the field can increase authenticity and the importance of the report and can remove the teacher from being the only evaluator.

Team Rotation Team A moves to Team B to present their ideas while members of Team B listen and ask questions. Teams then reverse roles.

Three Stay One Stray A person from Team A is designated to move to Team B to report while the other team members remain behind to hear from a traveling team member from Team C.

Rotating Trios From a group of four, one member stays behind as the "group expert" or "group reporter." The other three members move to a new station to learn from another group. If this procedure is repeated, the student who stays behind rotates, so that the student stays behind for only one rotation.

Poster Session Students meet in small groups to develop a visual product (for example, a concept map, graphic organizer, collage, or poster). Each group posts its product (such as taping it to the wall) so that all students can walk around and view each team's report. One student is assigned the role of spokesperson while other group members view other groups' posters. Students rotate roles so that all have the chance to be spokesperson. After a specified period of time, students return to their groups to discuss what they have learned, and the instructor may wish to have a full-class discussion about the representations.

Small-Group Stations The instructor sets up several stations around the room in which different questions or issues are posted on newsprint or whiteboard. Teams walk around, view the issue, and discuss their responses for a designated time period and post their response, leaving it behind for the next team to view. Teams use the preceding team's comments as a starting point for their discussion. At the end of the exercise, individual students move from station to station to view all responses.

Helping Groups Achieve Closure

Closure can be an important part of the collaborative learning experience. Without it, students may not see the interesting connections between different aspects of content or between their group work and prior learning. This can reinforce negative student perceptions of collaborative activities as being busy work and a way for instructors to avoid teaching responsibilities. Well-done closure can be motivating and prepare students for their next phase of learning. Therefore, after groups have completed their activities, consider implementing opportunities to synthesize information and celebrate accomplishments.

Helping Groups Synthesize Lessons Learned and Conclusions Reached

It is important to provide students with an opportunity to combine, integrate, and synthesize their small-group responses and understandings into a coherent whole that applies to the entire class. Many of the CoLTs in Part Three are useful for providing groups the opportunity to synthesize information, such as *Colt 1: Think-Pair-Share, CoLT 7: Note-Taking Pairs, CoLT 12: Test-Taking Teams, CoLT 22: Sequence Chains, CoLT 23: Word Webs,* and *CoLT 24: Dialogue Journals.* Yet even when students have multiple opportunities to synthesize information, they may not fill in all of the learning gaps or make all of the interesting connections. They may go into too much depth in some areas and treat other areas superficially. Instructor synthesis can be effective and may take several forms, including the following (Ventimiglia, 1995):

- Summarize salient points and recurring themes from the group reports
- Clarify details
- Point out misconceptions or inaccurate reports
- Add information where omissions occurred
- Address any unanswered or "nagging questions"
- Point out implications
- Help make connections to previous content and content yet to be addressed
- Review objectives with the group

However, it is important that the teacher refrain from taking control of the classroom at this late stage of the game. It is tempting to launch into an impromptu lecture to fill in what the groups missed. This could undermine the good effort thus far in enabling students to assume responsibility for their learning. In addition, if students anticipate that the teacher will "save them" in the end, they will be less likely to take the group work seriously and may instead wait until the "real teaching" gets started to become engaged in active listening and note taking. Thus it is important to find the balance that helps students achieve their own synthesis of the lessons they've learned.

Helping Students Celebrate Their Achievements

Celebration is part of a debriefing process that recognizes positive experiences and gains in learning that occurred during the collaborative experience. It is an important—but frequently ignored—aspect of closure. Celebrating group accomplishments honors students' achievements, holds successes up for public notice, and serves as a sincere signal of appreciation for hard work well done. There are a variety of ways to help groups celebrate. One way to celebrate is to throw a good old-fashioned class party. Ask everyone to bring something to contribute such as punch, cookies, chips, paper plates, cups, or napkins. Or just order pizza.

Another strategy is to create a "Gallery of Achievement" in which groups list their accomplishments (or the most important things they learned) on flip chart paper that is then posted on the walls. Ask students to walk around and look at the lists, and place a check next to achievements other than their own that apply to themselves as well. Survey the results and note the most popular, unusual, or unexpected accomplishments. Yet another way to celebrate is to take a photo of each group. Right before snapping the picture, consider expressing appreciation for the group's hard work and offer any specific observations about their accomplishments. Have the developed pictures available for students to pick up on the final day of class, and consider keeping and posting copies of all group photos as a "portrait gallery" for future classes. (Silberman & Clark, 1999, pp. 289–300).

Because students often remember praise long after a particular course has ended, celebrating and recognizing group successes can reinforce learning by helping to further cement ideas, concepts, and processes. Celebrating can be particularly effective when long-term, base groups have worked together over multiple sessions or even a semester.

Conclusion

Facilitating group work is a complicated task. It involves putting into practice the ideological role of teachers in the collaborative classroom. This means providing supportive rather than directive supervision, having high expectations of students, and helping and trusting groups to manage themselves.

Chapter 6

Grading and Evaluating Collaborative Learning

ALTHOUGH MOST TEACHERS HOPE to develop and capitalize on students' intrinsic motivations for learning, they also recognize that grades are the "coin of the realm." Grades determine who gets admitted into institutions, who graduates from them, who plays on athletic teams, and who qualifies for scholarships. It is partly *because* grades are so powerful that assigning them is a challenge. McKeachie observes the "heated discussion and cries of dismay" that surround grading (2002, p. 103). Millis and Cottell point out, "When teachers are asked what they most dislike about teaching, a majority of them answer, 'Grading'" (1998, p. 187). Walvoord and Anderson note, "Grading is the topic faculty most frequently choose when asked which issues they want to discuss in future workshops" (1998, p. xv). The problems and paradoxes of grading in general can be exacerbated when evaluating collaborative learning. This section, therefore, provides advice on how to evaluate group work and assign grades in the collaborative classroom.

Ensuring Individual Accountability and Positive Group Interdependence

The fundamental challenge in collaborative learning is ensuring individual accountability while promoting positive group interdependence. *Individual grades* provide a mechanism to ensure individual accountability, but they may minimize the importance of group effort. Individual grades can also be difficult to determine, as individual contribution and achievement within a group project is not always easy to identify. *Group grades* ensure that the group is held accountable and that members support each other's learning, but if individuals are not held accountable, group grades create opportunities for "easy riders" to avoid responsibility.

Furthermore, as Kagen (1995) argues, assigning group grades to individuals is unfair and unwise because (1) students may be penalized or rewarded by the performance of other students on their teams, (2) group grades that partially reflect the ability of other students undermine the validity of report cards (college transcripts), (3) students who are evaluated on forces beyond their control (the work of their teammates) may be frustrated; (4) group grades foster resistance to cooperative learning; and (5) undifferentiated group grades may be illegal (lawsuits have emerged when the grades of honor students were pulled down by less able teammates) (in Millis and Cottell, 1998, p. 191).

Since achieving individual accountability while still promoting group interdependence is a primary condition for collaborative learning, it is most effective if grades reflect a combination of individual and group performance. One way to achieve this is to (1) structure the learning task so that it requires both individual and group effort to accomplish, and (2) ensure that individual effort and group effort are differentiated and reflected in a product that can be evaluated. Many collaborative activities can be implemented in this way. Examples of how to achieve this in three CoLTs follow.

CoLT 12: Test-Taking Teams

There are three stages to this activity. First, student teams study a unit together. To help students prepare for studying together, consider asking them to bring a list of questions that they expect to be on the exam. Second, individual students take the teacher-prepared exam for individual grades. Third, teams discuss and submit team responses on the test for a group grade. The group response is generally superior to any individual scores. Thus, individuals receive a combination of individual and group scores, such as two-thirds individual and one-third group. The individual test taking emphasizes individual accountability. Studying together, retaking the exam as teams, and receiving the group score as part of the individual grade encourages group interdependence. There are many variations that place greater emphasis on either the individual or the group components. For example, the focus on group effort can be increased if groups with highest scores, highest combination of individual scores, or greatest collective improvement receive bonus points.

CoLT 20: Group Grid

Group Grid is one of the graphic organizer CoLTs intended to help students organize and classify information visually. Groups of students are given a grid in which the columns and rows are labeled with superordinate concepts, but the cells are left blank. Teams receive scrambled lists of subordinate pieces of information that belong in the cells, and students complete the grid by sorting the items into the correct grid categories. No item can be repeated. To emphasize individual accountability, each student is given different color sticky notes or colored pens to indicate his or her contributions. To grade the activity, teachers count the number of correct answers per individual for an individual score, and the total number of correct answers for the team score. Again, different weights, such as two-thirds individual and one-third group, are used to determine a composite individual grade.

CoLT 24: Dialogue Journals

Individual students keep a journal in which each page is divided by a vertical line. On the left side of the journal, the student records his or her thoughts about a reading assignment, lecture, task, or experience. Individuals then exchange journals with a partner who writes comments, suggestions, or questions on the right side of the journal. Both the original writer's and the peer's comments can be evaluated, and grades assigned for each student. Thus individual accountability is maintained in the original writer's grade, but the peer's comments are also graded, thus encouraging the peer to read carefully and comment thoughtfully.

By crafting the task to result in a product that includes differentiated individual and group components, teachers can help ensure individual accountability as well as promote group interdependence. The CoLTs in Part Three come from the existing literature and the wisdom of practice, and many have built-in strategies for combining group and individual grades.

General Guidelines for Grading Collaborative Work

As with grading in the traditional classroom, grading collaborative work is most effective when a teacher approaches grading as a process rather than isolated artifacts. Walvoord and Anderson (1998) sum up their view of grading as a

> *process by which a teacher assesses student learning through classroom*
> *tests and assignments, the context in which good teachers establish*
> *that process, and the dialogue that surrounds grades and defines their*
> *meaning to various audiences. Grading, then, includes tailoring the test*
> *or assignment to the learning goals of the course, establishing criteria*

and standards, helping students acquire the skills and knowledge they need, assessing student learning over time, shaping student motivation, feeding back results so students can learn from their mistakes, communicating about students' learning to the students and to other audiences, and using results to plan future teaching methods. (p. xi)

Not every activity needs to be graded, and not every activity needs to be collaborative. Fink (2003) offers a few simple rules to help guide decisions in putting together a course's grading system. First, make the list of graded items diverse, as students learn in different ways and differ in how they best show what they know. Second, ensure that the list reflects the full range of learning goals and activities. For example, if a teacher wants students to learn decision-making skills, then teachers should create an activity that requires students to make decisions. Finally, the course grade should reflect the relative weight of each component activity (pp. 142–143).

To help guide teachers in their overall approach to grading, Walvoord and Anderson suggest that teachers:

- *Appreciate the complexity of grading* and accept that any grading system will have flaws and constraints, so focus instead on grading as a tool for learning.

- *Recognize that there is no such thing as absolutely objective evaluation,* and that instead, a teacher's responsibility is to render an informed and professional judgment to the best of his or her ability.

- *Distribute time effectively,* understanding that other aspects of student learning also require time. Spend enough time to make a thoughtful, professional judgment with reasonable consistency and then move on.

- *Be open to change* and recognize that grade inflation is a national problem and must be addressed by institutions in concert at the national level. Individual teachers cannot address the problem in isolation.

- *Listen to and observe students* in order to understand and manage the meaning of grades to various students, as it is the meaning students attach to grades that will most affect learning.

- *Be very clear and explicit about the meanings* attached to grades and the standards and criteria on which grades are based.

- *Communicate and collaborate with students,* and try to build in the classroom a spirit of working together toward common goals.

- *Integrate grading with other key processes* such as planning, teaching, and interacting in the classroom.

- *Seize the "teachable moment"* and be alert and stay focused on what students should learn, especially in emotionally intense moments that may be the most powerful teaching opportunities all semester.

- *Make student learning the primary goal.* Grading is a powerful lever, capable of influencing the learning, and this should be its primary purpose.

- *Be a teacher first, a gatekeeper last*: school is the bridge between learning and gate keeping.

- *Encourage learning-centered motivation,* and work against negative attitudes toward grading. Instead, help students learn that they are empowered to affect what happens to them, that if they work hard it will pay off, that success comes from hard work rather than just luck, and that success is within their control. (Walvoord and Anderson, 1998, pp. 10–16)

Crucial to good grading is establishing clear criteria and standards. Walvoord and Anderson (1998, p. 65) point out that taking the time to clarify explicitly how students will be graded can

- *Save time in the grading process*

- *Allow you to make that process consistent and fair*

- *Help you explain to students what you expect*

- *Show you what to teach*

- *Identify essential relationships between discipline information and processes*

- *Help students participate in their own learning, because they know what they are aiming for*

- *Help students evaluate their own and each other's work*

- *Save you from having to explain your criteria to students after they have handed in their work (often as a way of justifying the grades they are contesting)*

- *Help student peers give each other constructive feedback on plans and drafts*

- *Help team teachers or teaching assistants grade student papers consistently*

- *Help teachers of sequenced courses communicate with each other about standards and criteria*

- *Form the basis for departmental or institutional assessment*

Therefore, regardless of the specific evaluative approach you use, identify your grading standards clearly and make the criteria by which students can achieve the standards explicit.

Important Decisions in Grading Collaborative Work

There is no single answer to the question of how to grade collaborate learning, because faculty, institutions, and courses have widely divergent value systems. Following are choices to consider as teachers make their decisions regarding the *what, how, why,* and *who* of evaluating collaborative learning and assigning student grades.

Deciding What to Evaluate

In collaborative learning, there are two things to evaluate: student achievement of course content and student participation in group process. Most teachers want to know how well students learned the discipline-related content of the course. Teachers emphasizing collaborative learning also believe that it is important to grade group process. The teamwork and social skills that constitute group process may be considered so important that they are part of the content goals of a course, such as in a business management or intercultural communication course. When group work skills become course content, grading group process is essential. Furthermore, as more faculty recognize the importance of collaborative skills for the workplace and good citizenship, these skills are becoming part of the teaching goals in many disciplines. Ways to grade achievement of content is well understood and accepted in higher education, but teachers are still developing effective ways to grade group process.

Deciding Whether to Evaluate for Formative or Summative Purposes

Evaluating students can be formative or summative. Formative assessments are intended to provide teachers and students with information on how well students are learning in order to help both improve. They are almost never graded. The aim of formative assessment is primarily to *educate and improve* student (or teacher) performance, not to *audit* it (Wiggins, 1998, p. 7). Most of the CoLTs in Part Three provide suggestions for formative assessment in each technique's "Observations and Advice" section. Summative assessments gather evidence to assign grades that will combine to form a course grade, becoming part of a student's official transcript. Formative and summative assessment reflect different primary purposes, but many of the same questions, tools, or strategies can be used in the evaluations. See Angelo and Cross's *Classroom Assessment Techniques* (1993), Grant Wiggins's *Educative Assessment* (1998), and Walvoord and Anderson's *Effective Grading* (1998) for further discussion and techniques for evaluation.

Deciding Who Does the Evaluating

Evaluating and grading students is one of an instructor's chief responsibilities, but students can provide useful insight, as they have had a firsthand view of the collaborative experience. In addition, involving students helps develop students' abilities to evaluate their own and others' work—important goals in collaborative learning. Student participation in evaluating themselves and others also underscores the importance of teachers and students sharing responsibility for learning in the collaborative classroom.

Instructor

There are many ways instructors can approach grading either individual achievement of course content or participation in group process. McKeachie, for example, identifies two main approaches: *contract grading* and *competency-based grading.* In contract grading, students and instructors develop a written contract that specifies the tasks a student will do to achieve different grade levels. Contract grading individualizes the process and empowers students because they can be directly in control of whether or not they complete the work requirements for any given grade level. McKeachie suggests instructors ensure that points are awarded not only for doing the activity, but also that the activity is linked to appropriate standards; otherwise contract grading can reward quantity rather than quality. In collaborative learning, contracts can be used to specify the content and group process learning activities to be undertaken, the criteria by which the work is to be evaluated, and the grade or amount of credit to be assigned upon completion.

In competency-based grading, students' grades are based on achievement of specified competencies. Instructors develop an appropriate definition of the competencies desired and then develop adequate criteria for assessing achievement of each competency. Competency-based grading is a large category that includes mastery, performance-based, and criterion-referenced systems. This approach ties grades to course goals, but it may be difficult to operationalize (McKeachie, 2002, pp. 107–108). One way to implement this approach is known as Primary Trait Analysis, abbreviated as PTA. To construct a PTA, the teacher (1) identifies the factors or traits that will count for the scoring, (2) builds a scale for scoring the student's performance on that trait, and (3) evaluates the student's performance against those criteria. Walvoord and Anderson (1998) and Fink (2003) describe this approach in detail and provide numerous examples using different kinds of traits and criteria to evaluate and grade both individual and group work.

Davis (1993) would add at least one more approach: assigning a grade based upon the amount of improvement a student has made in the class. Grading on progress avoids competition and emphasizes individual learning, but it can produce inequities: a student who enters a course with the least background can still be the poorest student at the end, but might get an A for progress. Conversely, an outstanding student with little growth may get a C for progress. As Davis notes, "'Improvement' grades are also difficult to interpret within established grading norms: does a B mean that a student's work is above average or that his or her *improvement* is above average?" (p. 290). In terms of collaborative work, using improvement in teamwork and group process skills may be an appropriate approach to evaluating learning.

Just as teachers can use any of these three approaches to grade work in the traditional classroom, so can they use any of the three approaches to grade collaborative work. It is often most effective to use a hybrid approach, or a combination of approaches throughout the term, in order to emphasize advantages while minimizing disadvantages of a single approach.

Student Self-Evaluation

Self-evaluation encourages students to take stock of their own efforts, weighing their work against their own goals and against the work of other students. Embedded within self-evaluation is the concept of "reflection." Reflection is important in collaborative learning because it gives students opportunities to think about what they have learned and how they have learned it. As Berthoff (1990) reminds us, "Our job as teachers is to devise sequences of assignments which encourage conscientization, the discovery of the mind in action" (p. 25). Reflection, whether written or oral, provides a nice balance with the activity of collaborative learning, building the bridge between experiences and learning. Reflection helps students be more self-aware as they discover their thinking processes and develop patterns of self-regulated learning (Paris & Ayers, 1996).

Reflection is mostly used for formative assessments, but many of the same questions could be asked as part of a self-evaluation for grades. The questions may be presented as open-ended, such as *In what ways did you help/hinder the group?* or they may be modified such that students answer based on a Likert scale rating. For example, *On a scale of 1 to 5, how would you rate how well you helped the group?* Self-evaluation can focus on subject matter, such as, *What did you learn about course content in this collaborative activity?* or process, such as, *What did you learn about how you interact with others?* A list of possible questions for reflection or self-evaluation follows:

- What have you learned about yourself as a learner? As a team player?
- How can you apply what you learned in this activity to new situations?
- Describe your most successful (or least successful) interaction with your peers.
- How did collaborative learning contribute to learning course content? What were the advantages and disadvantages?
- What connections do you see between this experience and your other college courses?
- How did this experience challenge your assumptions and stereotypes?
- How would you do this differently next time?
- What was the best/worst/most challenging thing that happened?

Although self-evaluation can help promote deep learning, students may be reluctant to negatively evaluate themselves, particularly if they believe they will be penalized for it. When using self-evaluation, it is important to establish trust in the classroom, to explain the benefits of the evaluation, and to make clear whether the evaluation will be used for formative or summative purposes. If the responses are used for grading purposes, self-evaluations might be compared or averaged with instructor or peer-evaluations. Exhibit 6.1 shows an example of a form that might be used for self-evaluation.

EXHIBIT 6.1

Sample Self-Evaluation Form

Name_____

Group Number or ID_____

Project Title_____

Rate yourself on your performance on the project using the following scale:

5 = Always   4 = Frequently   3 = Sometimes   2 = Rarely   1 = Never

I was prepared to contribute to the group	
I stayed on task	
I listened to others	
I participated in discussion	
I encouraged others to participate	
Overall I felt my performance in the group should be rated:	

Student Peer Evaluation

Peer evaluation can be an integral part of the assessment process for collaborative learning because peers have a firsthand view of what is going on during collaborative activities. Peers are therefore well positioned to identify each other's levels and degrees of competence. Although peer evaluation is primarily used to assess group process at either the group (see "Group Evaluations" following) or individual levels, teachers are increasingly using peer evaluation for content as well (such as in calibrated peer review). There are challenges inherent in using peer evaluation. It is not a skill that students have had experience with, and faculty must devote time to instructing the students on what and how to effectively assess the product or presentation. Students may lack confidence in evaluating other students and may not be prepared to be critical. Like the other kinds of evaluations, peer evaluation can be used for either formative or summative purposes. In either case, it is perhaps most effective if instructors work with students to develop a set of evaluation criteria, and then ask students to rate their peers according to those criteria. A sample peer evaluation form appears as Exhibit 6.2. (See Chapter Two, Orienting Students.)

EXHIBIT 6.2

Sample Peer Evaluation Form

	Needs Improvement = 1	*Adequate = 2*	*Outstanding = 3*
The team member . . .			
Prepares			
Listens			
Contributes			
Respects others			
Demonstrates the following skills . . .			
Critical thinking			
Problem solving			
Communication			
Decision making			
Subtotals			
Total			

Group Evaluation

Group evaluations are a subset of peer evaluations, and focus on group process. Evaluations of the group process by members can help identify conflicts early so that problems can be addressed and tensions ameliorated. It can also help students identify and then capitalize on their group's strengths while minimizing disadvantages. Group evaluations, however, can open up doors for students to undermine the collaborative learning process. For example, students may try to get the instructor involved in conflict resolution instead of working to negotiate the conflicts themselves. Or they may use the activity as an opportunity to "bash" the group work process itself. If used for summative assessment purposes, students may choose to answer dishonestly in hopes of obtaining a more favorable grade. Providing structure to the evaluation can help deter unproductive negative responses to the process. Angelo and Cross (1993, p. 350) provide the sample form shown in Exhibit 6.3.

EXHIBIT 6.3

Sample Group Evaluation Form

1. Overall, how effectively did your group work together on this assignment?

                    Poorly   Adequately   Well   Extremely Well

2. Out of the five group members, how many participated actively most of the time?

                  None   One   Two   Three   Four   Five

3. Out of the five group members, how many were fully prepared for the activity?

                  None   One   Two   Three   Four   Five

4. Give one specific example of something you learned from the group that you probably wouldn't have learned working alone.

5. Give one specific example of something the other group members learned from you that they probably wouldn't have learned otherwise.

6. Suggest one change the group could make to improve its performance.

Conclusion

Grading collaborative learning—like grading learning in the traditional classroom—can be challenging. In the collaborative classroom, where students are empowered to take responsibility for their learning and are encouraged to work collaboratively rather than competitively with their peers, a natural tension exists between the collaborative learning goals and having an instructor assign a final, individual grade. It is important to minimize this tension. In this section we provided a variety of strategies for assigning grades that help ensure both individual accountability and group interdependence. If approached thoughtfully, teachers can create grading systems for collaborative learning that are fair, contribute to the learning process, and are still educationally valid.

Part Three

Collaborative Learning Techniques (CoLTs)

THE THIRTY TECHNIQUES INCLUDED in Part Three of this handbook provide teachers with specific tools for engaging students in collaborative learning. In some ways, they are like a collection of well-tested recipes. Our goal was to make each CoLT clear and comprehensive so that teachers new to collaborative learning could follow the procedures precisely and be reasonably guaranteed good results. We hope, though, that teachers will use the "recipes" more as would accomplished chefs and consider the techniques as guidelines, as starting points that spark their own creativity. In this way, teachers are encouraged to substitute, combine, or add elements in order to adapt the CoLTs to best meet their unique instructional needs.

The CoLTs are similar to recipes in other ways. If teachers have been predominantly lecturing, adding even a few of these techniques can vary and enrich the menu of learning opportunities that instructors provide their students. Alternately, even a CoLT that was once a refreshing, new activity can become dull or stale if used excessively. Finally, the CoLTs resemble recipes in that they give only directions; like cooks, teachers must provide the actual "ingredients." These ingredients are the learning task itself, and just as flawed ingredients can ruin the best recipe, so can an ill-conceived learning task undermine the effectiveness of even the most basic CoLT. We recommend, therefore, that teachers refer to Chapter Four, Structuring the Learning Task, for additional ideas on how to construct creative task prompts that can be used in conjunction with the CoLTs presented in this part of the handbook.

Origin of the CoLTs

We have drawn from the existing literature and the wisdom of practice to collect techniques that have already been time and classroom tested. For further information, we have included in each CoLT a "Key Resources" section that contains two to three important references to works that describe the CoLT, with varying degrees of explication. For example, in *CoLT 14: Send-A-Problem*, we cite Millis and Cottell (1998), who fully explicate the CoLT, while in *CoLT 30: Paper Seminar*, we cite Habeshaw, Habeshaw, and Gibbs (1984), who include more broad, general descriptions. The Key Resources section is not intended to provide the original source; in some cases, the techniques have been shared among practitioners for decades and thus it is impossible to confidently identify an original source. In other cases, the original sources are not readily available should readers wish to examine them. Nor is the "Key Resources" section intended to provide the sole sources available that describe the technique, since multiple sources exist for several of the CoLTs—many of which, it can be argued, are of equal importance. Rather, the section provides resources we found to be the most useful in our synthesis.

How to Use the CoLTs

The easiest approach to incorporating collaborative learning is to look at what you do now and see whether one or more activities could be done collaboratively. The CoLTs in Part Three are organized into five categories of general learning activities: discussion, reciprocal teaching, problem solving, information organizing, and collaborative writing. An introduction for each category of CoLTs describes that category's unique pedagogical benefits and provides an exhibit with a brief description of each CoLT. Thus, if teachers are already using class discussion as a teaching strategy, they might look at the Discussion CoLTs and choose one or two techniques that can help make class discussions more effective. For example, *CoLT 1: Think-Pair-Share* is a very simple but effective technique for increasing the quantity and quality of discussion participation. If the course requires students to engage in a significant amount of problem solving, consider looking in the Problem-Solving Colts for ideas on how to use collaborative learning to help students learn these skills. For example, *CoLT 13: Think-Aloud Pair Problem Solving (TAPPS),* provides a structure for students to help each other practice specific problem-solving strategies. A brief review of the descriptive exhibits introducing each CoLT category might lead teachers to incorporate additional techniques, such as *CoLT 7: Note-Taking Pairs* or *CoLT 12: Test-Taking Teams.* Approached in this way, incorporating collaborative learning may require only minor adaptations of existing activities.

When planning the activity, take time to think through all of the stages. The CoLTs described in Part Three assist instructors in their planning for all phases of the learning task, but for additional information or ideas, refer to the chapters in Part Two of this handbook. Each chapter of Part Two examines various aspects of implementing collaborative learning. For example, Chapter Three contains a thorough discussion and offers many suggestions on how to form groups. Review Chapter Five, Facilitating Student Collaboration, for elements to consider including when introducing or closing the activity, and so forth. Although the five chapters of Part Two and the thirty CoLTs in Part Three provide detailed advice on all phases of the learning task, a general overview of the phases to consider follows:

- *Before:* Decide how to form the groups and how many students will be in each group. Gather adequate materials. Estimate the amount of time that the activity will take and then plan accordingly. Groups, like individuals, will complete tasks at different rates. Prepare extension activities (for example, additional questions) to keep groups occupied if they finish early.

- *Beginning:* Carefully explain the objectives of the activity and tell students how the groups will operate. Make sure that the task is clearly defined, with directions or prompts presented in a written handout or on an overhead transparency. Set up the expectation that cooperation is essential, and make sure that students know how both the groups and individuals will be evaluated and held accountable.

- *During:* If it takes more than one class session to accomplish a task, check in with groups regularly to monitor progress. If a group is not working well, don't simply break it up, but rather try to help groups learn to solve their own problems so that they can become productive and learn valuable teamwork skills.

- *Ending:* Structure closing activities so that groups present their findings to an interested and critical audience. This activity may be structured in a way that different student groups contribute their findings to make up a bigger learning outcome.

- *After:* Consider incorporating a "reflection" stage in which students analyze what they have learned, identify strengths and weaknesses in the collaborative learning processes, and offer constructive ideas on how their learning can be improved.

Categories of CoLTs

To reduce the effort required to locate an appropriate CoLT, we have organized the techniques into five broad categories:

1. Discussion	Student interaction and exchange is achieved primarily through spoken words.
2. Reciprocal Peer Teaching	Students purposefully help each other master subject matter content and develop discipline-based skills.
3. Problem Solving	Students focus on practicing problem-solving strategies.
4. Graphic Information Organizers	Groups use visual tools to organize and display information.
5. Writing	Students write in order to learn important course content and skills.

These categories represent our best attempt at sorting the techniques into sets that share fundamental commonalities, yet the dividing lines are not precise. For example, in the Writing CoLTs, we include *CoLT 27: Peer Editing.* This is a technique in which students critically review and provide editorial feedback on each other's essay, report, argument, research paper, or other writing assignment. One could make a case that this technique might be better included in Reciprocal Peer Teaching, but we included it in the writing section because students write a response to another student's paper and thus learn to evaluate their own written work.

Format Used to Present the CoLTs

Each CoLT is presented in a format that includes the following elements.

Number and Name

The thirty CoLTs are numbered sequentially and, within each category, appear in order from least to most complex. We identify each CoLT by a simple, descriptive name. In some cases, we have changed a name from the name as it appears in the literature. For example, we modified "Team Word Webbings" to "Word Webs" because it seemed simpler, and "Dyadic Essay Confrontations" to "Dyadic Essays" because one of our faculty colleagues asked, "For techniques intended to promote collaboration, why use the word *confrontation*?" Sometimes a technique appears in the literature under multiple names. Where possible, we have identified alternative names, usually in the "Variations and Extensions" section of that CoLT. For example, a variation of *CoLT 6: Critical Debate* appears in Millis and Cottell (1998) as "Structured Academic Controversy" (pp. 140–143).

Characteristics

At the beginning of each CoLT, we provide a quick overview of important attributes.

- *Group Size:* This indicates the number of group members we believe is optimal for that technique. Some of the CoLTs are designed for pairs or quads; most work best in small groups that range from four to six members.

- *Time on Task:* Although the time on task can vary widely based on the learning activity, we provide the estimated average length of time the activity requires. Some CoLTs can be completed in a few minutes; others take several hours.

- *Duration of Groups:* Most CoLTs can be done by an ad hoc group within a single class session. Others take longer and are best accomplished using base groups that work together for multiple sessions or throughout the entire academic term.

- *Online Transferability:* This is our assessment (low/moderate/high) of how well the CoLT can be adapted to the online environment given current technology.

Description and Purpose

This element includes a brief explanation of what the CoLT is, identifying its key characteristics and distinguishing features. It also includes an explanation of why the CoLT is useful.

Preparation

In this element, we describe what activities should be completed, or materials acquired, prior to implementing the CoLT. This advice most often centers on what the teacher should do, but occasionally we provide information about what steps students should take to be ready to actively participate in the CoLT.

Procedure

This section contains simple, step-by-step directions for conducting the CoLT.

Examples

Here we include examples that illustrate use of the CoLT in a wide range of disciplines. These examples have been pulled from the literature, shared with us by faculty colleagues, or drawn from our own experience as teachers. We hope that readers will learn from examples in all fields and adapt the ideas for their own academic areas. Examples are presented usually in order of simplest to most complex. A graphic indicates a description of this CoLT in an online or hybrid course.

Online Implementation

In this section, we describe how to adapt the CoLT for the online environment. Several factors made writing this component challenging. First, technology changes rapidly, and this speed is in direct conflict with the enduring nature of print. We recognize that information that is cutting edge at this moment will soon be out of date and advances that may eventually become commonplace are not yet even imagined. Second, the sophistication of online courses and the level of assistance provided online instructors vary widely across institutions, making it difficult to provide concrete ideas for application. Third, readers will have different levels of students (lower division or graduate seminar?) and sizes of class (12 or 120?), attributes that make it difficult to suggest specific online variations for collaborative activities. But, because of the growing importance of technology, we believe it is critical to offer some ideas in an Online Implementation section. We have therefore drawn from our own experience as online instructors and the experience of our colleagues to offer general guidelines for adapting the CoLT to the online environment. Advice concentrates on two broad categories of tools: synchronous (such as Chat or Instant Messaging) and asynchronous (such as e-mail and Threaded Discussion).

Variations and Extensions

This section includes ideas for ways in which the CoLT can be adapted, extended, or modified.

Observations and Advice

In this section, we include additional information we believe will help readers implement the CoLT successfully, such as caveats, ideas for closure activities, suggestions for grading and assessment, and so forth.

Key Resources

As we have described, this element contains the two or three most helpful sources for further information on that technique.

Chapter 7

Techniques for Discussion

EXCHANGING INFORMATION, IDEAS, AND OPINIONS in open and provocative discussion lies at the heart of collaborative learning. McKeachie describes discussion as the *prototypic* teaching method for active learning and one of the most valuable tools in the teacher's repertoire (2002, p. 30). Davis notes, "A good give-and-take discussion can produce unmatched learning experiences as students articulate their ideas, respond to their classmates' points, and develop skills in evaluating the evidence of their own and others' positions" (1993, p. 63). Use of discussion as an effective teaching tool is well established: class discussion has been and remains the single most popular instructional method in higher education, with 83 percent of all college teachers reporting that they use it in all or most of their classes (U.S. Dept. of Education, 2000).

Why is discussion so popular? Perhaps it is because teachers recognize that discussion helps students learn in many ways. Discussion helps students formulate their ideas and learn to communicate them clearly. It encourages students to think in the language and habits of the discipline. It exposes students to multiple perspectives, increases their awareness of ambiguity and complexity, and challenges them to recognize and investigate assumptions. It teaches students to be attentive, respectful listeners. It helps students learn more deeply and remember longer by requiring them to connect what they hear and what they say to knowledge that they already possess.

Yet getting students to participate in a really good discussion is difficult. If students have been sitting passively listening to a lecture, many are content to continue sitting passively when the lecture shifts to discussion, quietly listening to a few others contribute comments. Good discussion requires participants to speak and say what they truly think, feel, and believe, and many students are reluctant to take this risk. Students are afraid of being publicly embarrassed if their comments are viewed as incorrect or stupid. If a student is an immigrant or international student and English is not his or her primary language, or if a student is still struggling to become acculturated to modes of appropriate college classroom behavior, speaking in class is even more threatening. Whatever the reasons for student reticence to speak, many instructors find it challenging to generate stimulating classroom discussion.

The six Discussion CoLTs are good strategies for improving class discussion. Used as a small-group alternative or as a warm-up to whole-class participation, these CoLTS address many of the general problems of discussion by

- Dividing the class into pairs or small groups so that each individual has the opportunity to participate in the discussion

- Establishing a framework (such as giving each student a meaningful role) that requires every student to be engaged and to contribute

- Reducing the risk associated with speaking and saying what one really thinks because the discussion is occurring within a small group of peers rather than publicly in front of the whole class and teacher

- Allowing students to clarify their thoughts and rehearse their comments before speaking in the whole class

- Providing individual students the opportunity to find other students who may agree and support them in their opinion before they "go public"

Although the CoLTs in this chapter are joined by the commonality of communicating through spoken words, they also have unique attributes and functions. A brief description and the primary purpose of each of the Discussion CoLTs are provided in Exhibit 7.1.

EXHIBIT 7.1

Discussion CoLTs

This CoLT	Is a Technique in Which Students:	It Is Particularly Useful for:
1: Think-Pair-Share	Think individually for a few minutes, and then discuss and compare their responses with a partner before sharing with the entire class	Preparing students to participate more fully and effectively in whole class discussions
2: Round Robin	Generate ideas and speak in order moving from one student to the next	Structuring brainstorming sessions and ensuring that all students participate
3: Buzz Groups	Discuss course-related questions informally in small groups of peers	Generating lots of information and ideas in a short period of time to prepare for and improve whole-class discussions
4: Talking Chips	Participate in a group discussion and surrender a token each time they speak	Ensuring equitable participation
5: Three-Step Interview	Interview each other and report what they learn to another pair	Helping students network and improve communication skills
6: Critical Debates	Assume and argue the side of an issue that is in opposition to their personal views	Developing critical thinking skills and encouraging students to challenge their existing assumptions

COLLABORATIVE LEARNING TECHNIQUE

1

Think-Pair-Share

Characteristics

Group Size	PAIRS
Time on Task	5–15 MINUTES
Duration of Groups	SINGLE SESSION
Online Transferability	LOW

DESCRIPTION AND PURPOSE
In this simple and quick technique, the instructor develops and poses a question, gives students a few minutes to think about a response, and then asks students to share their ideas with a partner. Think-Pair-Share is particularly effective as a warm-up for whole class discussion. The "Think" component requires students to stop and reflect before speaking, thus giving them an opportunity to collect and organize their thoughts. The "Pair" and "Share" components encourage learners to compare and contrast their understandings with those of another, and to rehearse their response first in a low-risk situation before going public with the whole class. This opportunity to practice comments first with a peer tends to improve the quality of student contributions and generally increases willingness and readiness to speak in a larger group.

PREPARATION
Prior to coming to class, spend time developing an engaging question or problem that has many potential responses. Try responding to the question yourself. Decide how you are going to present the question (such as worksheet, overhead transparency, whiteboard) and how you are going to have students report out.

PROCEDURE
1. Pose the question to the class, giving students a few minutes to think about the question and devise individual responses.

2. Ask students to pair with another student nearby.

3. Ask Student A to share his or her responses with Student B, and then Student B to share ideas with Student A. Suggest that if the two students disagree, they clarify their positions so that they are ready to explain how and why they disagree. If useful, request that pairs create a joint response by building on each other's ideas.

•   •   •

EXAMPLES

English Composition

A freshman writing instructor planned to have students write argument essays throughout the semester, so he shared several passages from arguments for students to read as homework. In the next class meeting, he used Think-Pair-Share to help students examine features of a compelling written argument. The professor began by posing the following question to the class: *What makes a written argument effective?* The instructor asked students to think about the assigned passages individually and to consider the features that made those arguments effective. He waited two minutes and then asked students to form pairs with students seated nearby to compare and jot down ideas.

After giving students several minutes to exchange ideas, the instructor asked for responses from each pair, writing them on the board as students spoke. Next, students were given an instructor-generated list of features of effective arguments against which they compared their lists. Overall, the lists were similar, and the instructor commended the students for their ability to identify qualities of a good argument. The students and the instructor then worked together to combine and refine a set of criteria, with the instructor guiding the discussion by asking questions. Together, they developed a strong set of argument evaluation criteria used both by students in peer assessment of each other's writing and by the instructor in grading.

•   •   •

 ### Introduction to Physical Anthropology

This is a hybrid course, in which students attend classes on campus but do a considerable amount of work online. In this adaptation of Think-Pair-Share, Professor Sara McShards organizes students into pairs and then quads at the beginning of the semester. On

Thursday of each week, she posts three questions online that require students to read, understand, and apply concepts from readings that will prepare them for the next week's in-class activities. Before the class meets on Monday, partners must have worked together to create and write down joint responses to the questions. For the first ten minutes of each Monday class, the two sets of partners meet as a quad to discuss, compare, and contrast their responses before submitting a group worksheet.

• • •

ONLINE IMPLEMENTATION   Without adaptation, this CoLT does not transfer effectively to the online environment. Even in a synchronous activity such as a chat session, it would be impractical to interrupt the session, organize the students into pairs, and have them communicate together before returning to whole class discussion. If the online class is small and enrollment is stable, consider adapting Think-Pair-Share by assigning student pairs to work together over an extended period of time. Post the question on a discussion board and then ask students to communicate first with their partner in instant or private messaging, and then one student posts the joint response.

VARIATIONS AND EXTENSIONS

- Export the "think" step by posing a question for students to consider outside of class. When they return to class, ask students to pair and share their homework responses.

- Give students time to write their responses down before pairing; this variation is called Write-Pair-Share (Johnson, Johnson, & Smith, 1991; Lyman, 1981).

- Ask each pair to share and compare their "paired" ideas with those of another pair before, or instead of, the whole-class discussion; this variation is called Think-Pair-Square (Lyman, 1981).

OBSERVATIONS AND ADVICE   See Chapter Two, Structuring the Learning Task, for ideas on developing and presenting good prompts.

Give students sufficient time to think before pairing and responding; the time required will depend on the nature, scope, and complexity of the question, as well as on the students' level of familiarity with the topic. For a conceptual question, allow at least a minute for individual responses. This provides students time to formulate and rehearse ideas before sharing them. In addition to think time, plan enough time for both students to express and compare their responses. This "share" time will give students the opportunity to discuss well-thought-out answers with peers and to refine their answers before speaking to the whole class.

Announce a time limit, but gauge time needed by decibel levels as well. If the pairs are all still actively engaged, consider extending that limit by a minute or two.

If one student seems to be dominating the other in the pair, set time limits for each student response.

The simplest reporting out strategy is to have each pair share their most important point with the whole class. Limit the number of responses, repetition, and time required in the report out by asking each pair after the first to share only ideas not yet mentioned. Following the reports, conclude with a synthesis to validate student responses by highlighting the good points that students brought out. Gently correct any responses that are incorrect, and add any points that weren't covered. If appropriate, provide learners with an expert response, allowing them to check and revise their individual and pair responses. If time is limited or the class is large, randomly call on student pairs or collect a written version of the pair responses and review them outside of class.

To promote active listening during the report out phase, randomly call on students and ask them to summarize what the reporting student just said.

The reporting out usually provides instructors with sufficient feedback to assess student understanding. However, in cases where student pairs have exhibited a great deal of difficulty or confusion in their responses, it may be useful to do additional assessment. Consider using *Minute Paper* (CAT 6, Angelo & Cross, 1993, pp. 148–153) and ask students to write a Half-Sheet Response to a question such as, *What aspect of the prompt question was most difficult for you to answer?* or *On what points did you and your partner agree, or disagree?*

Think-Pair-Share is typically used as an informal strategy to stimulate discussion, and is not generally used for grading purposes.

KEY RESOURCES   Lyman, F. (1981). The responsive classroom discussion. In A. S. Anderson (Ed.), *Mainstreaming digest.* College Park: University of Maryland College of Education.

Lyman, F. T. (1992). Think-Pair-Share, Thinktrix, Thinklinks, and weird facts: An interactive system for cooperative learning. In N. Davidson & T. Worsham (Eds.), *Enhancing thinking through cooperative learning* (pp. 169–181). New York: Teachers College Press.

Millis, B. J., & Cottell, P. (1998). *Cooperative learning for higher education faculty.* American Council on Education, Series on Higher Education. Phoenix, AZ: Oryx Press, pp. 72–78, 115–116.

COLLABORATIVE
LEARNING
TECHNIQUE

2

Round Robin

Characteristics

Group Size	4–6
Time on Task	5–15 MINUTES
Duration of Groups	SINGLE SESSION
Online Transferability	LOW

DESCRIPTION AND PURPOSE Round Robin is primarily a brainstorming technique in which students generate ideas but do not elaborate, explain, evaluate, or question the ideas. Group members take turns responding to a question with a word, phrase, or short statement. The order of responses is organized by proceeding from one student to another until all students have had the opportunity to speak. This CoLT is especially effective for generating many ideas because it requires all students to participate, and because it discourages comments that interrupt or inhibit the flow of ideas. Round Robin also ensures equal participation among group members. The ideas that students generate can be compiled in a list that serves as the basis for a next-step assignment.

PREPARATION The purpose of a brainstorming session is to create an extensive list of ideas. Crafting a prompt that can generate a sufficiently rich array of responses that can be expressed quickly and succinctly is particularly important. Practice ahead of time by thinking of and listing as many possible responses as you can. You can use the length of your list to predict the duration of your in-class exercise and to decide whether or not groups should rotate through Round Robin more than once.

PROCEDURE 1. Ask students to form groups of four to six.

2. Explain that the purpose of brainstorming is to generate many ideas. Group members will take turns, moving clockwise, and respond to the question. Inform students that to prevent interrupting or inhibiting

the flow of ideas, they must refrain from evaluating, questioning, or discussing the ideas.

3. If it would be beneficial for students to assume a role (such as recorder or rule enforcer), allow a few moments for role assignment.

4. Tell students whether or not they will go around the group once or multiple times, announce a time limit, and pose the prompt.

5. Ask one student to begin the activity by stating an idea or answer aloud. The next student continues the brainstorming session by stating a new idea. The activity continues, moving from member to member in sequence, until all students have participated.

• • •

EXAMPLES

Survey of International Business

Professor Mark Etting decided to use Round Robin to generate ideas and enthusiasm for a unit on risk analysis. He organized students into groups of five or six and assigned one person in each group to be the recorder. He then asked the students to respond to the prompt, *Identify a force that influences the competitive business environment.* Students took turns responding, each student adding a new idea. After groups had generated ideas for about ten minutes, the professor moved from group to group asking the recorder to share one new idea, which he then wrote on the board under the rubrics of Political, Cultural, and Social Influences. The many ideas on the board led to a stimulating whole-class discussion on the relative importance and risk each of the factors might play in affecting the global commercial community.

• • •

Conversational French

In this language course, students engaged in intensive oral practice in order to increase their ability to apply the grammatical and syntactical structures they had studied in a previous course. The professor used Round Robin sessions to engage students in fun, fast-paced activities to increase communicative competency and vocabulary. Responding to prompts such as *Say words for different kinds of food*, individual students in succession contributed a French word, and the next student translated it into English. Students who could not respond within a few seconds lost a turn.

> The groups continued until they had exhausted their vocabulary, and then they would move on to another word prompt. As students became more fluent, the professor expanded the prompts to require responses in full sentences, such as *Describe your favorite restaurant.*

• • •

ONLINE IMPLEMENTATION Spontaneous brainstorming is possible in a synchronous environment such as a Chat session or Instant Messaging, but it is difficult to get online students together in real time, and if the software does not save text transcripts, brainstorming information will get lost. An adaptation that retains some of the Round Robin characteristics is to use an asynchronous environment like a Threaded Discussion, and establish ground rules such as (1) Each posting must present new ideas, (2) Students should not agree, disagree, or question what is already posted, and (3) Every student in the class or a base group should post a response before posting a second comment or response.

VARIATIONS AND EXTENSIONS
- Although Round Robin works best for brainstorming, its circular response organization can structure regular group discussion to ensure equal participation. To do this, explain to students that their discussion must move clockwise around the group, with each student giving an opinion or sharing an idea until all students have participated. Decide whether each student should be able to respond to a prior student's comments, or whether each student should express only new ideas until everyone has contributed to the discussion.

- Use this structure for learning activities other than brainstorming that still benefit from structured practice of quick responses. For example, organize Round Robin activities to recite words, phrases, or formulae until they become habitual (such as for ESL or foreign languages) or are memorized (such as for science or mathematics).

OBSERVATIONS AND ADVICE When the activity is simple (such as asking students to list answers in a word or short phrase), this activity is fast moving and may be conducted in as few as five minutes. If the activity is more complex and requires students to contribute longer responses, this CoLT can move slowly and lack energy, resulting in boredom and wasted time. Therefore, rather than asking students to engage in complex thinking and reasoning tasks, use this technique for straightforward tasks such as helping students generate lists, review material, or identify obvious applications of ideas.

Once several ideas are on the table, students may find themselves "stumped" and feel pressured if they cannot come up with new ideas. Ideally, team members should not skip turns, but it is better to pass than hold up the process. Set a time limit and establish some ground rules, such as allowing a student who has nothing to contribute to pass. When only a couple of students are left participating, the procedure should end.

Some students will find this activity difficult if they have trouble expressing themselves. Specify the type of responses expected in order to help alleviate anxiety. Also consider using written rather than oral responses (see *CoLT 25: Round Table*).

Controlling participation in this way has advantages and disadvantages. Requiring people to participate when they have nothing to contribute—or limiting the participation of those who want to contribute something additional until all others have participated—can be counterproductive. On the other hand, this strategy can address problems of inequitable participation because it provides the structure to ensure that everyone participates.

Brainstorming sessions generate ideas, but these ideas are not evaluated, sorted, or discussed. It is essential to use the students' ideas so that they see the value of their work and input. Therefore, decide how ideas will be used to structure an appropriate follow-up activity. Whole-class discussion is one option, but Round Robin is particularly effective linked with another CoLT. For example, students may prioritize the ideas, sort the ideas into categories using *CoLT 19: Affinity Grouping*, or graph the relationship of the ideas to each other, using *CoLT 23: Word Webs*.

KEY RESOURCES Kagan, S. (1992). *Cooperative learning*, 2nd ed. San Juan Capistrano, CA: Resources for Teachers, pp. 8:3, 8:9, 12:1, 10:12.

Sharan, S. (Ed.). (1994). *Handbook of collaborative learning methods*. Westport, CT: Greenwood Press, pp. 117–118, 228, 237, 257–258.

**COLLABORATIVE
LEARNING
TECHNIQUE**

3

Buzz Groups

Characteristics

Group Size	4–6
Time on Task	10–15 MINUTES
Duration of Groups	SINGLE SESSION
Online Transferability	LOW

DESCRIPTION AND PURPOSE Buzz Groups are teams of four to six students that are formed quickly and extemporaneously to respond to course-related questions. Each group can respond to one or more questions; all groups can discuss the same or different questions. Discussion is informal, and students do not need to arrive at consensus, but simply exchange ideas. Typically, Buzz Groups serve as a warm-up to whole-class discussion. They are effective for generating information and ideas in a short period of time. By dividing the whole class into small groups, more students have the opportunity to express their thoughts. Because students have had a chance to practice their comments and to increase their repertoire of ideas in the Buzz Group, the whole-class discussion that follows is often richer and more participatory.

PREPARATION Prior to coming to class, decide what the Buzz Groups will discuss. Craft one or more engaging discussion prompts that tend toward the conceptual rather than factual and that will stimulate an open-ended examination of ideas. Try responding to the questions yourself, so that you are confident that they will generate a variety of responses. Choose the manner in which you are going to present the prompt questions, such as on a worksheet, overhead transparency, or whiteboard.

PROCEDURE 1. Form groups; announce the discussion prompts and time limit.

2. Ask group members to exchange ideas in response to the prompts.

3. Check periodically to see whether groups are still actively engaged and focused on the assigned topic. If off topic, shorten the time limit. If on topic and the time has ended, consider extending the limit for a few minutes.

4. Ask the students to return to whole-class discussion and restate the prompt to begin.

· · ·

EXAMPLES

The Nature and Origin of Major Social Problems

Professor Jen Derr was frustrated with the superficial quality of discussion in her lower-division sociology class. Despite her efforts to engage students in meaningful dialogue about significant social problems, students avoided controversy and offered only safe, predictable comments. In an attempt to move a discussion on gender issues to a more meaningful level, she decided to experiment using Buzz Groups as a warm-up to whole-class discussion. To introduce the topic of gender discrimination, she divided the room into male and female students and then asked them to subdivide into groups of four of the same gender. Her hope was that at least some students might have personal experiences related to this topic, and that they would feel safe sharing these experiences in a small group of same-sex peers. On an overhead transparency, she posted the prompt, *Can you recall a situation in which you experienced or observed gender-based discrimination?*

The groups were soon engaged in spirited discussion. After fifteen minutes, she stopped the Buzz Groups and shifted the focus back to the whole class but asked students to remain in the male or female sides of the room. She alternated between male and female groups, asking a volunteer from each group to report out to the whole class one or two of the experiences their group found most compelling. Following each report, she invited comments from students on the other side of the room. Professor Derr found that students felt empowered and supported by the presence of their same-sex peers. The whole-class discussion proceeded at a level of depth and with a sense of immediacy that had been lacking when she had tried to generate whole-class discussion on this topic in previous semesters.

· · ·

Leadership Issues in Community Colleges

A professor of a graduate-level seminar containing students who were primarily upper-level college administrators had been accustomed to lecturing about a topic first and then moving to whole-class discussion. She decided to reverse this order and to use Buzz Groups to introduce students to the topic of mergers and consolidations in the community college sector. Among the list of questions she prepared for each group to discuss were, *What is the difference between a consolidation and a merger? Have you had any experience with consolidations or mergers? What are some of the issues that would attend a consolidation or merger?* These were open-ended questions, and she hoped that her students would be able to draw on their own experiences in college administration to respond to them.

It soon became apparent that several students within each Buzz Group had experienced consolidations and mergers on their campuses, and that they had strong opinions about those experiences. When Buzz Groups reported out, the professor used group comments as the basis for a whole-class discussion. She was able to integrate the information that she had intended to cover in the lecture by offering comments such as, *What Carol is describing is an example of what is called _____.* In the whole-class discussion, students explored the political issues, organizational problems, and personnel dilemmas associated with consolidations and mergers at a level that was deep and engaging. The Buzz Group discussions had provided a good introduction to the topic by allowing students to connect theoretical constructs to work-related situations that had occurred in their professional lives. Furthermore, by integrating what would have otherwise been her lecture on theory into the whole-class discussion, the professor was able to offer students a framework for understanding their personal experiences that illuminated the importance of connecting theory to practice.

• • •

ONLINE IMPLEMENTATION   Preserving the impromptu, spontaneous character of Buzz Groups is possible in a synchronous environment such as a Chat session. Or consider instead modifying this activity for an asynchronous environment. Form groups of eight to twelve at the beginning of the semester, identify each group (for example, Group A, Group B, and so forth), and create a forum for each group. Post discussion prompts on each group's forum and ask students (for example) to reply at least twice: once directly to the prompt, and once to another student's response.

VARIATIONS AND EXTENSIONS

- Assign the groups a task other than responding to questions. Instead, ask them to generate questions or ideas, share information, or solve problems.

- Hold the discussion without formal or structured questions, but rather as an opportunity to discuss the course texts in general or a specific assigned reading. This variation, called Relaxed Buzz Groups, is simply a conversation, and students do not report out. Students are required, however, to keep the discussion focused on issues from the readings. They can question, highlight passages, look for the thesis, and identify flaws (Brookfield & Preskill, 1999).

- After each Buzz Group has completed an initial discussion, have two Buzz Groups join together and continue the conversation as a single, larger group. Groups can combine again, with each group doubling in size at successive iterations. This variation, called Snowball Discussion (Brookfield & Preskill, 1999), is good for allowing students to network with their peers and to hear many diverse views and opinions. Furthermore, students generate additional ideas at each new combination, so the conversation becomes more complex.

OBSERVATIONS AND ADVICE

This is a good technique for introducing a topic and having students engage in semi-structured conversations about important issues in the field. However, the informal, minimally structured nature of Buzz Groups can allow students to get off task, and discussions to degenerate into aimless chitchat. Avoid this problem by creating engaging, open-ended, multiple-response discussion prompts and by enforcing a time frame. Walking around the room monitoring group progress and offering procedural guidance as needed may also help to keep discussion focused.

Because of the unstructured nature of Buzz Groups, students might miss important issues (Brookfield & Preskill, 1999), so be prepared to offer these ideas during the closure period.

In the Snowball variation, in which students combine groups multiple times, adding new students and new ideas each time, students may feel shaken up or disjointed by the process (Brookfield & Preskill, 1999).

Ameliorate this by alerting students to this in advance, and by emphasizing that the purpose is to meet many students and to generate lots of information in a short period of time.

For the reporting out stage, go around the room and ask a representative from each group to share one of the group's most important points with the whole class, contributing only ideas that have not yet been mentioned. Invite students to comment on how different groups' ideas compare and contrast.

If the Buzz Groups responded to different questions, an alternative report out strategy is to have each group serve as a panel. Each student who serves on the panel can share one of the major themes or discussion points generated in their Buzz Group. The whole class is then invited to ask panel members questions.

When Buzz Groups report out, instructors typically receive sufficient insight into how much or what students have learned in their discussions. To gain additional feedback, consider using *CAT 23: Directed Paraphrasing* (Angelo & Cross, 1993, pp. 232–235). Ask students to summarize and restate the most important ideas or information from their Buzz Group discussion, imagining that the paraphrase would provide a succinct summary for a student who was not able to attend class that day. These paraphrases will illustrate how deeply students have understood and internalized the information generated in the discussions. These written summaries may be used for grading purposes.

KEY RESOURCES Brookfield, S. D., & Preskill, S. (1999). *Discussion as a way of teaching: Tools and techniques for democratic classrooms.* San Francisco: Jossey-Bass, pp. 104–105.

McKeachie, W. J. (1994). *Teaching tips: A guidebook for the beginning college teacher,* 9th ed. Lexington, MA: D. C. Heath, p. 44.

COLLABORATIVE
LEARNING
TECHNIQUE

4

Talking Chips

Characteristics

Group Size	4–6
Time on Task	10–20 MINUTES
Duration of Groups	SINGLE SESSION
Online Transferability	LOW

DESCRIPTION AND PURPOSE In Talking Chips, students participate in a group discussion, surrendering a token each time they speak. The purpose of this CoLT is to ensure equitable participation by regulating how often each group member is allowed to speak. Because it emphasizes full and even participation from all members, this technique encourages reticent students to speak out and talkers to reflect. Talking Chips is useful for helping students discuss controversial issues, and it is also useful to solve communication or process problems, such as dominating or clashing group members.

PREPARATION Determine a question or problem for group discussion. Bring poker chips, playing cards, or simply gather a sufficient number of paper clips, pencils, chalk, or other available items to serve as tokens.

PROCEDURE 1. Form student groups.

2. Give each student three to five tokens that will serve as permission to share, contribute, or debate in the conversation.

3. Ask students to participate equally in the group discussion, specifying that as they contribute comments, they should surrender a token and place it in view of the other group members.

4. When all students have contributed to the discussion and all tokens are down, ask students to retrieve and redistribute the chips so that the procedure repeats for the next round of discussion, or end the discussion if the activity is complete.

• • •

EXAMPLES

Introduction to Social Welfare

This course was a historical overview of social problems and welfare, focusing on sociological theory to explain the development of social service systems. The professor wanted groups to discuss the pros and cons of various programs that had been established to deal with unwanted pregnancies. These programs varied in terms of their support of adoption, abortion, or birth mothers keeping and raising their babies. He felt that it was important for all students to speak so that groups could explore the issues thoroughly, evaluating the programs from the perspective of society, mother, and the unborn child. The professor knew that many students would have strong feelings about the topic and possibly even personal experience. He wanted to create a discussion structure that encouraged equitable participation, and decided to implement Talking Chips. After he had formed groups and given students the discussion prompt, he explained the process and gave each student four poker chips to use as tokens.

• • •

Calculus

Professor Anna Log decided to form groups to work together for the entire semester. About two weeks into the semester, she noticed that while most of the groups were working well, a few were not. For example in one group, one student seemed to dominate the discussion, while other members were often silent. The quiet members seemed to accept the dominant member's responses regardless of the quality of the response. In another group, two students consistently challenged each other's comments and the discussion frequently deteriorated into a debate on who was right. To address group process problems, she decided to structure the next discussion using Talking Chips.

Professor Log posed a problem for group work. She told groups that in order to ensure full participation from all group members, she was giving each student one poker chip and that after each student had made a suggestion, posed a question, or supported or refuted a point made by another member of the group, he or she should surrender the chip, placing it in the center of the table. Once a student's chip was gone, he or she should wait to speak again until all chips had been placed in the center, collected, and redistributed. Professor Log instructed the groups to begin their discussions. She found that students soon became accustomed to the tokens and observed that students were participating in all groups more equitably. As part of her closure comments, she asked students to use the discussion as a model for future discussions.

• • •

ONLINE IMPLEMENTATION

Although this CoLT could be adapted to monitor participation in Threaded Discussions (for example, by telling participants that once a group member has posted comments, the same group member should wait until all—or most—other members have contributed to the discussion before posting again), it would most likely be counterproductive. Students would become impatient logging on, checking in to the discussion, and finding repeatedly that it is not yet their turn to contribute additional comments. Consider instead simply establishing discussion ground rules regarding number and length of comments. If a student repeatedly violates the ground rules, send him or her a private message affirming the importance of providing other students with an opportunity to contribute, the difficulty of reading lengthy text, and so forth.

VARIATIONS AND EXTENSIONS

- Give each student several chips of the same color. For example, Student A receives blue chips, Student B receives yellow chips, and so forth. Allow the conversation to proceed for a while. Ask students to examine the surrendered chips and to reflect on how the conversation has gone. Ask them to continue with their discussion but to try to work toward an equal number of chips from each group member.

- To regulate the length of time each student speaks more than the number of times they speak, give each student several chips and instruct them to surrender a chip every three to five minutes that they have the floor.

- Give each student only one chip. When everyone has contributed, retrieve the tokens and start the process again. This variation could be useful in brainstorming or listing items.

- Instead of using chips, assign a group member the task of recording individual contributions to a conversation. Do this by creating a grid sheet with one column for student names and an additional column or columns for the recorder to note down when each individual speaks. The recorder can place a checkmark or simply keep a tally by each person's name. Explain that recorders will use the sheet for a set period of time and that the aim is to promote an even level of participation among group members. When time is up, ask group members to review the sheets and analyze the interaction.

OBSERVATIONS AND ADVICE   Talking Chips can help to build listening and communication skills because students who tend to "spout off" consider more carefully what they have to say, since it will require their surrendering a token. Reticent students feel encouraged to speak because the ground rules have created an environment that promotes participation by all (Millis & Cottell, 1998, p. 98).

Controlling participation in this way has advantages and disadvantages. It can inhibit the natural flow of conversation, making discussions feel stilted and artificial, and hence should not be overused. On the other hand, helping students to see how they participate during group work develops teamwork skills and self-awareness. In addition to providing a structure to discuss controversial items, this CoLT is probably best used to give students insight into effective teamwork and to solve problems of inequitable participation.

Consider asking students to engage in a closing activity in which they write a short reflective essay describing their participation in the discussion, their comfort during this activity, and their plans for improvement. This may be most effective if students reflect personally upon how their involvement in the discussion changed because of the use of tokens. Individual essays could be followed by a group assignment in which students discuss, write, and submit a group report on how they plan to improve group communication.

KEY RESOURCES   Millis, B. J., & Cottell, P. G. (1998). *Cooperative learning for higher education faculty.* American Council on Education, Series on Higher Education. Phoenix, AZ: Oryx Press, pp. 98–99.

Sharan, S. (1994). *Handbook of cooperative learning methods.* Westport, CT: Greenwood Press, p. 119.

COLLABORATIVE
LEARNING
TECHNIQUE

5

Three-Step Interview

Characteristics

Group Size	2, THEN 4
Time on Task	15–30 MINUTES
Duration of Groups	SINGLE SESSION
Online Transferability	MODERATE

DESCRIPTION AND PURPOSE In Three-Step Interview, student pairs take turns interviewing each other and then report what they learn to another pair. The three steps (Interview-Interview-Report) are

Step 1:   Student A interviews Student B.

Step 2:   Student B interviews Student A.

Step 3:   Students A and B each summarize their partner's responses for Students C and D, and vice versa.

The type of questions used depends upon the course goals and may probe for values, attitudes, prior experience, or comprehension of course content.

Three-Step Interview creates the opportunity for students to network and improve specific communication skills. Interviewers must listen carefully, concentrating on the interviewee's responses and encouraging elaboration but refraining from imposing their own thoughts and opinions. Interviewees practice expressing their thoughts succinctly. Because the spotlight is solely on them and they are not exchanging comments as in a discussion situation, their responses require a high degree of personal commitment. Finally, the interviewers must understand and incorporate the information gathered from their interviewees' responses at a deep enough level to be able to summarize and synthesize the responses effectively for other students.

PREPARATION   Develop a list of interview questions prior to the class session. Interview questions that are particularly effective ask a person about opinions or experiences related to course content. An example of this type of question is, *What was the most powerful scene for you from the film* Amistadt *that we watched in class, and why?* or *Describe a situation in which you had to either stay true to your personal ethics or bow to group pressure. What did you decide to do, and why?*

PROCEDURE   1. Students divide into groups of four, and quads subdivide into pairs A-B and C-D.

2. Student A interviews B and student C interviews D for a predetermined time. The interviewer asks questions, listens, and probes for further information but does not evaluate or respond.

3. Partners reverse roles and interview each other for the same amount of time.

4. Students A and B introduce each other with synthesized summaries of their partner's interview responses to Students C and D. Students C and D do the same for Students A and B.

• • •

EXAMPLES

Introduction to Music

On the first day of a general education music appreciation class, Professor Clara Nett wanted students to participate in an icebreaker, but she wanted the interaction to focus on course content rather than simply hobbies or how students spent their summer vacation. Before the class started, she wrote on the chalkboard: *Welcome to Music 1. What musician recording today (from any style) do you think people will still be listening to in fifty years, and why?* She asked students to reflect upon the prompt as she was calling attendance. She then formed quads, instructing students within each quad to pair up to participate in a Three-Step Interview. She asked students to interview each other to learn names, academic majors, and to share their responses to the question on the chalkboard. After the report out within the quads, Professor Nett asked each quad to share the names of their artists with the whole class, and she wrote the names on the board. She asked students to look at the cumulative list and to identify characteristics the musicians had in common. Professor Nett used their comments to illustrate the distinction between "classic" and "popular," closing by explaining that in this class, they would be studying music masterworks from a variety of genres that had stood the test of time and were now universally acknowledged as classics.

• • •

Calculus

In this calculus class, the professor knew that a majority of students had had difficulty with the most recent homework assignment. He also knew that some of the students struggled with math and were becoming increasingly anxious because they believed that they were falling far behind the other students in the class. Historically, this had been a point in the semester when a significant number of students dropped, and he was trying to improve course retention. He asked students to engage in a Three-Step Interview using the following prompt question: *What homework problem did you find most difficult and why?* He asked the quads to report out to the whole class which of the problems had been identified in their groups, and wrote the numbers of the problems on the board. It became evident that the majority of students had had difficulty with the same few problems, and he knew that this would be reassuring to the struggling students. He used the information generated in the quads to review the most challenging problems and to focus on the issues and steps that had been most troublesome. To help students help each other for the next homework assignment, he reserved the last few minutes of class and suggested that if they wished, they could use the time to make arrangements with one of the other students to work together for peer tutoring and support.

• • •

Patient Care in Radiation Oncology

The instructor of an advanced course in radiologic technology wanted to prepare her students for their clinical practicum. She decided to use a Three-Step Interview to help students anticipate and solve problems they might encounter in the clinics. She hoped that this preparation would increase her students' confidence, reduce their anxiety, and help them transition to the professional world more successfully. She created a series of *What would you do if…?* questions drawn from her medical experience that addressed the kinds of difficult situations her students were most likely to encounter. After partners had interviewed each other and summarized responses for the quad, she gave quads a few minutes to choose the question that had concerned them most. She used their responses as the basis for a whole class discussion on how best to handle the most anxiety-provoking scenarios.

• • •

ONLINE IMPLEMENTATION   Creating a sense of community in online classes is a challenge many instructors face. Implementing a modified Three-Step Interview can be an effective strategy to help students get to know other students in the class. Divide students into base groups of eight to twelve and subdivide each base group into pairs A-B, C-D, and so forth. Create a private forum for each group. Give partners a designated amount of time to interview each other through private messaging or e-mail. Give students additional time to synthesize responses and post an introduction of their partner on the forum to the other students in the base group. You may wish to retain these base groups and partnerships throughout the semester for other kinds of collaborative activities.

VARIATIONS AND EXTENSIONS
- Decide upon a general topic, and ask each student to develop interview questions themselves.

- Rather than asking questions that generate new information, use Three-Step Interview as an activity for students to review what they learned from a lesson.

- Have three teammates interview the fourth in depth; this variation is called a Team Interview (Kagan, 1992).

- Consider having interviewers write up their findings in a format appropriate for the course (for example, in an executive summary, descriptive essay, newspaper article, and so forth).

OBSERVATIONS AND ADVICE   Three-Step Interview is an effective strategy for drawing out students' experience and knowledge from outside of class. Used in this way, it can help motivate students because it bridges the gap between the academic and the "real" world.

Try to create interview questions that are likely to generate a wide array of interesting responses. If interview questions have predictable and similar answers, the interviews will lack energy and the reporting out within the quads will be boring.

Generally, students should interview students whom they do not know well so that the interview is fresh and generates information that is new to the interviewer. This CoLT also helps achieve the goals of exposing students to several views and ideas and of meeting other students in the class.

Establish a time limit so that student discussion does not drift into socializing that has nothing to do with course content.

An initial level of reporting out will have already occurred when student pairs introduce their partner to the next pair. If there is enough class time and the interview questions elicit responses that are important for everyone to hear, have quads report out to the whole class. First give each quad a few minutes to choose a spokesperson and to select one or two responses from their group that they think were most imaginative (or comprehensive, or humorous, for example). As each quad's spokesperson reports out, validate the group's efforts by commenting on what was particularly informative about their contribution.

As with many of the other discussion CoLTs, the built-in reporting feature gives faculty on-the-spot information about how students are connecting with course content. If additional assessment information is desired, conduct a variation of *RSQC2* (CAT 46, Angelo & Cross, 1993, pp. 344–348). This assessment technique provides a five-step structure for students to recall, summarize, question, connect, and comment on either the Three-Step Interview or the follow-up whole-class discussion. Use the entire sequence of assessment activities, or select one step. For example, ask students to *Recall the most important response from the interview you conducted of your partner* or, *Now that we have had a chance to discuss this as a whole class, what questions on this topic do you think would be interesting to ask students to use in next semester's interviews?* Ask students to write their responses in an essay that they submit for evaluation.

If the interview activity was particularly important, consider having students take notes or even record and transcribe the interview. Students could then analyze the interview or use the information to write a biographical essay about the person that they interviewed. Written assignments of this nature can be submitted for evaluation.

KEY RESOURCE   Millis, B. J., & Cottell, P. G. (1998). *Cooperative learning for higher education faculty.* American Council on Education, Series on Higher Education. Phoenix, AZ: Oryx Press, pp. 85–86.

COLLABORATIVE
LEARNING
TECHNIQUE

6

Critical Debate

Characteristics	
Group Size	4–6, THEN 8–12
Time on Task	1–2 HOURS
Duration of Groups	SINGLE SESSION
Online Transferability	MODERATE

DESCRIPTION AND PURPOSE   In a Critical Debate, individual students select the side of an issue that is contrary to their own views. They then form teams and discuss, present, and argue the issue against an opposing team. Preparing for, participating in, and listening to debates offers many benefits to students. Debates can increase motivation, enhance research skills, promote critical thinking, and develop communication proficiency. Debates expose the class to a focused, in-depth, multiple-perspective analysis of issues. Because Critical Debates have the added dimension of requiring students to assume a position opposite to their own, they encourage students to challenge their existing assumptions. This can move students beyond simple dualistic thinking, deepen their understanding of an issue, and help them to recognize the range of perspectives inherent in complex topics. In this way, Critical Debate may also build appreciation for diversity and develop tolerance for other viewpoints.

PREPARATION   Critical Debate is a fairly complex CoLT and thus requires ample preparation. First, spend sufficient time selecting a controversial topic in the field with two identifiable, arguable, and opposing sides that are appropriate to debate. Carefully craft the debate proposition into a one-sentence statement, such as, *Universities should use affirmative action policies to determine student admission.* Proposition statements should avoid ambiguity, yet be general enough to offer students flexibility in building arguments.

Second, determine whether students need any background information to address the proposition. Prepare students for the debate through lecture, assigned reading, discussion, or student research on the topic.

Third, identify ground rules. For example, allow students to use as many arguments as they wish, or have students spend five to ten minutes brainstorming all possible arguments supporting their position and then select their five best arguments. Consider whether each team should select one person as spokesperson, or whether each member of the team will be responsible for presenting at least one of the arguments. Thinking about ground rules ahead of time will also provide the opportunity to decide whether to assign team members specific roles, such as team leader or timekeeper.

PROCEDURE

1. Propose the motion and ask students to identify which side of the proposition they most support. They can indicate a preference by raising their hands or by writing their names and choice on a sign-up sheet or piece of paper.

2. Explain to students that they will argue the side that is contrary to their own beliefs, stressing the benefits of arguing against their personal views (for example, it helps them to clarify their own ideas and to deepen their understanding of the issue).

3. Divide students into four- to six-member teams, with half the teams assigned to one side of the argument and the other half assigned to the opposing argument. Try to get as many students as possible arguing for the side they disagree with, realizing that especially with complex issues, students will likely not divide evenly. A large group of students who "don't know" or who gravitate toward a middle position will provide a fair amount of flexibility in group formation.

4. Explain ground rules and give students time to assign roles and organize how they will prepare for and conduct the debate.

5. Give students time to prepare their arguments (such as fifteen to thirty minutes).

6. Pair teams representing opposing sides.

7. Announce and allow time to present arguments (such as five minutes each side, ten minutes total).

8. Give teams time to prepare rebuttals (such as ten minutes).

9. Announce and allow time to present rebuttals (such as five minutes each side, ten minutes total).

10. Hold a whole-class discussion to summarize the important issues and to give students the opportunity to discuss the experience of arguing opinions they do not hold.

• • •

EXAMPLES

Philosophy of Law

Due to an increase in illegal immigration, terrorist attacks, and Internet sabotage, Professor Lex Rex was starting the semester amid heightened publicity on the need to improve national security. One solution that received significant media attention was a proposal to implement an expanded, federally maintained and integrated individual identification system. Professor Rex believed that it was important for his law students to understand the complexity of the issues regarding individual versus national rights underlying proposals such as this. He therefore decided to add to his course a unit on privacy rights.

To introduce the unit, he had students complete a survey in which they rated from 1 to 5 their level of agreement with a series of statements on the national collection, maintenance, and disposal of personal records. During the weeks that followed, he took care to cover a wide range of examples of the basic conflict from several perspectives, including real-life scenarios concerning everything from financial and medical records to confidentiality of opinions expressed in e-mail and on the Internet. By the completion of the unit, students had at least a basic knowledge of the challenges from both the individual's and the government's perspectives.

To help students synthesize the information presented in the unit and to help them clarify their personal views, he closed the unit with a Critical Debate. Using the initial survey as a guide, he organized students into two groups based on their overall tendency to support individual or national rights. Professor Rex then assigned individual students to a team charged with arguing for or against the proposal, *The government is justified in collecting and maintaining personal information on private citizens.* Wherever possible, he assigned students to a team asked to argue the side contrary to their general beliefs. After the debate, he had students retake the original survey. He then had students compare their individual pre- and post-responses to the survey, noting any areas of change. As a final activity, he had students write an essay responding to the prompt by summarizing the issues using concrete examples and concluding with their personal viewpoints.

• • •

ONLINE IMPLEMENTATION Prepare as you would for a face-to-face (F2F) debate. Write a paragraph that explains the rationale behind Critical Debate, provides the discussion proposal, and gives assignment directions. Provide a deadline for students to choose the side they support least. Organize students into "Pro" or "Con" teams of eight to twelve students, and create a forum for each team. If possible, make the forums "protected access" so that only team members can access their forum. On the whole-class discussion board, inform students of their team assignment and give team members one or two weeks to research and post their arguments on the appropriate forum. After the deadline, open forums to all students, require students to read through the arguments on a forum from the side opposed to their own, and allow an additional week for students to formulate and post rebuttals. Consider summarizing and synthesizing the debate, or assign students to do this task. Although the online debate may lack the sense of immediacy achieved in an in-class debate, the essential characteristics of requiring students to assume, investigate, and debate a contrary perspective are preserved. Consider posting a follow-up Threaded Discussion, in which students can share how it felt to assume a position contrary to their beliefs and inviting them to say whether participating in the debate changed their viewpoints.

VARIATIONS AND EXTENSIONS

- Instead of forming teams, ask students to work in pairs to present opposing sides to each other.

- Identify a topic that has three clear sides, and set up a three-way debate.

- Use a within-team debate in which a team researches the topic. One student presents an argument for one side, and then another student presents an argument from the opposing side. The debate continues as various members within the team alternate between additional arguments and rebuttals.

- In a variation called Structured Academic Controversy (Millis & Cottell, 1998, pp. 140–143), student partners review material on an issue and then synthesize the information to support their position. Two pairs with opposing positions form a quad, and each pair presents the arguments supporting their position to the other pair. Pairs then reverse their positions and argue for the opposing position. The pairs work together to synthesize their findings and to prepare a group report. All four students must agree with the summary. To close the activity, teams make a presentation to the whole class.

- For a more comprehensive assignment, have students research the topic in preparation for the debate.

- If it is not necessary to have students do their own research on the topic, prepare background materials for them that can be distributed in advance or covered at the beginning of the class. This will allow teams to move quickly into the debate.

- Add a writing component by requiring students to work together to draft the four best arguments for their side. After the groups have had time to write out their arguments, ask groups to share their arguments supporting or opposing the proposition.

- Ask students to write a follow-up paper describing issues that they clarified or confirmed, surprises they encountered, new information they gained, or the sources they used to validate new information.

OBSERVATIONS AND ADVICE

This technique works best if students have a reasonably deep knowledge or understanding of the topic so that they can make better arguments and rebuttals. Critical Debate is therefore best used after students have had time to investigate a topic beforehand either through lecture, discussion, or reading assignments. Use this CoLT to introduce a new topic only if the topic can be addressed through common knowledge.

Try to pick a topic that has two appealing sides. Part of the purpose of this CoLT is to help students carefully consider a side of an argument that is contrary to their own beliefs. It is therefore best if the instructor does not have strong feelings of support for one or the other side themselves.

The topic must be one that is engaging. It is especially effective when topics address issues that are contemporary and connected to students' lives.

Try to select a topic that will generate opposing viewpoints. One way to determine this in advance is to use a preliminary assessment technique such as *Classroom Opinion Polls* (CAT 28, Angelo & Cross, 1993, pp. 258–262) to determine attitudes ahead of time.

In some contexts, students will tend to have similar opinions about issues or want to assume the side that they perceive is popular or "politically correct." They may not feel safe to argue a side that is in opposition to their own or that they know is generally unpopular. If one is careful to set up a nonthreatening environment and explain the purpose of Critical Debate, however, students can enjoy role reversal, and the activity can take on the qualities of a fun game.

Depending upon the importance of this CoLT to overall teaching goals, choose an additional follow-up activity. For example, use *Pro and Con Grid* (CAT 10, Angelo & Cross, 1993, pp. 168–171) and require students to list each argument and balance it with a competing claim or rebuttal. This assessment technique provides a quick overview of each student's final analysis and understanding of both sides of the issue. A more complex assignment for use after the debate is *Analytic Memo* (CAT 12, Angelo & Cross, 1993, pp. 177–180). For this activity, ask students to write a one- or two-page analysis of the issue, being careful to provide equitable coverage of both sides. Suggest that they select a role such as "policy analyst for a legislator" or "consultant for a corporation's chief executive officer." Taking on such a role may make it easier for them to assume a position and it also establishes the writing audience.

KEY RESOURCES Bean, J. C. (1996). *Engaging ideas: A professor's guide to integrating writing, critical thinking, and active learning in the classroom.* San Francisco: Jossey-Bass, pp. 6–7, 176–177.

Brookfield, S. D., & Preskill, S. (1999). *Discussion as a way of teaching: Tools and techniques for democratic classrooms.* San Francisco: Jossey-Bass, pp. 114–115.

McKeachie, W. J. (1994). *Teaching tips: A guidebook for the beginning college teacher,* 9th ed. Lexington, MA: D. C. Heath, p. 44.

Chapter 8

Techniques for Reciprocal Teaching

IN ANSWER TO THE QUESTION, "What is the most effective method of teaching?" McKeachie and his colleagues answered that it depends on the goal, the student, and the teacher. But the next best answer is, "Students teaching other students" (McKeachie, Pintrich, Lin, & Smith, 1986, p. 63). In Reciprocal Peer Teaching, students serve as both teacher and learner, and the CoLTs in this section emphasize mutual exchange through these dual student roles.

Reciprocal teaching puts into practice what researchers and scholars are finding about effective learning. It is active rather than passive, requiring students to both give and receive as they help each other gain knowledge or understanding. Students also enhance their own learning as they attempt to understand the subject well enough to coach others. Reciprocal teaching encourages interdependence. Students must make good use of the knowledge, skills, and understandings of their peers. They must cooperate rather than compete, as each student has a stake in the successful learning of others. Reticent or lazy students have a role to play; "easy riders" are discouraged, since their peers depend upon their performance as peer teachers. Reciprocal teaching also helps students retain information, because students synthesize, clarify, and rehearse ideas and receive immediate reinforcement of course concepts. The six CoLTs in this chapter, listed in Exhibit 8.1, provide frameworks for students to purposefully help each other master subject matter content and develop discipline-based skills—major instructional goals for most teachers.

EXHIBIT 8.1

Reciprocal Peer Teaching CoLTs

This CoLT	Is a Technique in Which Students:	It is Particularly Useful for:
7: Note-Taking Pairs	Pool information from their individual notes to create an improved, partner version	Helping students acquire missing information and correct inaccuracies in their notes and learn to become better note takers
8: Learning Cell	Quiz each other using questions they have developed individually about a reading assignment or other learning activity	Engaging students actively in thinking about content and encouraging them to challenge each other to pursue deeper levels of thought
9: Fishbowl	Form concentric circles with the smaller, inside group of students discussing and the larger, outside group listening and observing	Providing opportunities for students to model or observe group processes in a discussion setting
10: Role Play	Assume a different identity and act out a scenario	Engaging students in a creative activity that helps them "learn by doing"
11: Jigsaw	Develop knowledge about a given topic and then teach it to others	Motivating students to learn and process information deeply enough to teach it to their peers
12: Test-Taking Teams	Prepare for a test in working groups, take the test individually, and then retake the test in their groups	Helping students assess and improve their understanding of subject matter as they also teach each other test-taking strategies

**COLLABORATIVE
LEARNING
TECHNIQUE**

7

Note-Taking Pairs

Characteristics	
Group Size	PAIRS
Time on Task	5–15 MINUTES
Duration of Groups	SINGLE SESSION or MULTIPLE
Online Transferability	MODERATE

DESCRIPTION AND PURPOSE

In Note-Taking Pairs, student partners work together to improve their individual notes. Working with a peer provides students with an opportunity to revisit and cross-check notes with another source. Partners help each other acquire missing information and correct inaccuracies so that their combined effort is superior to their individual notes.

Being able to take good notes is an important learning skill, yet many students are poor note takers; their notes are incomplete and inaccurate. The purpose of this CoLT is to provide students with a structured activity to pool information, fill in gaps, check for and correct mistakes, and help each other learn to be better note takers. Although Note-Taking Pairs was originally designed to improve lecture notes, teachers now also use it to help students improve their notes on reading assignments and other kinds of learning activities.

PREPARATION

Consider providing students with guidance about how to take good notes in a mini-lecture, a handout, or by providing examples of effective notes. Also, present material in class in ways that encourage students to take detailed notes. For example, speak slowly; provide handouts of complicated graphs and figures so that students can keep up; and use the whiteboard or overhead projector to show overall structure by using titles and headings (Davis, 1993, p. 182).

PROCEDURE   1. Students individually take notes of the major points from a body of content, such as a lecture or a text chapter.

2. Students form pairs, at your direction or by choosing partners.

3. Partner A begins by summarizing the main points from a section of the content to Partner B, who offers corrections and additional information.

4. Partner B summarizes the next section, and Partner A offers corrections and additional information.

5. The partners continue to alternate sharing summaries, corrections, and additional information until they have completed checking their notes.

• • •

EXAMPLES

General Physics

A professor teaching a large introductory course knew that he would lecture frequently and that most of his students would not have good note-taking skills. At the beginning of the semester, he assigned students to pairs. He told students that the pairs would work together for ten minutes at the end of each major lecture to ensure that all students would have as complete and accurate a set of notes as possible. The professor reassigned pairs after each of the four major course examinations to give students the benefits of working with a number of their peers.

• • •

Geriatrics

Because many of her students were not scoring well on the weekly quizzes, Professor Penny Cillen believed that her students had not been reading their assignments thoroughly and critically. Her first solution was to ask students to take notes on their reading assignments and to submit these to her for review. As she reviewed the notes, she noticed that some students were much better note takers than others. She decided to use Note-Taking Pairs so that the better note takers could help the poorer note takers develop more effective note-taking strategies. She made a quick list organizing student names into two columns based on the quality of their notes. At the beginning of the next class session, she formed pairs based on her lists and asked students to take out the notes they took the night before. Without formalizing the tutoring process by asking the better student to help the poorer student, she simply asked students to compare notes, with each person adding something to his or her notes from the other student's notes. She used this technique for the next several weeks, noticing that students' notes gradually improved, as did the overall student performance on the quizzes.

• • •

Statics

Professor Alec Tricity covered extensive information in his lectures that was not yet available in print. It was critical that students take excellent lecture notes. Professor Tricity decided to require students to work with a partner to compile notes and submit both their individual and their collaborative notes as an in-class portfolio. The portfolio was due at the midterm and again at the end of the semester, and it constituted a significant proportion of the final grade. The professor organized the students into pairs, creating new pairs after the midterm. The pairs were told to take notes individually, and then to work collaboratively outside of class to combine their notes into a synthesized and typed single version. The synthesized version would serve as each student's exam study guide, and students were told to (1) create a subsection that included a lexicon of terms and definitions, (2) search out additional resources and expand upon any topics that they found particularly intriguing or unclear, and (3) write down questions or make any comments about the individual lectures or class in a "Feedback" section.

The professor also created an in-class portfolio cover sheet that the students filled out and attached to their portfolios when they submitted them for evaluation. The cover sheet included the rubrics by which the portfolio would be evaluated (thoroughness, clarity, followed directions, additional research, and so forth) along with a space for assigning points. Professor Tricity found a marked improvement on exam grades. The portfolio also provided him with an easy and useful class assessment since it included both individual and collaborative notes and a cover sheet with assessment rubrics. The portfolio had the unintended positive effect of creating a better sense of community, because each student now had a friend in class.

• • •

History of Western Civilization

> Professor Meg Nacarta had been posting text "lectures" in her online class, and students were required to complete worksheets covering the information in the lectures as one of their weekly assignments. She discovered that a significant percentage of her students were simply electronically copying segments of the lectures and pasting them in their assignments as the answers to the worksheet questions. For the next semester, she removed the posted lectures and published her lectures as a separate document that was sold along with the textbook in the college bookstore. This prevented students from simply copying and pasting the material. She also modified and expanded her worksheets to include questions requiring more critical interaction with the information as well as questions that asked for simple summaries of various portions of the readings. She organized students into pairs, and asked them to work first individually and then together to complete each worksheet. Students were given an initial deadline for their individual assignments, and a second deadline for a collaborative version of their assignment.

• • •

ONLINE IMPLEMENTATION Instructors in online classes can assign Note-Taking Pairs for reading assignments if the class is relatively small, enrollment is stable, and all students have access to and know how to use word processing attachments. Provide guidance on how to take good notes on reading assignments. Instruct students how to exchange notes (for example, through e-mail attachments) and a time frame for exchange. If you wish students to consolidate notes into a single partner version, different font styles or colors can distinguish individual contributions.

VARIATIONS AND EXTENSIONS
- Ask student pairs to sit together during the lecture. At various times throughout the lecture, stop and ask partners to participate in this CoLT. You can offer specific prompts, such as, *Ask each other what was the major point so far and make sure that that point is clear in your notes.* This technique keeps students' attention focused on the lecture and allows students to rehearse the information and to correct any misinformation or perceptions.

- Give students overnight to revisit their notes to make revisions and corrections and to add information before sharing the notes with a peer. This will allow students to clarify their own thoughts and to make their writing more legible before sharing their notes with another.

- Consider making your lecture notes available to student pairs after using this CoLT for students to recheck and thus revisit their notes a third time.

- If you do not wish to use in-class time for students to compare notes, tell students to share their notes outside of class through e-mail attachments. Students can copy and paste notes into a single partner version, using different font styles or colors to distinguish individual contributions.

- Use this CoLT for students to review homework assignments, check answers to homework problems at the beginning of class, or to review for a test.

OBSERVATIONS AND ADVICE

This technique can help reinforce course concepts, but it can also reinforce inaccuracy if both students in a pair have faulty information. Repeat and emphasize the main concepts frequently, and review and assess the notes periodically to make sure that students are learning the correct information.

It is important that each student take something from the other student's notes to improve his or her own notes. If only one student is taking good notes, that student will probably resent helping the student who is taking poor notes.

To assess learning, ask students to respond in writing to two questions: (1) *What is the most important suggestion you got from your peer?* and (2) *What do you think is the most helpful suggestion you gave to your peer?* (CAT 6: *Minute Paper*, Angelo & Cross, 1993, pp. 148–153). If the major purpose of the exercise is to improve written note-taking skills, occasionally collect notes before the peer conversation and again after. Or to simplify your review, ask students to highlight or indicate what changes they made as a result of discussion with a peer. If you are more interested in assessing the quality of the peer suggestions, ask students to hand in one set of their notes with suggestions by their peer made in a different color pencil.

KEY RESOURCES

Johnson, D. W., Johnson, R., & Smith, K. (1998). *Active learning: Cooperation in the college classroom.* Edina, MN: Interaction Book Company, pp. 2:28, 3:21–3:22.

Millis, B. J., & Cottell, P. G. (1998). *Cooperative learning for higher education faculty.* American Council on Education, Series on Higher Education. Phoenix, AZ: Oryx Press, pp. 113–114.

COLLABORATIVE
LEARNING
TECHNIQUE

8

Learning Cell

Characteristics	
Group Size	PAIRS
Time on Task	15–30 MINUTES
Duration of Groups	SINGLE SESSION, MULTIPLE, OR ALL TERM
Online Transferability	MODERATE

DESCRIPTION AND PURPOSE

In Learning Cells, students individually develop questions about a reading assignment or other learning activity and then work with a partner, alternating asking and answering each other's questions.

The purpose of this CoLT is to engage students actively in thinking about content, to encourage students to generate thought-provoking questions, and to teach students how to check their understanding. Creating questions about an assignment requires students to think about the content in a way that is different from simply taking notes on it. It provides an opportunity for students to think analytically, to elaborate as they put material into their own words, and to begin to use the language of the discipline. Responding to the questions of peers provides a platform for discussion based on student levels of understanding. Exchanging questions and answers with a peer can motivate students and challenge them to pursue deeper levels of thought.

In addition to developing content mastery, this technique motivates students to practice interpersonal skills such as giving feedback in nonthreatening ways, maintaining focus, and developing and sustaining mutual tasks. Students learn to question, explain, admit confusion, and reveal misconceptions—something that they are more likely to do with a peer than with the instructor. Finally, an effective partner can act as a role model for useful learning strategies.

PREPARATION   Prepare students by teaching them how to write good questions. See Chapter Four, Exhibit 4.1, and Observations and Advice in CoLT 26: Dyadic Essays for suggestions.

PROCEDURE   1. Ask students to individually develop a list of questions and answers dealing with the major points raised in a reading or other learning assignment.

2. Form student pairs, or simply ask students to partner with a student sitting nearby.

3. Explain the process by which you want partners to alternate asking and answering each other's questions.

4. Student A begins by asking the first question, and Student B answers the question. Student A offers corrections and additional information until a satisfactory answer is achieved.

5. Student B asks the next question and Student A answers, and the process repeats until all questions have been asked and answered.

• • •

EXAMPLES

Introduction to Art

In this art appreciation course, the instructor decided to use Learning Cells to help students review major schools of art in order to prepare for an upcoming examination. The instructor asked students to develop two questions for each of the following schools: Cubism, Dada, Expressionism, Fauvism, Futurism, Impressionism, Post-Impressionism, and Surrealism. One question was to address a defining feature, the other was to ask a more thought-provoking question emerging out of some aspect of the school that the student found particularly intriguing. After students finished asking and responding to each other's questions, they turned in their questions and answers to the instructor. He reviewed the questions, added a few questions that had not been addressed by the students, and then selected five questions for each school, transcribing them into a single document. At the next class meeting, the professor distributed the handout as a study guide, explaining to students that he would draw his exam questions from the guide.

• • •

Human Anatomy and Physiology

Professor Tish Oosells chose this CoLT to break up her three-hour class sessions and to deepen her students' understanding of the content she was presenting. She lectured on her first topic and then distributed a handout with a set of questions based on the lecture that were samples of the kind she would use on an exam. She next engaged students in a class discussion in which she guided them through the process of creating similar questions. After she lectured on her second topic, she asked students to write a set of questions on their own that addressed the material she had just covered.

She then asked students to find a partner and take turns asking and answering the questions. She used this technique throughout the semester, and as students became more proficient with practice, the activity took less time. Professor Oosells believed that the process of creating the questions provided a clear framework for focusing students' attention on the lecture. She also thought that responding to another student's questions provided the opportunity for each student to recall, rehearse, and check their understanding of key concepts in a way that kept students engaged and motivated during the long class session.

• • •

Race and Ethnic Relations

This professor organized his online class into three segments. At the beginning of the semester, he assigned students to work in pairs for the first course segment, and then reassigned new pairs for the next two segments. For each of the three segments, he asked students to prepare two questions that particularly intrigued or puzzled them. Since the course focused on racial relations, he encouraged students to use the assignment to ask questions that were appropriate to segment topics but that students might otherwise feel uncomfortable about asking. For example, one student asked, "Should I be using the terms 'Black' or 'African American'?" Partners then exchanged questions. This format gave students permission to pursue answers outside of class (for example, "I'm in a class and was asked to find out whether 'Black' or 'African American' was the preferred term. Can you help me?"). Students returned their answers to the partner who had created the questions. The partner added any comments or follow-up questions, and submitted it to the professor. The professor evaluated both partners' contributions, added his own comments, and assigned each student a grade that took into consideration the thoroughness and thoughtfulness of their work. For each segment, he selected several of the best questions and answers and posted them in a forum on the course's discussion board.

• • •

ONLINE IMPLEMENTATION A modified version of this CoLT is an effective strategy for enhancing community and promoting reciprocal teaching in online classes. Organize students into pairs and ask them to e-mail exchanges of questions and answers.

VARIATIONS AND EXTENSIONS
- Instead of using this activity only sporadically, use the technique regularly as an opening activity for class sessions (McKeachie, 2002).

- Vary this CoLT by having each student in the pair read different materials. Rather than asking questions about the reading, have them "teach" the essentials of their reading to the second student (McKeachie, 2002).

- Provide students with generic question stems to guide their question writing (for example, *Explain why ____. Why is ____ important? Compare ___ and ___. Summarize ____.*). This variation is called Guided Reciprocal Peer Questioning, and a fuller list of generic question stems may be found in Chapter Four, Structuring the Learning Task.

- Vary the type of question. On one assignment, have students create an essay question. On the next assignment, have students create five multiple-choice questions or five True/False questions. Or ask students to create one of each kind for the assignment.

- Rather than having students asking and answering questions orally, have students write out questions and answers.

- Have long-term student pairs meet frequently to administer questions under test-like conditions. This variation is called Reciprocal Peer Tutoring (Fantuzzo, Dimeff, & Fox, 1989; Fantuzzo, Riggio, Connelly, & Dimeff, 1989).

- Ask students to write more open-ended questions that may not have a single "right" answer. Students may then pose questions that interest, puzzle, or inspire them.

OBSERVATIONS AND ADVICE The time this CoLT takes up in class can vary widely depending on the kinds of questions students will develop (questions that can be answered in a word or phrase, or questions requiring more elaborate responses). Asking students to prepare questions in advance can save class time.

Both students must prepare and participate for this activity to work well. If students are not prepared with thoughtful questions, time is wasted and nonproductive. Therefore, consider using an "entry ticket" approach (see Chapter Two, Orienting Students), requiring students to be prepared in order to participate and allowing pairs to re-form if a student comes unprepared. Students who are unprepared lose participation points.

To assess this CoLT, ask students to write out, on a single sheet of paper, two questions that their peer should be able to answer, leaving space on the page for their peer to provide brief written answers. Collect the papers. This assessment should be sparingly used, perhaps once in the beginning of the term to alert students to the importance of the exercise and again later to note improvement in questions and answers. Or in a report out to the class, ask a few students to volunteer an especially interesting, creative, or provocative question posed by their peer. Ask other students in the class to respond to the question.

KEY RESOURCES Johnson, D. W., Johnson, R., & Smith, K. (1998). *Active learning: Cooperation in the college classroom.* Edina, MN: Interaction Book Company, pp. 2:28, 3:21–3:22.

McKeachie, W. J. (2002). *McKeachie's teaching tips: Strategies, research, and theory for College and University Teachers.* Boston: Houghton Mifflin, pp. 190–191.

COLLABORATIVE
L E A R N I N G
T E C H N I Q U E

9

Fishbowl

Characteristics

Group Size	3–5 INSIDE, REMAINING STUDENTS OUTSIDE
Time on Task	15–20 MINUTE DISCUSSION, 10–15 MINUTE DEBRIEFING
Duration of Groups	SINGLE SESSION
Online Transferability	MODERATE

DESCRIPTION AND PURPOSE

In Fishbowl, an outer circle of students sits around a smaller, inner circle of students. Students in the inner circle engage in an in-depth discussion, while students in the outer circle consider what is being said and how it is being said. This CoLT has also been called Inside Outside Circles. Inner circle students are challenged to participate in a high-level discussion while the outer circle is able to listen to the discussion and critique content, logic, and group interaction. This technique therefore serves two purposes: to provide structure for in-depth discussion and to provide opportunities for students to model or observe group processes in a discussion setting.

PREPARATION

Decide whether you want to facilitate the inner circle discussion, sit with the outer circle, or separate yourself so that you can observe both circles.

In class, preparation time involves having students move into the circles and giving students instructions. You will need moveable chairs and sufficient classroom space to form the circles. If the physical constraints of the classroom do not allow movement of chairs into circles, consider having the inner circle of students simply sit in chairs and participate in the discussion at the front of the classroom.

PROCEDURE 1. Ask a small group of students (generally three to five) to form a circle in class, and ask the remaining students to form a larger circle around the first circle.

2. Give students the following guidelines: Only inner circle students will speak; outer circle students will be "observers" and will take notes on both content and group process; although observers will not speak during the Fishbowl discussion, they will have the opportunity to address any issues that arise in the follow-up discussion.

3. Give students the prompt question for discussion.

4. Ask students to report out in a whole-class discussion, requesting that they address the content issues that arose and that they comment on group processes.

• • •

EXAMPLES

General Biology

Professor Ann Virement structured her large lecture class to include regular small-group break-out sessions. As she observed the small-group discussions, she noticed that student participation was uneven: some students within each group contributed while others remained silent. She decided to use a Fishbowl discussion to model effective group interaction as well as bring together all of the elements of a unit that the course had just covered on the causes and effects of ozone depletion. She selected a group of five students she believed would be comfortable in the spotlight and asked them before class if they would be willing to participate in a discussion while other students observed. She then had them move chairs to form a circle at the front of the room, prompting discussion with the following question: *Why are we worried about changes in the ozone layer?*

The five students engaged in a discussion of the topic while the other members of the class listened and observed. When the group had completed its discussion, she asked the observers to volunteer any additional insights about the content. She then asked the inner circle students to comment on their interactions, asking them what went well with the process and what could have been improved. She also asked the observers to comment on the group process. To close the activity, she asked all students to reflect on their own participation in groups, and to jot down in their notes the good discussion practices they learned from the Fishbowl activity. She asked them to put a star next to at least one strategy they planned to implement in future group work.

• • •

Administration of Higher Education

In this graduate-level seminar, the professor engaged students in whole-class discussion on a regular basis, but she wanted to vary the form of the discussion to keep the course interesting. After several weeks exploring the origins and purposes of higher education, the professor divided the class in half and asked the students in one half of the room to form pairs and participate in *CoLT 1: Think-Pair-Share,* responding to the prompt, *In what ways is higher education an industry?*

She had the students in the other half of the room also form pairs, but they responded to the prompt, *In what ways is higher education not an industry?*

After students had shared and discussed their ideas, she selected four students (two students from each side) to participate in a Fishbowl discussion in the center of the room while the remaining students critiqued discussion content and group processes. The professor then engaged the class in whole-class discussion, asking observers to contribute additional insights on either content or process.

• • •

 ### American Cinema

In an online undergraduate film history course, the professor required students to participate in weekly Threaded Discussions, but he was frustrated with the superficial level of most of the postings. He found that only a few students posted insightful, thorough responses to the prompts; the majority of students seemed to be in a hurry, posting quick comments such as "I agree" or "Good point," without seeming to read all the preceding remarks and without contributing in such a manner as to move the discussion forward. The large number of cursory comments in between more thoughtful comments tended to dilute the quality of the whole discussion. Several students complained that reading the discussion was a waste of time. The instructor therefore decided to use a series of Fishbowls to ensure more focused, in-depth discussions. As a culminating exercise for a unit on the role of music in films, he selected five of his best students and told them that he would like them to participate in—and model—a thoughtful discussion, responding to the prompt, *In what ways do film score composers use music to support plot development?*

He asked the remaining students to "lurk" and read the postings, but not respond to them. When the discussion had unfolded to a satisfactory level, the professor gave the "lurkers" an opportunity to post any comments that they might like to contribute that were significant and new. Using the film score discussion as a model, he selected a new group of five students to participate in the inner circle discussion of the next unit's Threaded Discussion, and another five students for the following week's discussion, systematically moving through the remaining students. This technique helped to create Threaded Discussions that were thoughtful, thorough, and focused. Additionally, it helped make the discussions more manageable and easier to read. To ensure that lurkers read the discussion thoughtfully, he added questions to his worksheet assignments that asked students various synthesis and evaluation questions on the discussion postings.

• • •

ONLINE IMPLEMENTATION   Because whole-class discussions can become unwieldy and often repetitive, Fishbowl is a useful discussion-structuring technique in online classes. In a synchronous environment such as a Chat session, assign individual students to "virtual" inner or outer circles. Inner circle students participate actively, responding to the prompt, while outer circle students lurk and observe the discussion. After the inner circle discussion is finished, outer circle students are invited (or required) to comment.

Fishbowl is probably more effective, however, conducted asynchronously. To do this, create the prompt, explain the grading criteria, identify which students will participate in the inner circle, and determine the time frame. (For example, inner circle students will discuss for one week; outer circle students will discuss the following week.) Create two forums, one labeled Inner Circle, the other labeled Outer Circle. If the forum software allows it, consider making the inner circle a protected forum such that only inner circle students can post responses. If students in the inner circle need prodding or if the discussion needs redirecting, consider sending the participants a private message. During the outer circle discussion segment, leave both forums open so that students can switch back and forth to read postings.

VARIATIONS AND EXTENSIONS

- Instead of one large Fishbowl, consider multiple small Fishbowls of four to six students, with two or three students in each of the inner and outer circles.

- After the initial Fishbowl discussion, ask students to switch places, with the outer circle assuming the inner circle role, and vice versa.

- Allow students from the outer circle to join the inner circle by tapping a student on the shoulder and exchanging places with him or her. This is a fun strategy for creating enthusiasm, and it keeps more students active and engaged. Be aware, though, that some students and some cultures and religions are not comfortable with being touched, so consider as an alternative telling students who wish to join or exit a group to simply raise their hands. Or give an entry/exit token such as a slip of paper.

- Have students perform a task, such as solving a problem or learning a new skill, instead of discussing an issue.

- Bring in a group of experts to form the inner circle.

OBSERVATIONS AND ADVICE

Because you are putting students on the spot, it is important to have established a level of trust in the classroom and to know that students are ready and prepared to be the center of attention. Ensure that students are prepared for this task by giving them an out-of-class reading assignment, by using this technique at the end of a unit, or by allowing them a few minutes in class to think before beginning the technique.

Since some students are more comfortable than others speaking in a public forum, ask for volunteers, or solicit participation from students that are likely to be at ease in this format. On the other hand, this strategy may continue to reward the same students who always speak in class; instead try to provide less verbal or vocal students an opportunity to share their thoughts.

Participate in the discussion only if it becomes necessary in order to stimulate conversation or to steer discussion back on target.

Consider creating a handout with specific questions for observers to answer either during or after the Fishbowl activity. For example, ask students to track the order, type (new information or elaboration), and duration of student participation. Follow-up questions could ask students to contribute their own insights or to synthesize the discussion, pretending the "audience" is a student who was not able to attend class that day.

KEY RESOURCES

Kagan, S. (1990). The structural approach to cooperative learning. *Educational Leadership, 47*(4) 12–15.

Tiberius, R. (1995). *Small group teaching: A trouble-shooting guide.* Toronto: OISE Press, p. 25.

**COLLABORATIVE
LEARNING
TECHNIQUE**

10

Role Play

Characteristics	
Group Size	2–5
Time on Task	15–45 MINUTES
Duration of Groups	SINGLE SESSION
Online Transferability	HIGH

DESCRIPTION AND PURPOSE   A Role Play is a created situation in which students deliberately act out or assume characters or identities they would not normally assume in order to accomplish learning goals. Role playing provides an action environment for students to experience the emotional and intellectual responses of an assumed identity or imagined circumstance. At its essence, Role Play is an example of "learning by doing." The word *role* indicates that students must actively apply knowledge, skills, and understanding to successfully speak and act from a different, assigned perspective. The term *play* indicates that students use their imaginations and have fun, acting out their parts in a nonthreatening environment. Role Play thus engages students in a creative, participatory activity that requires them to apply course concepts as they assume fictional identities or envision themselves in unfamiliar situations.

PREPARATION   It is critical to spend thoughtful time designing the scenario for your Role Play. Appropriate scenarios require interaction from stakeholders with multiple perspectives. Therefore, identify the perspectives and define the type and number of characters and the framework for their actions. In addition to the roles for persons who are participating in the action, consider assigning group process roles such as moderator (who can, for example, intervene if a person is falling out of character) or observer (who interprets and comments on the action). When crafting the basic story line, it is best to initiate the action through a critical event that the players must respond to, such as a comment by one of the actors or an incident that has just occurred.

Identify resources (if any) for each of the playing roles, and decide how the activity will end. For example, will you set a time limit, or will you let the scenario end naturally?

PROCEDURES

1. Ask students to form groups with enough members in each group to assume each stakeholder role.

2. Present the scenario and allow time for discussion of the problem situation. It is important to allow sufficient time for students to ask questions on any aspects of the scenario that are unclear.

3. Assign or ask students to each assume a stakeholder role. If assigning group process roles such as moderator or observer, make sure students are clear on their tasks.

4. Inform students of the time limit or other parameters that will signify the end of the activity.

5. Instruct students to enact the role play. The role play should run only until the proposed behavior is clear, the targeted characteristic has been developed, or the skill has been practiced.

6. Follow the role play with a discussion within the small groups and/or with the whole class. Discussion should focus on the students' interpretations of the roles and the motivations for and consequences of their actions.

7. Consider asking students to reenact the role play, changing characters or redefining the scenario and then holding another discussion.

• • •

EXAMPLES

Psychology of Prejudice

The purpose of this course is to help students understand the complex psychological patterns that develop among different majority and non-majority groups resulting from the effects of overt and covert discrimination. In order to increase his students' awareness of the nature of prejudiced interactions as well as help them to identify appropriate ways to respond, Professor Watts D. Matta uses Role Play frequently in his class. Professor Matta typically organizes his students into groups of three and assigns group members one of three roles: prejudiced speaker, responder, or social observer. Throughout the academic term, he crafts a variety of simulated situations and creates characters representing multiple perspectives that his students assume (such as ethnic, racial, gender, socioeconomic background, physical disabilities). For example, in one situation he creates a business meeting scenario in which the speaker is a manager who makes an offending racist remark, the responder is a subordinate representing the targeted race who must determine an appropriate response, and the social observer describes his or her feelings when watching the scene. At the end of the activity, the students share their reactions first with their groups and then with the whole class, critiquing the response and the reaction. The class then participates in a post-exercise discussion that focuses on a range of topics that emerge from the exchange (Plous, 2000).

• • •

ESL Oral Communication Skills I

Professor Ann Glish knew that many students were self-conscious about speaking in her beginning ESL class. As non-native speakers, they came from countries around the world, and feared that they would make mistakes and that other students would not understand them. Yet it was essential that students practice extensively in order to develop vocabulary, grammatical accuracy, and clear pronunciation. She discovered that if she asked students to pretend they were someone else, it ameliorated some of their anxiety. Furthermore, if they assumed a role in a scenario that she created based on everyday situations, it motivated them because they immediately saw the usefulness of the exercises. She created scenarios such as ordering dinner at a restaurant, or asking for directions to the main campus library, that emphasized everyday English. She then formed small groups so that students had more opportunities to practice speaking and so that the context would be less threatening than speaking in the whole class.

• • •

 ### History of the Vietnam War

In this hybrid class on the Vietnam War, the professor believed it was important to use classroom time for lecture, but he also wanted his students to understand the war's complexity and to be able to empathize with the viewpoints of the war's various stakeholders. This goal was particularly important to him since he knew that his class attracted many students who had had personal experience with the war. For example, there were Vietnam vets, immigrant students from Vietnam, returning adult students who had actively protested the war, or parents whose children had died or been injured in the war. Thus many of the students had strong feelings and preformed beliefs about the war's issues. He worked with his institution's technology department to establish a Virtual Reality Environment (VRE) for his class and then created scenarios that correlated with his lecture topics. Rather than establishing individual roles, he developed generic role categories, such as American Soldier and South Vietnamese Villager. Each student selected a role and then adopted an appropriate name. He retained for himself the role of moderator so that he could intervene if exchanges became too emotional or inappropriate. He provided students with the option of entering the VRE anonymously, but if they wished to earn participation credit, they messaged him privately with the moniker they had assumed in the Role Play. At regular, scheduled intervals throughout the term, he devoted class time to discussion of the themes that emerged.

• • •

Business Management Practices

A professor teaching an online course decided to use a role-play game to teach concepts and content. He formed six groups of four students each, with each group representing a company and with each student assuming one of the following roles: CEO, financial officer, operations chief, or marketing executive. The companies competed against each other, completing the game that extended for three phases of the companies' life cycles (start-up, growth, and independence). The game simulated nine years during nine weeks of the course. Each year the students "employed" in each company established crucial input data, such as price, advertising, purchase, production, size of sales force, and so on. The instructor collected data and compiled them for the game, creating output data for each company that consisted of units sold, back orders, market share, operating income, income tax, net income, and so forth. The professor evaluated the companies based on results after nine years. Each company met in regular conference, during which the employees discussed data. In another conference, called Managers' Corner, the students participated in management-related discussions (adapted from Hsu, 1989).

• • •

ONLINE IMPLEMENTATION   Chat sessions or Virtual Reality Environments offer ideal frameworks for implementing role playing online. A Chat session typically occurs in real time, while VREs offer the option of either synchronous or asynchronous interaction. Because teachers can provide students with the option of assuming roles anonymously, the self-consciousness that sometimes accompanies face-to-face (F2F) role play is eliminated. If this CoLT is one that seems to fit well with your teaching goals, consider investigating software products that have been developed for designing and delivering online role plays. The commercial market in this area is dynamic, and hence the best strategy is simply to conduct a Boolean search online (starting with simple keywords such as "role play" + "teaching") using a standard search engine such as Google.com, or consult the technology advisors for teaching on your campus.

VARIATIONS AND EXTENSIONS

- Allow students to help determine the scenario, identify the major stakeholders, and create the roles.

- After practicing, have student groups perform the role play in front of the class. Or, instead of having multiple groups participating in multiple role plays, consider having one group role-play in front of the rest of the class. Assign observers specific tasks for interpreting the action and dialogue of the role play.

- Combine this activity with a Fishbowl, by having one group perform the role play while another group watches, and then have the groups trade places.

- Especially in VREs, consider creating roles that allow students to manipulate the environment. For example, a Manipulative Devil sets up obstacles and creates challenges for the characters; the Improvising Storyteller creates extensions to the scenario, adapting to unforeseen twists in the action (No author cited; retrieved December 4, 2003, from http:// adulted.about.com/library/weekly/aa092502b.htm.)

- Use Role Play to help students develop speaking and listening skills in a technique called Triad Listening (Luotto & Stoll, 1996). Groups of three students take turns performing specific roles (Speaker, Reflective Listener, and Referee). Speakers talk first, trying to state their ideas as concisely as possible and then amplifying and clarifying the idea with an example. Reflective Listeners say back to the Speakers what the Speaker has said, but using their own words. Reflective Listeners try to be as thorough and accurate as possible. They try to avoid simply repeating the same words, but instead use their creativity to capture the essence of what the Speaker has said. Referees make sure that group members stick to the rules. If the Referee (or the Speaker) feels that the Reflective

Listener's summary is inaccurate, the Referee interrupts and helps clear up the misunderstanding.

OBSERVATIONS AND ADVICE Spend sufficient time prior to the activity to ensure that students understand the purpose of the role play. If they don't understand the learning goals, students may get off track, or the role play may fall flat and seem artificial.

Students must also understand the nature and character of the roles they are assuming. If they know who they are, then they will be more effective in the role. If the role is a complicated one, then they may need time to reflect or conduct research prior to enacting their role.

Although many students will be drawn to this CoLT with enthusiasm, others will feel self-conscious and uncomfortable about assuming a role. They may resist this activity, protesting that it seems silly. To reduce their discomfort, take care to create a nonthreatening environment and consider preparing students earlier in the term with icebreaker activities (see Chapter Two, Orienting Students). Also, reassure students that while acting is important in this CoLT, you are not trying to develop acting ability but rather to achieve specific learning goals. Finally, consider allowing these students to assume observer roles.

The closure stage of this activity is very important. Take time to debrief on the lessons learned through the experience. Don't expect students to develop deep understanding of human situations after a limited exposure in a single role play. Help students relate the role play to their own lives using an assessment technique such as *Application Cards* (CAT 24, Angelo & Cross, 1993, pp. 236–239).

The real value of Role Play occurs when students form general opinions about course concepts that they developed and internalized as a consequence of assuming a new identity or acting in a new situation.

This CoLT can be effective, but as with any teaching strategy, be careful not to use it excessively. If it is overused, it can become tedious and feel artificial or silly.

To assess or grade Role Play, consider videotaping the role plays or having students create their own videotape. Groups can view the videotape and discuss the specific problems or general principles revealed in the tapes, perhaps summarizing and synthesizing their observations into an essay. Alternatively, the whole class can watch one or more of the films and discuss the critical issues or themes that emerge.

KEY RESOURCES Naidu, S., Ip, A., & Linser, R. (2000). Dynamic goal-based role-play simulation on the Web: A case study. *Educational Technology and Society* 3(3), 190–202.

Plous, S. (2000). Responding to overt displays of prejudice: A role-playing exercise. *Teaching of Psychology* 27(3), 198–200.

**COLLABORATIVE
LEARNING
TECHNIQUE**

11

Jigsaw

Characteristics	
Group Size	4–6; RECOMBINE TO 4–6
Time on Task	VARIES
Duration of Groups	SINGLE SESSION or MULTIPLE
Online Transferability	MODERATE

DESCRIPTION AND PURPOSE   Students work in small groups to develop knowledge about a given topic and to formulate effective ways of teaching it to others. These "expert" groups then break up, and students move to new "jigsaw" groups, each group consisting of students who have developed expertise in different subtopics. Jigsaw is helpful in motivating students to accept responsibility for learning something well enough to teach it to their peers. It also gives each student a chance to be in the spotlight. When students assume the role of teacher, they lead the discussion, so even students who are reticent to speak in class must take on leadership roles. This CoLT is also an efficient strategy for extending the breadth, depth, and scope of learning because students learn and teach multiple topics simultaneously during the same class sessions.

PREPARATION   Spend sufficient time designing the learning task. The topic should be simple enough for students with a good grasp of the subject to teach it to their peers, but complex enough to require discussion and the design of interesting strategies for instruction. The topic should divide usefully into a number of expert groups of equal numbers of students. Be aware that the number of subtopics dictates the number of students in the second jigsaw group. Also, students who are not familiar with collaborative learning and are not comfortable in being so self-directed may complain that they are "doing the teacher's work." Explain the purpose of this collaborative technique to students before the exercise, and have a closure activity for reflection on what students have learned (see Chapter Six, Grading and Evaluating Collaborative Learning).

PROCEDURE 1. The instructor presents a list of possible topics for developing expertise, making the division of the material into component parts clear.

2. Either through teacher assignment or by interest areas, students form groups charged with developing expertise on a particular topic.

3. Students work in these expert groups to master the topic. They also determine ways to help others learn the material, exploring possible explanations, examples, illustrations, and applications.

4. Students move from their expert groups to new jigsaw groups in which each student serves as the only expert on a specific topic. In these groups, experts teach the material and lead the discussion on their particular topic. Thus each new jigsaw group consists of four to six students, each prepared to teach their subject to their peers.

5. The whole class reflects on the group discoveries in a closure activity.

•   •   •

EXAMPLES

Masterpieces of American Literature

Professor Paige Turner taught a Southern writers course. Toward the end of the semester, she decided to have her class examine the topic of how Southern writers used people and events from their own lives as elements in their fiction. She selected five authors for the assignment: William Faulkner, Flannery O'Connor, Eudora Welty, Walker Percy, and Thomas Wolfe. Each student selected one author to research for homework. At the next class, students worked in small expert groups organized by author to develop a list of biographical facts that appeared in the short stories of their author. Each group created a comprehensive list of information about their author and also determined how to present the material to other students so that it could be learned within a ten-minute small group discussion. In the subsequent class session, Professor Turner formed new jigsaw groups, each with one expert representative for each author who took turns leading the discussion. For closure, Professor Turner conducted a whole-class discussion in which students compared the amount and type of biographical facts that they found in each of the author's short stories.

•   •   •

Introduction to Cultural Anthropology

Wanting his students to gain an understanding of several primitive cultures, this professor decided to have his students participate in a Jigsaw. He believed that this collaborative technique would give students an opportunity to learn by engaging in research, by interacting with each other, and by teaching other students. He divided the class into six groups of six students each, informing students that they would be responsible for studying one culture, and then teaching their peers about that culture. Teachers would also conduct follow-up evaluations of their peers' understanding of the material that they taught them by creating, administering, and correcting a practice quiz. At the conclusion of that segment of the course, all students would take a comprehensive examination testing and grading them on all six cultures.

The professor advised students to consider the major religious beliefs, economic practices, governance structure, and class systems that produced each culture. To prepare them to assume the teaching role effectively, he led a class discussion about various teaching methods (including the use of outlines, definition pages, worksheets, and sample quizzes). After the groups became knowledgeable about their assigned culture, he reassigned students to new jigsaw groups, with one member from each of the first teacher groups. Each teacher took a turn providing information and leading a discussion in which they asked and answered questions about their culture. To close the group activity, each teacher gave the practice quiz to the students in the jigsaw group. After the teachers had evaluated the quizzes, they submitted them to the professor, who reviewed them and used them to guide the development of his study guide for the comprehensive exam.

•   •   •

Web Site Publishing Tools: Dreamweaver

This online course is an introduction to Web site design and management, and one of the course objectives is for each student to create a professional, functioning Web site using JavaScript, cascading style sheets, and techniques of authoring Web pages for different browsers and different end-use platforms. Halfway through the term, the instructor assigns each student to an expert team and a jigsaw team. There are six expert teams, based on six features of the Dreamweaver Web site design software program that she has not covered in class: Frames, Templates, Libraries, Timeline, e-Commerce, and Extensions. Although it is possible for students to create fully functioning Web sites without these features, implementing them into their final sites will enhance their projects and add to the professionalism of their e-Portfolios.

Students can select which expert team they would like to join on a first-come, first-served basis, but she assigns students to the jigsaw team so that she can ensure one expert is on each team. Each expert team is given their own private forum on the course's discussion board and one week to do a "knowledge quest" in which they research their specific feature. Team members can use Web resources, books, or external Dreamweaver discussion boards or listservs to research their topic, using their expert team's in-class forum to pool their information. At the end of one week, they take their shared knowledge and develop a strategy to teach their topic. Expert teams have one more week to create a learning unit to present to the jigsaw teams. These presentations must include screenshots, incorporate the researched Dreamweaver feature, list references, and recommend the two best resources for further information.

At the end of the third week, everyone on the jigsaw team has learned basic information about each of the six features of Dreamweaver, and the professor opens up all forums and presentations to the entire class. Students are then required to include one of the new features that they learned in the expert group and another feature that they learned in the jigsaw into their final projects.

• • •

ONLINE IMPLEMENTATION Identify four or five specific topics students should teach each other. Identify each topic as Topic A, Topic B, and so forth, and create an Expert Group Forum for each of these topics. Thus Expert Group Forum A will be for students who will become experts in Topic A. Determine possible ways the topics could be taught online, such as through text documents, Web pages, or forums on a discussion board. Part of the CoLT is having students determine the best way to teach it, which deepens their knowledge of it. Assess the skill level of students and the ease with which these teaching strategies could be incorporated into the class. For example, know how many students possess the skills and resources to create Web pages—and know whether or not the course management system allows you or students to upload

Web pages relatively easily—before offering this as an option for the teaching stage of this activity.

The simplest and most generally accessible format is to have students create instructional modules from text documents. These decisions and the size of the class will help determine the parameters to establish for the assignment. Provide sufficient time for expert groups to work on their assignments individually, to pool their ideas, to ask questions of each other, to become experts on that topic, and to determine and develop their teaching materials. Form jigsaw groups that include one expert for each of the topics. Thus individual members of Expert Groups A, B, C, D, and E will form into multiple jigsaw groups, each with ABCDE membership. Create separate forums for each jigsaw group and have each expert teach their topic to other group members.

VARIATIONS AND EXTENSIONS

- Consider using this technique for complex problem-solving tasks and have expert groups learn a skill necessary to solve the problem.

- Increase student interest in this exercise by asking students to help generate the lists of topics.

- Instead of calling students "experts," call them "teachers."

- Instead of asking students to work in two different groups (the expert one for mastery, and the jigsaw one for teaching), have students work with only one group, with pairs forming and breaking off to develop expertise on a specific topic, and then rejoining the full group for teaching. This variation is called Within-Team Jigsaw (Millis & Cottell, 1998, pp. 133–134).

- Ask groups to choose a spokesperson for an all-class review. The spokespersons make a presentation to the whole class, and remaining group members can elaborate or contribute additional views.

- Give students an individual quiz on the topics. Consider grouping individual scores into team scores. This variation is called Jigsaw 2 (Slavin, 1986).

- One way of assuring preparation for Jigsaw group work is to test individually for content knowledge prior to the discussion in the expert group, and retest after expert group discussion (see *CoLT 12: Test-Taking Teams* for a technique to implement this).

OBSERVATIONS AND ADVICE

Experienced teachers know that teaching something to others requires an understanding of the subject matter beyond surface learning. As students develop strategies for teaching to their peers, they may discover examples, anecdotes, or analogies that enhance their comprehension. They may design charts or graphs that illustrate relationships visually. They may create quiz questions or discussion questions that probe for new levels of meaning. These are learning activities that deepen the teacher's understanding and also benefit the learners.

Acquiring expert knowledge also encourages interdependence. In the initial expert group assignment, students must take advantage of the knowledge, skills, understanding, and creativity of their fellow students since this will benefit them in their role as teacher. In their role as teachers in the jigsaw group, peers reward their classmates for good teaching, or rebuke students who don't know their subject well enough to teach it.

If students are to realize the advantages of the peer-teaching role, they must take the challenges of teaching seriously. Consider engaging students in a preliminary whole-class discussion about what good teaching entails: clear explanations, practical examples, visual aids, provocative questions, and the like. Take time to present the challenges of teaching explicitly so that students can come up with creative ideas for communicating effectively with their peers about academic subject matter.

Any peer-teaching technique depends on how well prepared students are for their assignment. The focus of Jigsaw is to learn something well enough to teach it. But the learning group may also need advance preparation. For many topics, one cannot expect a peer teacher to work with a group that has not done any background reading or preparation. Thus, it may be important to assign homework that prepares students for both roles: teachers and learners.

Providing closure for this activity is essential. If lacking a good closing activity, students may believe that the instructor is shirking his or her duty by making the students teach themselves and providing them with no feedback. One possible closing activity is to give students a list of the key points to address. Hold a whole class discussion on how they fulfilled the assignment, where they fell short, and where they exceeded the learning requirements. An additional or alternative activity is to ask groups to reflect on, and then share, something that members did that helped the group to learn. Or give students a quiz or test on the material to stress its importance.

Jigsaw has been used effectively across a wide spectrum of levels, from K–12 to university. Because of its highly contrived structure, however, this technique should not be overused. Once or twice a semester preserves the novelty and freshness.

Since Jigsaw tends to be a time-consuming technique and includes a variety of purposes, it is important to evaluate the process. The most direct assessment might be to solicit student answers to a brief survey. Survey questions should be those that really concern you, derived from your experience in preparing the exercise and from your observations of the group process. Questions might be both specific and general. For example:

- On a scale of 1 to 10, how helpful was this exercise in deepening your understanding of _____?

- Did you find this an effective use of class time?

- How well was the "teaching" role performed in your group?

- What were the major advantages of Jigsaw to you? Major disadvantages?

- What did you learn from assuming the role of "teacher"?

- How could the exercise be improved?

You will receive the most candid answers if survey responses are anonymous.

Directed Paraphrase (CAT 23, Angelo & Cross, 1993, pp. 232–235) is often used in applied fields such as marketing, public health, education, and law, where students are expected to be able to explain often complex or technical information to the public—essentially a "teaching" function. Since Jigsaw is distinctive for its emphasis on students assuming the role of teacher for their area of expertise, an assessment technique such as *Directed Paraphrase* can focus on how well they perform the teaching function. Consider stopping after the first small-group session to ask a few students who will serve as experts in their next group to paraphrase briefly for the entire class their introductory statement. The paraphrase should be brief, hit the high points of the past discussion, and be understandable to their peers new to the concepts. This CAT provides an opportunity for the instructor to make any necessary corrections as well as to gain insight into the discussions taking place in the groups.

KEY RESOURCES   Aronson, E., Blaney, N., Stephan, C., Sikes, J., & Snapp, M. (1978). *The jigsaw classroom.* Beverly Hills, CA: Sage.

Aronson, E. (2000). *The jigsaw classroom.* Available: http://www.jigsaw.org/

Johnson, D. W., Johnson, R., & Smith, K. (1998). *Active learning: Cooperation in the college classroom.* Edina, MN: Interaction Book Company, pp. 2:24–2:25.

COLLABORATIVE LEARNING TECHNIQUE

12

Test-Taking Teams

Characteristics	
Group Size	4–6
Time on Task	PROPORTIONAL TO EXAM
Duration of Groups	PROPORTIONAL TO EXAM
Online Transferability	MODERATE

DESCRIPTION AND PURPOSE Students work in teams to prepare for instructor-created exams and then take the exams first individually and next as a group. This CoLT thus involves three steps: (1) the group studies for the exam together, (2) individuals take the exam, and (3) the group takes the exam. By working together to prepare for the exam, students help each other deepen their understanding of the content. Because each student first takes the test independently, this CoLT emphasizes individual accountability. By retaking the test as a team, individual students benefit from the collective knowledge of the group. Since the group score is generally superior to the individual scores, Test-Taking Teams is useful for demonstrating the value of collaborative learning. This CoLT may be used for short quizzes within a single class period or for tests covering larger amounts of material.

PREPARATION Once you have determined the content that students should master and you have presented it in lecture, reading assignment, or other activity, the preparation for this CoLT is the same as preparing a good examination for individuals. Refer to a source such as Davis's (1993) or McKeachie's (2002) chapter on testing and grading for tips on developing a good test. Consider creating a test study guide to provide students with a focused framework for preparing for the test.

PROCEDURE   1. Ask students to form groups of four to six members. Consider one of the instructor-determined stratification methods for forming groups described in Chapter 3 to ensure that each team contains diverse or ability-balanced membership.

2. Depending on the size and complexity of the material to be mastered, the groups may meet for fifteen minutes, for a full class session, or longer.

3. Administer the test for students to complete individually and to submit to the instructor for grading.

4. Before returning the graded individual tests, ask students to rejoin their groups to reach a consensus on the answers and submit a group response to the test.

5. Consider averaging individual test grades and group test grades to determine individual grades. Weight scores, as, for example, two-thirds for individual plus one-third for group.

• • •

EXAMPLES

General Psychology

Following three class sessions on cognitive learning theories in which students had read assignments, listened to lecture, and participated in discussion, Professor Sara Bellum decided to use Test-Taking Teams. She informed students that in the next class session they would be reviewing for and then taking a short-answer test. They should come prepared with questions that they thought would be on the test and plan to discuss them in a group session with three other students from the class. At the beginning of the next class, Professor Bellum asked students to form groups of four and spend fifteen minutes working together to review for the test. She then administered the test she had created, telling students that they must take it individually within a twenty-minute time limit. After students handed in their test papers, Professor Bellum asked them to return to their original groups to prepare a group response to the test. As she expected, the group test scores were superior to individual test scores. She assigned individual grades by giving a composite of two-thirds individual and one-third group score.

• • •

English Poetry of the Romantic Period

In this graduate-level course, Professor Cole Ridge knew that students were anxious about the upcoming master's degree comprehensive examination. He believed that this anxiety was distracting them from focusing on what they needed to learn specifically in his course. He decided to use Test-Taking Teams to address both issues: he used the content of his course to help prepare students for the type of questions they would be asked on the comprehensive exam. Professor Ridge designed a sample test focusing on English Romantic poetry and explained to students that the test included identification and essay questions similar in style to the comprehensive exam. He then asked students to work in groups to share study strategies as they reviewed the material and prepared to take the sample test. He gave individual students the test first, and then he gave the groups the test. By working in groups, students were able to fill in their knowledge gaps regarding his course while they learned additional passage identification techniques that prepared them for the comprehensive exam.

• • •

Elementary Statistics

This professor forms student pairs to work together until the midterm, and then forms new pairs to work together until the final. Pairs study together for each of the weekly quizzes. They take each quiz individually during the first thirty minutes of the class, and then retake it together during the last twenty minutes of class. The professor assigns each student a grade that is a combination of individual and partner scores.

• • •

 ### Music Composition and Theory

In order to transfer to a four-year institution and be placed at the junior level, community college music majors needed to pass a comprehensive exam at the receiving institution assessing their knowledge of music theory. Despite what many faculty and students felt should be appropriate preparation, students were not doing well and were often required to repeat second-year theory at the transfer institution. This was frustrating and discouraging, and the music theory faculty decided to work together to help students become more successful. They created an extensive bank of multiple-choice exam questions focusing on the kind of information they knew would be on the placement exam. They then worked with their college's instructional technology department to set up a test bank that was self-grading and accessible online.

During the last course of sophomore music theory, students were assigned to small groups to work together throughout the term. On a weekly basis, students went to the computer lab to take a practice exam first individually and then retake it as a group. While taking the exams as a group, students helped each other review material, such as the steps they needed to take to identify intervals or the chords within a harmonic progression. The testing software maintained a record of both individual and group scores that faculty took into account for the course grades. The following autumn, the community college theory faculty contacted faculty members at the local university to track placement of that year's transfer students. Scores and placement were so markedly improved that both institutions' faculty decided to work together to enhance the breadth and depth of questions in the test bank and to develop strategies for improving articulation in the music history and music performance courses.

• • •

ONLINE IMPLEMENTATION Due to issues of academic honesty, it is best to create essay or problem-solving exams if you wish to use this CoLT in an online course. Organize students into groups of ten or twelve, identify as Group A, Group B, and so forth, and create a forum for each group. Give groups time to work together to pool information, resources, and ideas to prepare for the test. Have students take the exam as individuals and then submit it to you for grading. Before you return the graded version back to them, ask all students to work together in their designated forum to create collaborative exam responses to submit. Assign (or have students select) a group leader who will submit the group test for his or her group. An alternative technique at this point is to do a variation of *CoLT 25: Round Table:* one student starts a response and sends it to another in the group as an e-mail attachment. This next student adds to it using a different font or color, and then sends it on to a third student, and so on until all members of the group have contributed to the test. As with the on-campus version of this CoLT, consider combining individual and group test grades to ensure individual accountability as well as promote positive interdependence.

VARIATIONS AND EXTENSIONS

- Have students work in pairs rather than in a group.

- Make two copies of the exam, one copy to distribute to the teams to use to review and the other copy to be submitted for grading.

- Ask groups to submit the materials that they created to prepare for the exam. For example, they can turn in a brief summary of each answer they formulated, a copy of the outline and material they used to organize their discussion, or a description of the procedures they adopted to prepare for the exam.

- Do a simple statistical analysis of test scores to show differences between individual and group test scores. Use the averages of all individual and all group scores (announcing to students, for example, "The average individual scored x and the average team scored y") or do this for each group.

OBSERVATIONS AND ADVICE

Test-Taking Teams can be a single activity (working together to prepare for and take one test during the semester), but it can also be effective when groups work together for several tests. This allows students to form strong bonds and to begin to feel responsible for each other's successes.

If you believe students would benefit from group-to-group competition, consider announcing the highest scoring group. Additionally, if comfortable with the concept of bonus points, consider rewarding bonus points to the most improved or highest scoring teams.

Design a grade structure that integrates individual and group scores (for example, average the individual and group scores, or assign two-thirds for the individual score and one-third for the group score).

To encourage individuals to make a best effort and to assess progress over time, have individuals take quizzes to score against their own previous averages; award points for the degree to which they meet or exceed their own performances.

KEY RESOURCES

Michaelsen, L. K., & Black, R. H. (1994). Building learning teams: The key to harnessing the power of small groups in higher education. In S. Kadel & J. Keehner (Eds.), *Collaborative learning: A sourcebook for higher education, 2* (pp. 65–81). State College, PA: National Center for Teaching, Learning and Assessment.

Michaelsen, L. K., Fink, L. D., & Knight, A. (1997). Designing effective group activities: Lessons for classroom teaching and faculty development. In D. DeZure (Ed.), *To improve the academy: Resources for faculty.* Instructional and organizational development, 16 (pp. 373–397). Stillwater, OK: New Forums Press.

Chapter 9

Techniques for Problem Solving

ALMOST ALL TEACHERS ARE interested in developing the ability of their students to solve problems. Although problems can be generally described as "puzzles"—difficult matters that exercise the mind—the precise definition of *problem* varies widely across the academic disciplines. There are well-defined problems with correct answers, as well as loosely defined problems that Donald Schön has described as "confusing messes incapable of technical solution" (Schön, 1983, p. 42). These latter kinds of problems may include a huge array of relevant variables, both known and unknown. They may require exercising judgment, making trade-offs, and considering values. They may have alternative solutions. Whether problems are straightforward tasks designed to produce a specified result, or seemingly insoluble quandaries posed for endless academic discourse, problem solving is at the core of most disciplines.

Presenting students with a problem to solve is also an effective teaching strategy. As McKeachie points out when talking about problem-based learning, "Problem-based education is based on the assumptions that human beings evolved as individuals who are motivated to solve problems, and that problem solvers will seek and learn whatever knowledge is needed for successful problem solving" (McKeachie, 2002, p. 197). Presenting problems to students that offer a challenge but are still solvable can be an important motivating strategy. Additionally, students need to "practice thinking" in order to learn to think more effectively. McKeachie concludes, "Cognitive theory provides good support for the idea that knowledge learned and used in a realistic, problem-solving context is more likely to be remembered and used appropriately when needed later" (McKeachie, 2002, pp. 196–203). Although McKeachie is referring to problem-based learning—a specific instructional strategy that uses complex problems as a catalyst for learning—the benefits he identifies apply to problem solving in general.

The six CoLTs in this chapter, summarized in Exhibit 9.1, are designed to help students learn and practice problem-solving strategies. The techniques provide frameworks for solving problems that range roughly in order from highly structured to loosely structured problems. CoLTs such as *Structured Problem Solving* and *TAPPS* walk students through a set of procedures designed to teach students how to identify relevant information and apply it in the solution of the problem. At the other end of the continuum is *Group Investigation,* in which students select their own topic and work with fellow students to assign tasks, conduct research, and prepare a report. Although all six CoLTs deal with problem solving, each CoLT is unique in that it focuses on different aspects of the process, concentrates on a specific type of problem, or offers a specialized approach to teaching a problem solving strategy.

EXHIBIT 9.1

Problem-Solving CoLTs

This CoLT	Is a Technique in Which Students:	It Is Particularly Useful for:
13: Think-Aloud Pair Problem Solving (TAPPS)	Solve problems aloud to try out their reasoning on a listening peer	Emphasizing the problem-solving process (rather than the product) and helping students identify logic or process errors
14: Send-A-Problem	Try to solve a problem as a group, and then pass the problem and solution to a nearby group who does the same; the final group evaluates the solutions	Helping students practice together the thinking skills required for effective problem solving and for comparing and discriminating among multiple solutions
15: Case Study	Review a written study of a real-world scenario and develop a solution to the dilemma presented in the case	Presenting abstract principles and theories in ways that students find relevant
16: Structured Problem Solving	Follow a structured format to solve problems	Dividing problem-solving processes into manageable steps so that students don't feel overwhelmed and so that they learn to identify, analyze, and solve problems in an organized manner
17: Analytic Teams	Assume roles and specific tasks to perform when critically reading an assignment, listening to a lecture, or watching a video	Helping students understand the different activities that constitute a critical analysis
18: Group Investigation	Plan, conduct, and report on in-depth research projects	Teaching students research procedures and helping them to gain in-depth knowledge about a specific area

COLLABORATIVE
LEARNING
TECHNIQUE

13

Think-Aloud Pair Problem Solving (TAPPS)

Characteristics	
Group Size	PAIRS
Time on Task	30–45 MINUTES
Duration of Groups	SINGLE SESSION OR MULTIPLE
Online Transferability	LOW

DESCRIPTION AND PURPOSE

In Think-Aloud Pair Problem Solving (TAPPS), student pairs receive a series of problems as well as specific roles—problem solver and listener—that switch with each problem. The problem solver "thinks aloud," talking through the steps of solving a problem. The partner listens to the problem solver, following the steps, attempting to understand the reasoning behind the steps, and offering suggestions if there are missteps.

Articulating one's own problem-solving process and listening carefully to another's process helps students practice what they have read about or heard in a lecture. This CoLT places the emphasis on the problem-solving process rather than the product, helping students diagnose errors in logic. Depending upon the problems used, it can also help increase student awareness of the range of possible successful (and unsuccessful) approaches to problem solving. TAPPS improves analytical skills by helping students to formulate ideas, rehearse concepts, understand the sequence of steps underlying their thinking, and identify errors in someone else's reasoning. Since it requires students to relate information to existing conceptual frameworks and apply existing information to new situations, it can also promote deeper understanding.

PREPARATION   To prepare for this CoLT, spend sufficient time developing an appropriate set of field-related problems that students can solve within a limited time frame. The problems should engage students in basic problem-solving skills such as identifying the nature of the problem, analyzing the knowledge and skills required to reach a solution, identifying potential solutions, choosing the best solution, and evaluating potential outcomes. To be most effective, the problems should challenge students, requiring them to concentrate and focus their attention, whether they are solvers or listeners.

PROCEDURE   1. Ask students to form pairs and explain to students the roles of problem solver and listener. The role of the problem solver is to read the problem aloud and talk through the reasoning process in attempting to solve the problem. The role of the listener is to encourage the problem solver to think aloud, describing the steps to solve the problem. The listener may also ask clarification questions and offer suggestions, but should refrain from actually solving the problem.

2. Ask students to solve a set of problems, alternating roles with each new problem.

3. The activity concludes when students have solved all problems.

• • •

EXAMPLES

English as a Second Language (ESL)

An English professor was teaching a course in grammar to ESL students. He decided to use sentence diagramming to help students understand the relationship of the various parts of speech. First he explained diagramming to the students, demonstrating the process by parsing and graphing several sample sentences on the board. When students indicated that they understood the steps, he formed pairs and gave each pair a set of several sentences. He asked students to alternate taking turns diagramming the sentences, talking out loud to explain why they were making their choices while their partner listened, and offered suggestions when necessary. The professor closed the activity by asking each pair to select a sentence from the set that was most challenging and go to the board, sharing both their diagramming and the reasoning behind the diagramming with the whole class.

• • •

Elementary Statistics

Professor Marge N. O'Vera decided to use TAPPS in an introductory statistics class to have students practice regression analysis. She prepared a handout that included problems with an attached printout of data. She then asked students to use this data to solve ten problems. Professor O'Vera asked students to pair with the student sitting next to them. She explained the roles of problem solver and listener. The students worked on the problems, alternating between problem solver and listener until all of the problems were completed. She then held a full-class discussion to review the answers and to clarify questions regarding the problem solving process.

• • •

Programming in BIOPERL

The purpose of this course was to teach students to create utility software programs using a specific scientific programming language. To achieve this goal, students needed to become competent in a complex problem-solving process of retrieving, manipulating, and analyzing sequences from a variety of databases. The instructor noticed that some of his students "caught on" and were able to go through the steps relatively easily. Others tended to make process mistakes that resulted in programming errors that were time consuming and frustrating to find later. Historically, these struggling students simply dropped the course at this point, so the instructor was searching for ways to reduce attrition and alleviate student anxiety. He decided to use TAPPS to structure practicing the problem solving process with a peer, and to use recent quiz scores to partner a student who was having difficulties with a student who was doing well. The result was that students not only gained competence sooner than in the previous semester when they had worked independently, but it also significantly improved student retention.

• • •

ONLINE IMPLEMENTATION   The need for synchronous communication between pairs makes this CoLT cumbersome online. However, if modeling and receiving feedback on problem solving is absolutely essential to the course, consider asking students to teleconference. An alternative would be to organize students into pairs, have them individually work through a problem (or problem set), explain their thinking at each step, and then send their assignment either as an e-mail attachment or post on a discussion board for feedback.

VARIATIONS AND EXTENSIONS

- This CoLT is typically used for a series of problems with single answers, but it can also be used for more open-ended problem solving. The activity may take more time, so plan for fewer problems.

- If all pairs have worked on the same problem set, select pairs at random to report out their solution or take a vote on the most challenging problems and share and examine solutions along with tips for improvement as a class.

OBSERVATIONS AND ADVICE

Many students, especially new students, will not have highly developed problem-solving skills. Consider preparing students by having students practice problem solving as a class prior to this activity.

Student problem solvers may not be comfortable having their logic exposed to other students. Student listeners may not be trained in logic, so they may not be able to note difficulties. Because of the level of risk students may feel, it is important to have established a high level of trust in the class prior to using this activity. Thus, it may also be a good idea to use this technique with pairs who work together throughout the term or at least over several sessions.

Students will solve problems at different speeds. In this CoLT, it is particularly important to have an additional problem (an extension or "sponge") on hand for students who complete the problems quickly, so that they do not sit around bored, waiting for the other students to finish. Consider crafting a particularly challenging "bonus" question for extra credit.

We recommend using assessment techniques with TAPPS, since students can reinforce faulty—as well as correct—information and problem-solving processes.

Either to get a rough measure of students' problem-solving ability prior to implementing TAPPS, or as a follow-up activity to assess how much they have learned, consider using *Problem Recognition Tasks* (CAT 19, Angelo & Cross, 1993, pp. 214–217). Provide students with a few examples of common problem types and ask them to recognize and identify the particular type of problem each example represents. This CAT can help assess how well students recognize various problem types, which is the first step in matching problem type to solution method.

If interested in assessing how students solve problems and how well they understand and can describe problem-solving methods, consider using *Documented Problem Solutions* (CAT 21, Angelo & Cross, 1993, pp. 222–225). After they have participated as partners in TAPPS, have them individually track the steps that they take in solving a problem and submit this for review. Angelo and Cross also suggest ideas for adapting and extending the assessment (pp. 224–225):

- Use Documented Problem Solutions as a pre-assessment by giving students two problems: one of low and the other of medium difficulty. The results of their efforts to solve the problems can help to gauge the best level at which to begin whole-class or small-group instruction.

- Ask students with elegant, well-documented responses to explain their solutions to a partner, a small group of students, or even to the whole class.

- Since most students have little experience or no experience reflecting on their own problem-solving processes, students may need help learning how. To ensure that peers give each other thoughtful and thorough responses, give students credit for this activity.

To grade this CoLT, students can submit a record of the solutions with the solver for each problem identified (such as by initials). Consider having the listener identified and having the listener include his or her suggestions for problem-solving improvement.

KEY RESOURCES   Lochhead, J., & Whimbey, A. (1987). Teaching analytical reasoning through thinking-aloud pair problem solving. In J. E. Stice (Ed.), *Developing critical thinking and problem solving abilities* (pp. 72–93). New Directions for Teaching and Learning, No. 30. San Francisco: Jossey-Bass.

MacGregor, J. (1990). Collaborative learning: Shared inquiry as a process of reform. In M. D. Svinicki (Ed.), *The changing face of college teaching* (pp. 19–30). New Directions for Teaching and Learning, No. 42. San Francisco: Jossey-Bass.

Millis, B. J., & Cottell, P. G. (1998). *Cooperative learning for higher education faculty.* American Council on Education, Series on Higher Education. Phoenix, AZ: Oryx Press, p. 114.

COLLABORATIVE
LEARNING
TECHNIQUE

14

Send-A-Problem

Characteristics	
Group Size	2–4
Time on Task	30–45 MINUTES
Duration of Groups	SINGLE SESSION
Online Transferability	MODERATE

DESCRIPTION AND PURPOSE   Each group receives a problem, tries to solve it, and then passes the problem and solution to a nearby group. Without looking at the previous group's solution, the next group works to solve the problem. After as many passes as seems useful, groups analyze, evaluate, and synthesize the responses to the problem they received in the final pass and report the best solution to the class. Send-A-Problem thus involves two activity stages: solving problems and evaluating solutions. The purpose of the first stage is to provide students with an opportunity to practice together and learn from each other the thinking skills required for effective problem solving. The purpose of the second stage is to help students learn to compare and discriminate among multiple solutions.

PREPARATION   Determine the number of problems you will need in order to have all groups working simultaneously. Decide how to present the problem. Consider attaching each problem to the outside of a file folder or an envelope into which groups can then insert their solutions. Also think carefully about the instructions regarding time limits and the order in which students should pass the problem (for example, clockwise). Being clear with students can help to reduce any confusion.

PROCEDURE   1. Form groups of two to four students, and take time to describe the activity, give instructions, and answer questions.

2. Distribute a different problem to each group, asking each group to discuss the problem, generate possible solutions, choose the best solution, and record and place their response in the folder or envelope.

3. Call time, and instruct teams to pass to the next group; each group receives a new folder or envelope.

4. Upon receiving new problems, students again brainstorm responses and record results until time is called and they again pass the problem to a new group.

5. Repeat the process for as many times as seems useful and appropriate for the problem.

6. Students in the final group review the responses to the problem, analyze, evaluate, and synthesize the information, adding any additional information they wish.

7. The activity concludes as teams report on the responses contained in the folder they evaluated. As groups report out, add any points that groups missed and reinforce correct processes and solutions.

• • •

EXAMPLES

Urban Planning

This professor decided to use Send-A-Problem so that students could evaluate different groups' solutions to a residential rezoning problem. She gave each group a manila envelope that included the data required to solve the problem and two 5 x 7 index cards. She asked students to discuss and agree upon a solution, write the solution on the card and place it in the envelope, and pass the envelope to the next group. The next group also discussed a solution, recorded their responses on an index card and placed it in the envelope. This group sent their solution to a third group, who reviewed the responses from the first two groups and selected what they believed was the best solution. The instructor asked these third, final groups to report on which solution they felt was best and to describe why.

• • •

Advanced Pathophysiology and Patient Management

To review assessment and treatment of patients with respiratory disease, Professor Xavier Breath divided the class of twenty students into three groups. He then gave each group an envelope with a patient's specific symptoms written on the outside. Professor Breath asked groups to review the symptoms, diagnose the disease, and recommend and write down appropriate treatment and therapy. After each group had discussed their first problem for fifteen minutes, the instructor asked students to put their responses in the envelope and pass it to a group sitting nearby who repeated the process. After another fifteen-minute discussion, students sent the envelopes to a final group. When the final group received the envelope, they synthesized the responses from the two previous groups and added additional responses. They then selected the most likely disease causing the patient's symptoms and selected the best treatment. The professor called on each group and wrote their best responses on the board, incorporating a review of diagnosis protocol, symptoms, diseases, and treatment.

• • •

 English Literature

In this online class, Professor Fitz William wanted students to think deeply about cultural and social conditions surrounding the development of the novel *Pride and Prejudice*. He decided to have students participate in an online adaptation of Send-A-Problem. He organized students into three groups and created a forum for each group. He then developed three questions relating the text to the historical context of the nineteenth century and posted one of the questions on each of the group forums. He gave students in each group one week to respond to their first question and a second week to respond to their second question. During the third week, he gave students access to all forums, and asked groups to evaluate the responses to their final question.

• • •

ONLINE
IMPLEMENTATION
An adaptation of this CoLT can be effective in the online environment. Determine problems and organize students into as many groups as you have problems. Create a protected-access forum for each group. Post problem prompts, and ask students to solve the appropriate problem as listed in Exhibit 9.2 for Stage 1.

During Stage 2, permit forum access to all students to respond to the solutions that were posted in the preceding two weeks.

EXHIBIT 9.2

Sample Problem Solving and Evaluation Schedule

	Stage 1: Problem Solving		Stage 2: Solution Evaluation
	Time Frame 1	Time Frame 2	Time Frame 3
Group A	Solve problem 1	Solve problem 2	Evaluate solutions for problem 3
Group B	Solve problem 2	Solve problem 3	Evaluate solutions for problem 1
Group C	Solve problem 3	Solve problem 1	Evaluate solutions for problem 2

VARIATIONS AND EXTENSIONS

- Consider allowing students to generate their own list of problems that they would like to see the class solve. For example, individuals may wish to have additional coverage of a certain type of problem that they find consistently confusing. Or perhaps there are issues in a reading assignment that they found particularly intriguing and would like to hear what other students think. While you may have specific topics that you must cover, giving students some control over the problems or topics can generate more engagement and investment in this CoLT.

- Consider using this CoLT as a review before an examination. Bring in copies of old tests for students to take and compare their answers.

- For closure, have groups write the numbers of the problems on the board, and ask the evaluating teams to report which group's solution they determined was best, recording the team's name under the problem's number. Then ask the evaluating team to summarize the "winning" team's solution and state why they felt that solution was best. Offer the winning team the opportunity to add any additional comments.

OBSERVATIONS AND ADVICE

Interpret *problem* to include a variety of complex questions and issues (for example, text, diagnosis, and identification of a physical element).

Send-A-Problem is most effective for developing several thoughtful solutions for more complex problems that do not have a single right answer. In some situations, it may be effective for single-answer problems that students just learned in a lecture or reading assignment. In this way, it can replace traditional drill-and-practice exercises by adding in higher-order thinking skills during the solution-evaluation stage.

Prepare the problems and work through the solutions to determine the amount of time it will take groups to solve the problems. Depending on the complexity of the problem, estimate how long each stage of this activity will take to allow enough time for thinking and reflection. Be sure to select problems that are roughly equal in complexity and that take approximately the same amount of time to solve.

If teaching a large class, consider having several groups work on the same problem, but this works better if groups with the same problems are not seated next to each other.

Be fairly specific about time limitations, and be thorough in the instructions introducing the activity. This will give students an idea of how much thought they can give to their responses, and it will help ensure that the activity proceeds smoothly. Be prepared to extend the time limit if the majority of the groups seem to still be on task or to call time sooner than you anticipated if the majority of the groups seem to be wrapping up.

Despite efforts to develop comparable problems and setting time limits, groups may well work at different rates, and they need sufficient flexibility to do that. In order to prevent any group from having to sit idle or from having to pass the problem before they are ready, be sure to have several extensions (additional problems) ready to fill in. Final groups can report on more than one problem, or you can pick up the additional problems and respond.

Having participated in Send-A-Problem, students should be relatively skilled at solving specific problem types and evaluating problem solving processes. If students have been working on different types of problems, *What's the Principle?* (CAT 20, Angelo & Cross, pp. 218–221) is an especially useful assessment technique, as it quickly gathers useful information as to how well they have accomplished this goal. Rather than emphasizing identifying the type of problem or solving the problem, this CAT focuses on the middle step: deciding the principle or principles needed to solve the problem. Provide students with a few problems and ask them to state the principle that best applies to each problem. This will help you evaluate student ability associated with specific problems, with the general principles used to solve them, and in determining student skill at transferring what they have learned to new problem situations.

KEY RESOURCES   Kagan, S. (1992). *Cooperative learning,* 2nd ed. San Juan Capistrano, CA: Resources for Teachers, pp. 10, 11.

Millis, B. J., & Cottell, P. G. (1998). *Cooperative learning for higher education faculty.* American Council on Education, Series on Higher Education. Phoenix, AZ: Oryx Press, pp. 103–105.

COLLABORATIVE
LEARNING
TECHNIQUE
15

Case Study

Characteristics	
Group Size	3–6
Time on Task	VARIES
Duration of Groups	SINGLE SESSION or MULTIPLE
Online Transferability	MODERATE

DESCRIPTION AND PURPOSE In this CoLT, student teams review a written study of a real-life scenario containing a field-related problem situation. These "cases" usually include a brief history of how the situation developed and present a dilemma that a key character within the scenario is facing. Team members apply course concepts to identify and evaluate alternative approaches to solving the problem. Although case studies originated in the fields of business, law, and medicine, they are now used in many disciplines.

A major challenge to many teachers is how to present abstract principles and theories in ways that students find relevant. Case studies are inherently appealing to students because they have a "true to life" feel; thus they help to bridge the gap between theory and practice and between the academy and the workplace. Case studies engage students in critical reflection, and because they typically involve multiple alternatives to solving problems, they can help students develop analysis, synthesis, and decision-making skills.

PREPARATION Writing a good case is an extremely complex task. Use research in your field or current events as stimulus ideas. The case can be real or hypothetical. Although classic or historical cases engage scholars, students are most intrigued by situations that deal with current issues. Whether creating your own or pulling from a collection, the case is usually written and distributed as a handout, often with a series of questions to guide students in their analysis.

PROCEDURE　1. Form student groups and distribute identical or different cases to each team.

2. Allow time for students to ask questions about the process they are to use to clarify the problem presented in the case.

3. Students work in groups (anywhere from one class session to a few weeks, depending upon the complexity of the assignment) to study the case in depth from the protagonist's point of view and to become familiar with the issues and decision options.

4. Students sort out factual data, apply analytic tools, articulate issues, reflect on their relevant experience, draw conclusions, and recommend actions that resolve the dilemma or solve the problem in the case. McKeachie (2002, p. 200) suggests the following questions to guide students in their approach to the case:

   - What is the problem?
   - What might have caused the problem?
   - What evidence can be gathered to support or discount any of the hypotheses?
   - What conclusions can be drawn? What recommendations?

5. Sometimes students prepare a written or oral statement describing their assessment of the case, the decision options as they see them, and their recommendations for a decision.

6. Students discuss the cases with the entire class as the teacher debriefs on the experience. If the case really occurred, students will want to know what happened, so be prepared to share this with them after they have reported and to allow a few more minutes for discussion of what actually transpired.

• • •

EXAMPLES

Issues in Contemporary Art

Throughout their undergraduate education, art department students concentrated on developing their personal artistic vision and style. Professor Neil Politan now wanted to help prepare them for the issues they would face trying to make professional careers as artists. He chose to use mini-case studies, and in this example he drew upon the experience of one of the school's recent graduates. The Chamber of Commerce had offered this graduate a commission to create a monument that would honor the contributions of the eighteenth-century missionary Father Serra to the city's heritage. The commission promised the young artist significant local and statewide exposure and a substantial payment. The artist accepted and spent considerable time thinking about and then creating a model to present to the committee for approval.

Several community members attended his presentation and voiced opinions that Father Serra and the California missions had enslaved and brutalized the Native Americans. Others believed that the missionaries' work had been essential in the effort to assimilate Native Americans into mainstream society. Both sides felt that the monument should reflect their views. As the subject of the sculpture generated increasing debate and controversy, the committee members started to align along various viewpoints, and the commission was in danger of being cancelled. The professor asked groups to discuss the case, asking each group to identify what steps this young artist might take to move the project forward while staying true to his own artistic vision. The professor used the teams' recommendations as the basis for a whole-class discussion on the challenges artists face reconciling their personal artistic ideals with the need to compromise in order to earn a living.

• • •

International Relations

Professor Warren Piece wanted to provide students in his advanced course the opportunity to pull together different aspects of their academic studies in an engaging, real-world scenario. He prepared a case study in which conflict between two countries had escalated to the point that war was imminent. In a period of heightened world tensions, the pressure was strong to find a diplomatic resolution. Professor Piece divided the class into six groups of five or six students, and assigned each group the task of providing support to an ambassador charged with resolving the conflict. He told the groups they would have three class sessions to analyze the historical, political, and economic roots of the conflict and propose a solution.

The professor told the groups that they would need to develop a Learning Plan (identifying their knowledge gaps and determining how they were going to go about filling those gaps), and a Work Plan (identifying how the group was going to go about the task of formulating their diplomatic resolution). To facilitate the process, he distributed to each group a template of both plans that groups could use or modify to suit their own needs.

After all teams had completed their proposals, he asked each team to evaluate the proposals of two other groups and select the most appealing one. An "ambassador" from each of the teams that had created the top three proposals presented their proposal to the class, and the whole class voted on the most persuasive proposal. The team with the most votes won the Nobel Pizza Prize (a coupon for a free pizza). The students found the contextualized, realistic scenario compelling, and the professor found that the case study had significantly enhanced student understanding of the complexity of factors underlying international relations.

• • •

Introduction to Teaching Online

This mini-course is part of an online training program for community college faculty who are preparing to teach online courses. It is designed to bring teachers together to learn from each other, explore teaching innovations, and search for solutions to the unique challenges of the online learning environment. The course's instructor frequently uses scenarios posted on a Threaded Discussion forum to help faculty "students" discuss effective teaching strategies. For example, one scenario provides details about an actual case in which a student who had failed an online class complained to the college dean that the grading procedure was unfair. The mini-course instructor divides students into two groups and assigns them to look at the case from the perspective of either the student or the online instructor. After students have posted their comments, she asks them to look at the case from the perspective of the dean and make a recommendation for how to resolve the dilemma, and to make suggestions on how the instructor might prevent similar problems in future classes.

• • •

ONLINE IMPLEMENTATION Organize students into teams, and create a closed-access forum for each team. Team members communicate through this forum to discuss and analyze the case. When they have completed and written up their analysis (or by a specific deadline), each group posts their analysis in a separate, whole-class case studies forum. Once every group has posted their analysis, open the forum up for comments.

VARIATIONS AND EXTENSIONS

- Instead of a written case study, use videotape or role play to present a problem situation (McKeachie, 1999, p. 178).

- Create a simpler mini-case that can be presented orally and that teams can analyze and propose solutions for in a short period of time.

- Present complex cases in several stages in a progressive disclosure format, asking teams to make decisions based on the limited information they have at each stage.

- Partner with professionals in your field (such as nurses, educators, small business owners) to craft real cases from personal experience, and consider inviting these professionals to share with students their decisions and the consequences of their choices after students have analyzed the case.

- Symposia and simulated business meetings are particularly appropriate for providing closure with case studies. See Chapter Five for additional ideas and for further explanation of reporting out and closure strategies.

- Pair Case Study with another CoLT for a more extensive collaborative experience. For example, use *CoLT 28: Collaborative Writing,* and have students develop a formal paper containing their analysis of the case.

OBSERVATIONS AND ADVICE

When writing or selecting cases, consider the following list of features (Davis, 1993, p. 162). Good cases

- Tell a "real" story with an interesting plot

- Focus on an interest-arousing or thought-provoking issue

- Often contain elements of conflict

- Promote empathy with the central characters

- Lack an obvious or clear-cut right answer

- Encourage students to think and take a position

- Demand a decision

- Are relatively concise

As an alternative to creating your own case studies, consider selecting cases from a case bank if your field has such a resource. For example, Harvard Business School publishes cases in accounting, finance, general management, organizational behavior, marketing, and other areas in its *HBS Case Services.* The National Center for Case Study Teaching in Science offers an extensive collection of science-based case studies online (http://ublib.buffalo. edu/libraries/projects/cases/case.html). Christensen (1987) and Cross and Steadman (1996) present case studies depicting classroom teaching situations. These may be especially helpful for faculty workshops.

In order to make cases realistic, teachers often include so many details that students lose the principles or points the case was intended to demonstrate. On the other hand, one of the goals of case study methods is to teach students to select important factors from a complicated mesh that includes less important factors. Although the factors are not critical, they still need to be considered to understand fully the context of the case. It is crucial, therefore, to match the cases and the amount of detail to the ability of your students. As McKeachie observes, "One does not learn such skills by being in perpetual confusion, but rather by success in solving more and more difficult problems" (McKeachie, 2002, p. 199).

Case studies can be particularly motivating when they involve scenarios that seem real to students and that may have application beyond school. These kinds of case studies produce discussions with a high level of student involvement. However, student learning can take many different directions, not all of which will be relevant. McKeachie offers this observation: "The major problem in teaching by cases involves going from the students' fascination with the particular case to the general principle or conceptual structure. In choosing a case to discuss, the teacher needs to think, 'What is this case a case *of?*'" (McKeachie, 2002, p. 199). It is important, therefore, to provide teams with well-crafted case study assignments and to close the activity by summarizing the key points and ensuring that students are clear on the principle or principles involved.

When facilitating the whole-class discussion after this CoLT, be careful to adopt a nondirective role. Pose questions and guide the discussion toward points of major importance, but avoid telling students the "right" answers. Students should feel encouraged and comfortable to speak openly about what is on their minds (Davis, 1993, p. 164).

If your groups have prepared a written statement that includes their analysis of the case and their recommended solutions, this can be submitted for assessment and grading.

KEY RESOURCES Christensen, C. R. (1987). *Teaching and the case method.* Boston: Harvard Business School.

Herreid, C. F. (1994). Case studies in science: A novel method of science education. *Journal of College Science Teaching, 23*(4), 221–229.

Olmstead, J. A. (1974). *Small group instruction: Theory and practice.* Alexandria, VA: Human Resources Research Organization, pp. 24–44, 96–102.

COLLABORATIVE
LEARNING
TECHNIQUE

16

Structured Problem Solving

Characteristics	
Group Size	4–6
Time on Task	1–2 HOURS
Duration of Groups	MULTIPLE SESSIONS
Online Transferability	HIGH

DESCRIPTION AND PURPOSE   Structured Problem Solving provides students with a process for solving a complex, content-based problem within a specified time limit. All members must agree to a solution and must be able to explain both the answer and the strategy used to solve the problem.

Students with poor problem-solving skills have difficulty at one or more stages of the problem-solving process. This CoLT helps students because it breaks the process apart into specific steps. Thus, students learn to identify, analyze, and solve problems in an organized manner. Rather than feeling overwhelmed by the magnitude of a problem, this activity gives students a format so that they have a place to begin. By providing them with a series of manageable steps, it keeps students from going astray or engaging in irrelevant steps.

PREPARATION   Create a problem that is complex enough to require students to use sophisticated problem-solving skills. Use research and current questions in the field as a resource. Identify a problem-identification and -solving procedure that is appropriate to the type of problem selected. Solve the problem yourself using the problem-solving procedure to uncover any difficulties or errors. You may wish to create a handout that includes both the problem and the problem-solving steps.

PROCEDURE   1. Organize students into teams and assign students a complex problem to solve.

2. Ask students to solve the problem using the specific steps you have identified as a problem-solving technique. The following is an example (The Dewey Six-Step Problem Solving Technique, Luotto & Stoll, 1996, pp. 91–92):

    a. Identify the problem.

    b. Generate possible solutions.

    c. Evaluate and test the various solutions.

    d. Decide on a mutually acceptable solution.

    e. Implement the solution.

    f. Evaluate the solution.

3. Ask teams to report out their solutions, describing to the rest of the class the steps they took and the solution they developed.

• • •

EXAMPLES

Music History and Literature

In a capstone course for music history majors, Professor Amanda Lin wanted to design a collaborative activity that would require students to pull together and apply what they had learned throughout their undergraduate courses in music. She also wanted to prepare them for graduate work and to create an assignment that would help them experience the excitement of research. She decided to use Structured Problem Solving as the basis for a game she called "Musical Sleuth." Professor Lin divided the class into teams of five and used instructor-stratification methods to make sure that each team had at least one advanced student in it. Each team was given a handout with generic problem-solving steps along with the initial pages of a musical score that had had the title, composer, and opus number removed. The teams were charged with trying to discover the missing information and identify the composition.

Although students were initially confused, they followed the problem-solving strategy and began to uncover clues. For example, in one team, a student pointed out the unusual instrumentation, deducing that it would probably have had to be written in the nineteenth century or later. Another student noticed that the performance markings were in German as opposed to the earlier standard of Italian, while others looked for clues in the harmony and form. Additional clues helped them to propose a list of possible composers, and combing through the detailed lists of works for those composers in library references and then the department's collection of orchestral scores, they were able to identify the work (in this case, the fourth movement of Mahler's Fourth Symphony). Each team made a presentation to the class revealing the name, composer, and opus number of their manuscript and explaining how they had discovered the composition's identity.

• • •

General Chemistry

In a chemistry class designed for non-majors, Professor Molly Cule knew that many of her students did not see how chemistry could be useful in their everyday lives. She decided to use Structured Problem Solving to help students understand chemistry's application beyond the classroom. She organized teams, and challenged the students to select the best antacid from a variety of products. To help students get started, she gave them a problem-solving strategy in which they responded to prompt questions. Using these prompts, they were able to identify that the problem was to evaluate the effectiveness of the antacids, and that the initial information they needed to solve the problem was provided in the list of active ingredients displayed on the boxes. They were able to add information from a previous lecture on acids and bases to recognize that they needed to determine which tablets neutralized the most acid. The students then designed an experiment they would use to test the antacid. Teams presented their ideas at the next class session, including a list of the materials they needed to conduct the experiments, the procedure they would follow, and the data they would collect. The following session, the professor had the materials for them to conduct their experiments. Students used the data gathered from the experiments to solve the problem and to identify the best antacids available over the counter.

• • •

ONLINE Organize students into teams, and provide each team with its own private
IMPLEMENTATION threaded discussion forum. It is also possible to use a synchronous tool such as teleconferencing or a Chat session so that students can confer and solve the problem in real time. However they choose to solve the problem, post the solutions in a Threaded Discussion area so that the entire class can view the solutions and offer comments.

VARIATIONS AND
EXTENSIONS

- Structure a multilayer discovery task in which you provide the students with data, a variation called Discovery Learning (Bruner, 1966) or Discovery Method (Millis & Cottell, 1993). Students identify problems, generate hypotheses, test hypotheses, and apply conclusions to new situations. This method provides a framework so that groups that work faster than other groups can delve more deeply into the problem.

- Have students write responses to the *What do you know? What do you need to know?* and *Where can you find out?* steps so that they do not lose track of their logic.

- Have students use *CoLT 22: Sequence Chains* to flow-chart the steps as they develop the plan to solve the problem.

- Angelo and Cross (1993, pp. 213–230) offer several techniques for assessing problem-solving skills. Depending on what aspect or stage in Structured Problem Solving will be assessed, consider one of the following variations.

- *CAT 19: Problem Recognition Tasks* asks students to review examples of different kinds of problems and then identify the particular type of problem each example represents. This helps students to determine which kinds of problems are best solved by which methods.

- *CAT 20: What's the Principle?* focuses on the second step in problem solving: it asks students to decide what principle or principles to apply in order to solve the problem.

- *CAT 21: Documented Problem Solutions* asks students to keep track of the steps they take in solving a problem. This helps teachers to assess how students solve problems and to assess how well students understand and can describe their problem-solving methods.

- *CAT 22 Audio- and Videotaped Protocols* asks students to record their talking and working through the process of solving a problem. Although time consuming and complicated, this technique can provide a wealth of useful information to teachers and students alike.

OBSERVATIONS AND ADVICE   This CoLT can be an effective way to introduce new students to the problem-solving process within the structure of a disciplinary context. Students will be able to adapt and reapply these processes to new situations as well as carry problem-solving structures between and among disciplines.

By explicitly guiding students through the problem-solving steps, this activity also helps students to develop discipline-specific meta-cognitive skills. Students are required to step back and observe their own thinking processes and hence become more aware of how they solve problems.

Advise students that during the initial stages of brainstorming possible solutions, they should allow creativity to flow by not evaluating, judging, or criticizing proposed solutions.

Written documents or audio- or videotapes that record group problem-solving processes provide teachers with an artifact for assessing and grading this CoLT.

KEY RESOURCES   Bruner, J. (1966). *Toward a theory of instruction.* Cambridge, MA: Harvard University Press.

Millis, B. J., & Cottell, P. G. (1998). *Cooperative learning for higher education faculty.* American Council on Education, Series on Higher Education. Phoenix, AZ: Oryx Press, pp. 95, 101, 103.

COLLABORATIVE
LEARNING
TECHNIQUE

17

Analytic Teams

Characteristics	
Group Size	4–5
Time on Task	15–45 MINUTES
Duration of Groups	SINGLE SESSION
Online Transferability	HIGH

DESCRIPTION AND PURPOSE In Analytic Teams, team members assume roles and specific tasks to perform when critically reading an assignment, listening to a lecture, or watching a video. Roles such as summarizer, connector (relating the assignment to previous knowledge or to the outside world), proponent, and critic focus on the analytic process rather than the group process (which entails roles such as facilitator, timekeeper, and recorder).

This technique is useful for helping students understand the different activities that constitute a critical analysis. It can be particularly effective when the teacher assigns roles that exist within the norms of the discipline. By dividing the process into parts and assigning these parts to individuals, students are able to focus on learning and performing one aspect at a time, thus preparing students for more complex problem-solving assignments in which they must assume multiple roles.

Listening to a lecture, watching a video, or reading an assignment can be passive activities. Forming teams in which each member is assigned a distinct task to perform may increase engagement because each student can say, "My job is to be a critic" (or to think of questions, or to look for examples, and so on). Assigned roles can increase participation among all members and equalize participation between active and less active contributors.

PREPARATION   Select an assignment that requires use of a complex analytical process and break the process down into component parts or roles. Although there are a variety of roles from which to choose, depending upon the specific analytic process and learning goals, the following are examples that can be applied to several kinds of assignments.

Proponents	List the points you agreed with and state why.
Critics	List the points you disagreed with or found unhelpful and state why.
Example Givers	Give examples of key concepts presented.
Summarizers	Prepare a summary of the most important points.
Questioners	Prepare a list of substantive questions about the material.

To ensure that the assignment is appropriate for team analysis, take the time in advance to determine whether you could perform each of the assigned roles and that each role has a sufficiently challenging task.

PROCEDURE   1. Form student groups of four or five, assigning each individual in the team a specific role and "job assignment."

2. Present the lecture, show the video, or assign the reading.

3. Give teams class time for individual members to share their findings and to work together to prepare to present their analyses in oral or written presentations.

4. Consider a closure strategy that emphasizes roles and component tasks. Stand-Up-and-Share would be particularly appropriate for a fairly short activity, whereas a Panel or Poster session would be appropriate for more complex assignments.

• • •

EXAMPLES

History of the Americas

In this online class, Professor A. Joe Vexploration wanted students to understand different stakeholders' perspectives in the European conquest of the Americas. He did not believe that he could achieve this effectively through narrative text alone, so he decided to assign students to watch the film, *The Mission*. Professor Vexploration knew that because the film was readily available at most local libraries and at video retail and rental stores, all of his online students would have access to it, regardless of their geographical location. The film, based on historical events that occurred in the borderlands of present-day Argentina, Paraguay, and Brazil around 1750, depicts the conflicts between the Spanish and Portuguese governments, the Roman Catholic Church, and the indigenous Guarani Indians. Based on his experience showing the film to students in his on-campus classes, Professor Vexploration knew that the film engaged students on the dramatic level. But he wanted to deepen the learning by helping his students to view the film more critically. He decided to structure the experience by creating Analytic Teams.

He organized students into groups of five, and created specific critical roles with assigned tasks:

- *Visual Analysts* focused on how the film's director used camera angles, European and Indian clothing, physical settings, and props to underscore the contrast in cultural views and social status.
- *Music Analysts* paid special attention to how Enrico Morricone's film score heightened viewers' perception of the culture clash between the indigenous and European traditions and the tensions between the sacred and secular.
- *Character Analysts* concentrated on how individuals within the drama changed throughout the film, and how the changes mirrored changes in the relationships between Spain, Portugal, the Guarani, and the Roman Catholic Church.
- *Historical Researchers* investigated the accuracy of the film's representation of the conflicts and also provided additional historical context.
- *Connectors* looked for similarities between the film's South American circumstances and the situation in North America, and also connected the historical events to contemporary cultural and political events.

Each team was given a private discussion board to talk about the film in general and the specific findings of each task member. By a specific date, each team was required to send to Professor Vexploration their team's comprehensive analysis of the film. The professor read the reports, collated the important points, added points that students had missed, and posted his synthesis along with team reports for general class viewing.

• • •

General Biology

> Professor Jenn Ettics wanted to help her students think critically about the connections between biology and sociology. For each unit, she identified a particular topic and located three to five articles addressing the topic from different perspectives. For example, for a unit on development and reproduction, Professor Ettics gave her students a collection of articles describing new technology that made it possible for doctors to save babies born sixteen weeks prematurely. She explained to students that babies born this early weighed about one pound, and faced months in an intensive-care nursery at the cost of hundreds of thousands of dollars per infant. The articles came from a variety of sources (including religious, medical, and insurance organizations) and represented a range of viewpoints.
>
> Professor Ettics formed groups of four and assigned each student a specific analytic role while reading the articles. Each student was responsible for looking for errors in one of four categories:
>
> 1. *Perspective*: Looked for unwarranted assumptions, an either/or outlook, absolutism, relativism, and bias.
> 2. *Procedure*: Looked for considerations of evidence, double standard, hasty conclusions, overgeneralization, stereotyping, and oversimplification.
> 3. *Expression*: Looked for contradiction, arguing in a circle, meaningless statements, mistaken authority, false analogy, and irrational appeals.
> 4. *Reaction*: Looked for changing the subject, shifting the burden of proof, creating a "straw man," and attacking the critic.
>
> During class, teams met for thirty minutes to discuss their analysis of the articles. Professor Ettics believed that using Analytic Teams helped students to read the articles critically and on multiple levels, laying the groundwork for a rich follow-up whole-class discussion. Team members rotated roles with each new set of readings.

· · ·

ONLINE IMPLEMENTATION   Form student groups, create a separate forum for each group with the posted prompt, assign individual roles, and have students respond to the prompt from their respective roles. Consider having groups write a team analysis that presents their findings that can be posted in a whole-class Threaded Discussion, or create a Web page for group viewing.

VARIATIONS AND EXTENSIONS

- Assign the different roles to teams instead of individuals.

- Give each group a different assignment to critique that is related to the same issue. The follow-up whole-class discussion will be particularly engaging if students read critiques that represent different sides of the issue.

- Extend this activity for more than one class session. For example, teams can read an entire book with individuals rotating roles such as summarizer, character analyst, and question developer every chapter.

OBSERVATIONS AND ADVICE

The most challenging aspect in preparing for this technique is selecting an assignment that is complex enough to yield a useful analysis when divided into component tasks. If the task is not sufficiently complex, one or more of the individual team members will be bored or unable to participate fully.

Giving students structured roles can help them develop and expand their repertoire of analytic thought patterns.

To reduce the amount of time required for this activity in class, have the actual listening, viewing, or reading take place out of class.

One of the significant challenges of this CoLT is determining how to follow up on the group work in a way that will help students meaningfully synthesize the various information and opinions they have heard. Consider one of the reporting out and closure strategies described in Chapter Five.

Students typically prefer some roles to others. They may even resist being assigned certain roles and request that they be assigned roles with which they have already developed both comfort and skill. Yet it is important that students develop their abilities in multiple roles.

To encourage students to develop their abilities and to move out of their comfort zone, consider adapting and implementing *Self-Assessment of Ways of Learning* (CAT 36, Angelo & Cross, 1993, pp. 295–299). In its original form, this CAT prompts students to describe their general approaches to learning, or their learning styles, by comparing themselves with different profiles and selecting the profiles that most closely resemble their own. It requires that faculty adopt specific theoretical frameworks that describe learning styles and to use this as the basis for creating their learning profiles. To modify this CAT to suit the needs of Analytic Teams, replace profiles of learning styles with profiles of analytic process roles. Each profile can consist of brief descriptions of the kinds of skills each role requires. Create two or three questions that will assess students' affinity for the various roles and ask each student to answer these questions for themselves. Awareness and class discussion of this may also motivate students to stretch and increase their analytical skills by working to develop their abilities in less comfortable or more challenging roles.

KEY RESOURCE   Johnson, D. W., Johnson, R., & Smith, K. (1998). *Active learning: Cooperation in the college classroom.* Edina, MN: Interaction Book Company, p. 3:23.

COLLABORATIVE
LEARNING
TECHNIQUE

18

Group Investigation

Characteristics	
Group Size	2–5
Time on Task	SEVERAL HOURS
Duration of Groups	MULTIPLE TO ALL-TERM
Online Transferability	MODERATE

DESCRIPTION AND PURPOSE   In Group Investigation, student teams plan, conduct, and report on in-depth research projects. These projects provide opportunities for students to study a topic intensely and gain specialized knowledge about a specific area. Allowing students to select topics of special significance to them, to form interest groups, and to carry out their own research can be very motivating. This CoLT also helps students recognize that research does not always follow the same series of steps but instead is context dependent. Students learn that good research is a logical, well-organized endeavor that differs from one discipline to another, from one project to another, and even from one researcher to another. When students complete a Group Investigation, they enhance their understanding of the importance of discovery. When they participate in peer and teacher review of their projects, they gain practical experience in both giving and receiving constructive criticism. Finally, because in conducting the investigation, the group follows a series of steps and is working within a time frame, it discourages the plagiarism sometimes associated with the conventional term paper assignment.

PREPARATION   Prepare for this CoLT as you would to assign a term paper. Decide what parameters you want to establish in terms of topic choices. Decide what kinds of resources you will accept: popular and scholarly sources? Information retrieved online as well as from library books and periodicals? Interviews with experts? Select the methods for students to report their findings. For example, some teachers allow students to choose whether they will construct a model, act out a skit, give a presentation, create a video, build a Web page, create a CD-ROM, and so forth. Other teachers specify the reporting method. Also, decide whether you want to assign individual group process or task roles or allow students to determine and distribute roles themselves.

PROCEDURE

1. Have students brainstorm potential topics that fit within your parameters.

2. Select the topics for investigation from the list that students have generated. You can make these choices, or you can have students participate in the selection. One method is to type out or write on the chalkboard all of the potential choices and then ask individuals to vote for their top three choices. The class's most popular topics can then be the available choices.

3. Form teams based on topic interest.

4. Give teams time to organize their efforts such as preparing a prospectus in which they formulate their research questions, identify goals and the resources they will need to carry out their investigation, choose their methods of investigation, and divide up and assign the tasks.

5. Ask groups to begin their investigation, gathering information, reviewing it, deciding whether more information is needed, and analyzing and interpreting the information.

6. Have groups prepare their final report.

• • •

EXAMPLES

Introduction to Research Methods

In her English course on argument, critical reading, research, and documentation, Professor Clara Fie decided to use Group Investigation. She explained to students that the purpose of the assignment was for teams to identify a policy problem and suggest a solution. This solution was to be a specific action or set of actions that the intended audience was capable of carrying out. Goals for teams included convincing an audience that there was a problem, getting the audience to agree that the proposed solution was the most effective means of solving the problem, and motivating the audience to implement the solution. Professor Fie formed teams and had students participate in *CoLT 2: Round Robin* to brainstorm ideas for problems. Each team then chose the one problem that they wished to investigate. Teams investigated their problem and worked together to collect resources and develop a solution. Each team made a formal presentation to the class using whatever visual aids they felt would strengthen their proposal, and also distributed an annotated bibliography of all the resources they had used. Teams provided students in the audience the chance to ask questions and to complete a brief peer evaluation form ranking various aspects of the group's presentation. (Adapted from http://users.mhc.edu/facultystaff/jpierce/spring02/eng112/gp_prelim.asp)

• • •

Plant Biology

Professor Phil O'Dendron wanted students to investigate a contemporary issue related to plants, people, and the local environment. He decided to use Group Investigation in lieu of a traditional term paper and gave students several possible general topic areas from which to choose. The topic areas included invasive weeds in California; fire management in California forests; pesticides in California agriculture; organic farming in California; laws protecting rare and endangered plant species; and native Californians' access to traditionally used plants. Students communicated via e-mail to identify others with similar interests and schedules. They formed groups of three or four people and informed the instructor of their group's membership. Groups worked together to focus their topic, identify goals, create an investigation plan, and determine the division of labor. They submitted an outline of their project to Professor O'Dendron and the teaching assistant (TA) for review and feedback. Groups determined references (including articles, books, and local experts) and then worked together to conduct the research. Individual team members were required to submit interim progress reports to the group leader and to the professor and TA. Each group wrote a formal final report and gave a brief oral presentation of their investigation during the last week of classes. (Adapted from http://www.plb.ucdavis.edu/Courses/f02/plb11/syllabus%2002.htm)

• • •

 ## *Music of Multicultural America*

This online course is a comparative and integrative study of the multicultural music styles of the United States. It traces the development of uniquely American music genres such as blues, jazz, Cajun, Zydeco, Tejano, Salsa, Anglo folk music, and hip-hop/rap from their historical roots to their influence on contemporary American music. The professor was finding it increasingly challenging to keep informed about current music, but wanted her students to be able to recognize the influence of these historical genres in the popular music to which they listened. She also wanted students to understand how their favorite musicians' individual styles had been shaped by the social, historical, racial, and ethnic context in which they had grown up. To accomplish this, she decided to implement term-length Group Investigation projects.

The first semester she implemented the projects, she worked with students to identify several popular musicians who had clear roots in ethnic music traditions, including artists such as Bob Dylan, Buffy Sainte-Marie, Carlos Santana, Gloria Estefan, Selena, Aretha Franklin, and Tupac. Students signed up for membership in the team assigned to investigate each artist, or they could propose an artist of their own and form their own team. The Group Investigation project was a Web page portrait that would be part of the course's online Performing Artists Portrait Gallery. The investigation needed to contain the following components:

- *Visual Representation:* A visual identity such as a copyright-free photo, a student drawing, or a photo that has been manipulated by the students to a significant enough level to constitute fair use.
- *Biography:* A narrative section that addressed both the social/historical context in which the artist grew up, artist-specific information including ethnic/racial roots, the styles and artists that had influenced them, and their influence on subsequent artists.
- *Discography:* An annotated list of recordings.
- *Music Examples:* Three representative listening excerpts that had been recorded on to a CD and converted to MP3 for delivery on the Web.
- *Liner Notes:* Analysis of listening examples for structural components (rhythm, melody, harmony), genre and/or genre influences (blues, jazz, gospel, folk), and ethnic influences (Latin clave rhythms, African melodic ornamentation).
- *Lyrics:* The lyrics and the team's interpretation of the lyrics.
- *Personal Significance:* Each individual team member's explanation of why the artist and music examples had been chosen.
- *Web Search:* Three to five Web sites that provide additional information on the artist, genre, social context, and so forth.

> The Group Investigation project engaged students, provided a framework for bringing together several aspects of the course, helped to keep the professor informed of current styles, and made a significant contribution to the learning repository for the class because the gallery was cumulative, with new artists added each term.

• • •

ONLINE IMPLEMENTATION   To be successful with online students, this activity must be highly structured. Form groups and assign each group its own threaded discussion area so that members can communicate aspects of the investigation privately. Break down the research process into its various parts and outline tasks so that each student is clear on their responsibilities. Establish a time framework with clear deadlines. Have final text reports or Web pages posted in a public forum for all members of the class to view. For closure, create an assignment that requires all students to view the various reports and, for example, to answer specific content questions or compare and evaluate the investigation results.

VARIATIONS AND EXTENSIONS

- Consider using *CoLT 2: Round Robin* to structure a collaborative activity in which students brainstorm ideas for investigation topics.

- Keep the reporting out engaging by asking students to be creative in the way that they present their findings. For example, suggest that students use animation, videotapes, simulations, role plays, and so forth as alternatives to traditional lecture presentations or written reports.

- Consider creating a Knowledge Repository that contains the results of consecutive terms' students. Written reports can be collected and placed in binders. Web pages can be housed in a single location.

OBSERVATIONS AND ADVICE   Davis (1993, pp. 219–221) offers some additional suggestions for assigning research papers that, with minor adaptation, also apply to Group Investigations:

- *Clarify what skills you expect students to develop.* For example, do you want students to gain experience in using the library and finding and retrieving information online? In locating and evaluating information to support a thesis? In synthesizing disparate material?

- *Check with your library to make sure it can support your research requirements.*

- Invite a librarian to make a presentation to your students on library skills, resources, and online search strategies.

- *Do not send an entire class in search of the same information.* If certain sources are applicable to all projects, consider putting these materials on reserve or duplicating them and making them available to students for purchase.

- *Break the assignment into manageable chunks.* Establish interim due dates to help teams structure the investigation process and learn from each step. The following critical points can have deadlines:

  1. Identifying a topic
  2. Preparing a prospectus that states the investigation's title, purpose, intended audience, major points, and a schedule of group and individual tasks
  3. Gathering sources, data, references
  4. Developing an outline
  5. Planning the presentation (skit, model, paper, and so forth)
  6. Revising the final report or presentation

It is important to keep track of group progress during this activity. Use the steps suggested in the preparation for this CoLT to establish deadlines and request interim progress reports. This will help groups pace themselves so that they are successful and don't feel overwhelmed. It will also give you a chance to provide feedback so that students can adjust their investigations and revise their work if it is needed.

If your schedule permits, you can meet with each team (or a team spokesperson) to check on progress, discover and discourage any potential plagiarism or academic dishonesty, and provide encouragement, guidance, and advice.

Give students time in class for teams to discuss, plan, and implement their investigations. If all of the work is done out of class, students will see it as an add-on and not as an integral and essential part of the course.

Upon completion of the investigation and report, provide time so that each team may present its findings to the other teams. Rotating Trios (see Chapter 5) is an interesting technique for having multiple teams report out.

KEY RESOURCES   Sharan, S., & Hertz-Lazarowitz, R. (1980). A group investigation method of cooperative learning in the classroom. In S. Sharan et al. (Eds.), *Cooperation in education.* Provo, UT: Brigham Young University Press, pp. 14–46.

Sharan, Y., & Sharan, S. (1994). Group Investigation in the cooperative classroom. In S. Sharan (Ed.), *Handbook of cooperative learning.* Westport: Greenwood Press, pp. 97–114.

Chapter 10

Techniques Using Graphic Information Organizers

"A PICTURE IS WORTH A THOUSAND WORDS" is the premise that underlies graphic organizers. Graphic organizers are powerful tools for converting complex information into meaningful displays. Because information can be arranged spatially, graphic organizers can help students discover the patterns and relationships among ideas that are sometimes impossible to convey in text alone. Because they can show the interrelationships among parts as well as the relationship of the parts to the whole, they help students view information on both holistic and detailed levels. Because they can compress and focus information, they can make interpretation, understanding, and insight easier. Finally, because graphic organizers use single words or short phrases and combine these with an illustration or diagram, they are ideal for many types of learners, including visual learners and those with limited English proficiency (Retrieved December 21, 2003, from http://www.fno.org/oct97/picture.html.)

Graphic organizers are flexible tools that can be used for many different instructional purposes. They can provide a framework for gathering and sorting ideas for discussion, writing, or research. This framework can help students focus their ideas. It can show different aspects of a concept. It can reveal what information is known and highlight what is still missing. Graphic organizers can serve as study guides, providing structures that help students to summarize text or to sort and remember key facts and ideas. They can also be used for assessment and grading, efficiently displaying the order and completeness of an individual or group's thought processes and the strengths and weaknesses of their understanding.

The five CoLTs in this chapter all use a graphic to organize information, but each technique is especially well suited for a specific conceptual task. Affinity Grouping is particularly useful for classifying ideas that have been generated in a brainstorming session. Group Grid and Team Matrix help to compare, contrast, and differentiate between closely related ideas. Sequence Chains focus on series of items or events. Word Webs—the group equivalent of an individually created Concept Map—can be simple or complex, and may be best used to uncover and display composite, multifaceted relationships. The Graphic Information Organizing CoLTs are summarized in Exhibit 10.1.

EXHIBIT 10.1

Graphic Organizing CoLTs

This CoLT	Is a Technique in Which Students:	It Is Particularly Useful for:
19: Affinity Grouping	Generate ideas, identify common themes, and then sort and organize the ideas accordingly	Helping students "unpack" a complicated topic and identify and classify its constituent parts
20: Group Grid	Are given pieces of information and asked to place them in the blank cells of a grid according to category rubrics	Clarifying conceptual categories and developing sorting skills
21: Team Matrix	Discriminate between similar concepts by noticing and marking on a chart the presence or absence of important, defining features	Distinguishing among closely related concepts
22: Sequence Chains	Analyze and depict graphically a series of events, actions, roles, or decisions	Understanding processes, cause and effect, and chronological series, and organizing information in an orderly, coherent progression
23: Word Webs	Generate a list of related ideas and then organize them in a graphic, identifying relationships by drawing lines or arrows to represent the connections	Figuring out and representing relationships; like maps, they can show both the destination and the sites and sights along the way

COLLABORATIVE
LEARNING
TECHNIQUE

19

Affinity Grouping

Characteristics	
Group Size	3–5
Time on Task	30–45 MINUTES
Duration of Groups	SINGLE SESSION
Online Transferability	LOW

DESCRIPTION AND PURPOSE Students individually generate ideas about a topic and write each item on a slip of paper. Groups sort and organize the slips into categories as they identify common themes. Affinity Grouping can help students unpack a complicated issue and build groupings from the separate pieces. Because students identify clusters of ideas and information shared by several people, this CoLT can help build group consensus.

PREPARATION Think of a complex topic for students to explore. Brainstorm yourself to check that the topic stimulates a sufficient number of ideas and that these ideas can be organized into clusters. Identify a physical area where all groups of students have a flat surface with ample room to move slips of paper around: the board or wall space with taped-up flip-chart paper works well for sticky notes; large tables can be used for slips of paper or index cards.

PROCEDURE 1. Distribute enough 3 x 5 cards, slips of paper, or sticky notes so that each student can have several slips for brainstorming ideas.

2. State the category, issue, or problem to be explored and provide a time limit for the activity.

3. Organize the students into groups, but then ask each student to separately and silently brainstorm ideas, writing one idea per slip of paper.

4. When time is up, ask one team member to collect the cards or sticky notes, mix them up, and spread them out (or stick them) on a flat surface.

5. Instruct the teams to discuss and arrange the cards or sticky notes into related groups.

6. Have students create a title or heading for each grouping that best describes the theme of each group of items.

• • •

Orientation to Environmental Horticulture

Professor Rhoda Dendron wanted to introduce students to the terminology used in the identification of plants. She formed groups and had students brainstorm lists of terms and ideas, and then had groups organize the lists into categories. Groups came up with categories such as families of plants, characteristics of plants, habits of growth, environmental requirements, and so forth. The activity helped students develop a conceptual framework for starting to learn plant identification and taxonomy.

• • •

Research Methods

Professor Anna Littical taught an educational research course and decided to use Affinity Grouping to teach students how to code qualitative data. She organized individuals into student teams and gave each individual a transcript of a recent interview with students regarding successful completion of the dissertation. She asked students individually to read through the transcripts, writing on sticky notes as many themes as they saw, one theme per note. Teams then worked together to sort the notes into categories and identify a category name. Professor Littical asked teams to write rules for what should be included or excluded in each of the categories and to develop category codes. When teams had finished the activity, she used their categories and rules as the basis for a whole-class discussion on the challenges to coding qualitative data.

• • •

English Literature

A professor teaching a composition course used Affinity Grouping to help students brainstorm and organize ideas for an upcoming writing assignment. All students were to write an essay responding to a work of literature, in this case Kate Chopin's

The Awakening. The professor asked students to form groups of five or six and individually brainstorm ideas about significant changes in the novel's characters, conflicts between characters, major developments in the plot, and so forth, and write each idea down on a separate slip of paper. She then asked three students from each group to sort the ideas into categories while others watched and eventually made suggestions. When students had completed the sorting step, she asked teams to create identifying phrases for each group of ideas. The phrases describing the categories of ideas fell naturally into the themes of the novel, such as the need for individual freedom, women's roles in the nineteenth century, and the development of personal identity. As each team reported out their categories with a few examples of supporting ideas, she wrote their thoughts on the board and used this as the basis for a discussion on what constituted the novel's various themes. By participating in this activity, she believed students were able to identify, explore, and select themes for their individual writing assignment.

•   •   •

ONLINE IMPLEMENTATION

Because the effectiveness of this CoLT is largely based on students being able to physically handle cards or pieces of paper, this technique does not transfer well to the online environment. If generating and sorting ideas is important to your teaching goals, consider asking students to write each idea as a single, new thread (analogous to writing each idea on a single piece of paper) and create a title or heading for each posting that best describes his or her idea. Have students review the list of titles and read the postings so that they can see other students' ideas. Ask students to reply with suggestions for groupings. If desired, use the editing function of the discussion board management to move the titles to groupings recommended by the students.

VARIATIONS AND EXTENSIONS

- This CoLT can be especially effective when groups have a complex decision to make, such as determining a topic to research as a group, and are experiencing difficulty reaching consensus. Have students brainstorm ideas for the topic, write them on the slips of paper, and then sort them into categories. Then use a decision-making strategy, such as one described in Chapter Five, Facilitating Student Collaboration, to select the final topic.

- If there are multiple teams, have teams review each other's categories; sometimes a fresh eye can bring clarity.

- Rather than the whole group, have only a few of the team members arrange the cards or sticky notes into related groups while other team members observe without commenting. When they are finished, ask other team members to review the groups and make suggestions for any reorganization.

- Extend this CoLT by using it as preparation for another CoLT, such as Group Investigation or Paper Seminar.

OBSERVATIONS AND ADVICE

Students will likely want to include multiple ideas on the pieces of paper. They need to limit their ideas to one per slip, but they need to include enough information so that the idea is understandable. Ask them to describe ideas with only a few words or short phrases.

Sorting is a complicated task. This phase should not begin until all team members are ready.

Teams may struggle with categories. The categories should generally be mutually exclusive. However, if an idea fits in more than one category or group and the group cannot reach consensus about placement, suggest that they make a separate card for each category.

Depending upon the purpose for having students generate and organize ideas, consider moving to whole class discussion with team spokespersons explaining their group's categories of ideas, or have students wander around to view other teams' efforts.

Teachers often use Affinity Grouping to generate and organize a large number of ideas that they then want students to prioritize. One strategy to help students reach consensus is to give each student three slips of five or so different colored label dots and explain a color-coded system for prioritization of ideas. For example, red is highest priority, blue is medium, and yellow is low. All students can wander among posted groupings and put a dot next to the item that reflects his or her personal assessment of the value of that item.

KEY RESOURCES

Brassard, M. (1989). *The memory jogger II.* Methuen, MA: Goal/QPC, p. 12.

King, R. (1989). *Hoshin planning: The developmental approach.* Methuen, MA: Goal/QPC, pp. 4:2–4:5.

**COLLABORATIVE
LEARNING
TECHNIQUE**

20

Group Grid

Characteristics	
Group Size	2–4
Time on Task	15–45 MINUTES
Duration of Groups	SINGLE SESSION
Online Transferability	LOW

**DESCRIPTION
AND PURPOSE**

This CoLT is probably most useful in introductory-level courses where students are building basic schema, learning a large number of new terms, and trying to understand the categorization rules of the discipline. Organizing and classifying information helps students to clarify conceptual categories and to develop categorization skills. By making students' conceptual organization explicit and graphic, Group Grid also helps students remember the information. In this activity, students sort pieces of information by placing them in the blank cells of a grid. The grid's columns and rows consist of superordinate concepts, and student groups receive scrambled lists of subordinate terms, names, equations, images, or other items that belong in the categories. Teams sort the subordinate items into the correct grid categories.

PREPARATION

Select two or more related categories that organize course information. The simplest grid sorts information into two or three columns. More complex grids have more columns, or they may contain a second level of sorting where the top horizontal row identifies one level of organization and the far left vertical column identifies another level of organization. The item placed at the point of intersection must meet both column and row classification criteria. Write out a list of items that belong in each category.

Make a grid by drawing a large rectangle and dividing it into as many smaller rectangles as you have categories and items of information. Write the name of the categories in the top row and/or left column, leaving the remaining cells blank. Either write out the items that teams are to sort in a scrambled list on the side of the grid, or write the list on a separate piece of paper, an overhead transparency, or the board. Check to make sure you can fill out the grid yourself. You may use your grid to evaluate students' grids or to have students check the accuracy of their grids.

PROCEDURE   1. Form groups and distribute the blank grid as a handout, or have students copy it from one that you project in an overhead transparency or draw on the chalkboard.

2. Give students the list of scrambled items of information.

3. Have students fill in the blank cells of the grid. Groups can discuss and come to consensus about how the items should be sorted, and fill out the grid as a group project. Or individual students can take turns in a Round Robin order, filling in one cell per turn. Each person within the group, or each pair within a quad, can have their own writing style (cursive versus printing) or colored markers to distinguish their contributions.

4. Students submit completed grids for assessment and evaluation, or you post a correctly completed grid for them to check for accuracy.

• • •

EXAMPLES

Introduction to Art

Professor Allie Gorical taught an introductory-level art appreciation course that was a survey of the major visual arts from the ancient world to the present day. The list of artist and artwork names was extensive, and students had traditionally felt overwhelmed trying to understand and remember *who* and *what* went *where*. Professor Gorical decided to use Group Grid as a technique to help students sort and remember the information. The course focused on four time frames: the Ancient World, the Middle Ages, the Renaissance, and the Modern World.

As a closing activity for each section of the course, she divided students into groups of four and gave each group a handout that contained a blank grid and each individual student a scrambled list of the most important artworks of that period. For example, for the Middle Ages, she gave students a list of fifty terms, such as the *Utrecht Psalter*, the *Gero Crucifix*, the *Bayeaux Tapestry*, and so forth, and asked them to write the terms into a larger version of the grid that appears as Exhibit 10.2.

EXHIBIT 10.2

Group Grid for the Middle Ages

	Two-Dimensional (Painting, Mosaics, Tapestries . . .)	Three-Dimensional (Sculpture, Bas Relief . . .)	Architecture
Early Medieval			
Romanesque			
Gothic			

After sufficient time had passed for teams to fill in the grids, she projected her own completed grid on an overhead transparency so that groups could check their grid for accuracy. The grids were one of several tools students used as study guides for examinations.

• • •

Physical Anthropology

This professor uses Group Grid periodically throughout the semester to help students organize critical units of information. For example, he wanted his students to be able to distinguish between important anthropological finds of *Homo erectus* fossils in China. He created a grid in which across the top row he wrote five categories of characteristics (the name of the site where the fossil was found, the estimated age of the fossil, the material of the fossil, the year that it was found, and any comments that further described the fossil). In the left column, he wrote the fossil designation (for example, *Hexian, Zhoukoudian, Yunxian,* and *Lantian*). Students formed teams, received a scrambled list of elements of information (such as *1980–81* or *mandible*), and worked together to fill in the grid, using the information provided and accessing their notes or text as needed.

• • •

Principles of Business

> Managerial decision making is one of the key topic areas in this introductory business course taught by Professor Owen Cash. Professor Cash uses mini-case studies throughout the term to provide his students with real-world scenarios that include problems teams must examine and for which they then propose a solution. To help students organize and evaluate the arguments for different decisions, Professor Cash asks teams to construct and fill out a simple, two-column pro-and-con grid for each course of action (CAT 10, Angelo & Cross, 1993, pp. 168–171).

• • •

ONLINE IMPLEMENTATION

Using synchronous tools such as teleconferencing or Chat sessions that also have whiteboard tools offer one possibility for using this CoLT in the online environment. Or consider giving students blank grids as a word processing document, as an e-mail attachment, or to download. Either have each individual member of a group complete a grid to compare with their teammates and reach consensus on a single grid, or assign each individual member responsibility for specific columns or rows. Completed grids can be uploaded as Web pages into forums that can be viewed by other students.

VARIATIONS AND EXTENSIONS

- Provide students with grids that include only the categories, and have them generate the items to write in the cells.

- Provide students with grids that include only the cell items and ask them to identify category names.

- Simple, two-column grids can be very effective using a variety of superordinate categories. Consider using the following: pros and cons, costs and benefits, advantages and disadvantages, problems and solutions, or cause and effect (Angelo & Cross, 1993, pp. 168–171).

- Consider having students fill out a two-column pro-and-con grid from different perspectives. For example, three separate grids can analyze the benefits and detriments of online course delivery from the student's perspective, the teacher's perspective, and the institution's perspective.

OBSERVATIONS AND ADVICE

If the grid is not complex enough either in terms of the categories or the cell items, this activity will feel like busy work.

Group Grids are useful to help students prepare for more complex activities. For example, pro-and-con grids can be used to organize arguments for debates or to evaluate decisions in case studies.

Ask students to report out on their grids. Have them make comparisons between their grids, asking them to explain why they sorted the items as they did. Having groups report on their grids gives you immediate information about how clear students are on the organization of concepts.

When groups have been given both the categories and a scrambled list of terms to sort, their completed grids are easily scorable.

KEY RESOURCES Angelo, T. A., & Cross, K. P. (1993). Categorizing Grid. *Classroom assessment techniques,* 2nd ed. San Francisco: Jossey-Bass, pp. 160–163.

Moore, D. W., & Readence, J. E. (1984). A quantitative and qualitative review of graphic organizer research. *Journal of Educational Research, 78*(1), 11–17.

**COLLABORATIVE
LEARNING
TECHNIQUE**

21

Team Matrix

Characteristics	
Group Size	PAIRS
Time on Task	10–20 MINUTES
Duration of Groups	SINGLE SESSION
Online Transferability	LOW

DESCRIPTION AND PURPOSE   In Team Matrix, students discriminate between similar concepts by noticing and marking on a chart the presence or absence of important, defining features. Unlike *CoLT 20: Group Grid*—which asks students to sort items by set criteria—Team Matrix asks students to differentiate between concepts by determining whether criteria are present or not. This CoLT is useful for tasks in which students mix up shared and uncommon attributes because it requires students to identify and make explicit critical distinctions of closely related concepts. Making the differences evident and graphic on a chart also helps students to understand the distinction.

PREPARATION   Choose two or three related concepts. Identify and make a list of the elements or the features that differentiate the concepts. Consider also making a list of the features that both concepts possess and that perhaps contribute to students' confusion. Create a matrix with the concepts in the top row, and either the categories for comparison or the identifying features in the left column (or vice versa). Check to make sure you can fill out the matrix yourself, so that you can uncover and correct any problems. Create a blank matrix for students to fill in as groups.

PROCEDURE   1. Form pairs and distribute the blank matrix as a handout, have students copy it from an overhead transparency, or draw it on the board.

2. If you want to grade completed matrices, ask individual students to select a way to distinguish their contributions (for example, colored markers or writing hand, such as cursive, printing, or block).

3. Have partners come to consensus and complete the matrix.

4. Move to whole-class discussion to compare group matrices with instructor matrix, or ask partners to submit completed matrices for evaluation.

• • •

EXAMPLES

Music of Multicultural America

To assist students who were consistently confusing blues and jazz, Professor Grace Note used a Team Matrix that required students to identify the shared and distinctive features of both genres. She organized students into pairs, gave them a chart listing various features, and asked students to decide whether each feature best described blues, jazz, or both. A filled-out excerpt from the matrix appears as Exhibit 10.3.

EXHIBIT 10.3

Team Matrix

Put a checkmark in the column indicating the genre that is most clearly defined by this feature.

Defining Features	Blues	Jazz	Both
Originated in urban areas		✓	
Originated in rural areas	✓		
Originated in the Mississippi Delta region			✓
Merged European and African traditions			✓
Developed earlier	✓		
Represented considerable interaction between Whites and Blacks from beginning		✓	
Interaction between Whites and Blacks not pronounced until later	✓		
Basis of rock 'n' roll	✓		
Uses African-based melodic ornamentation and rhythmic traditions			✓
Improvisation in melody and in harmonic substitution		✓	
Improvisation mainly in melody over standard progression	✓		
Uses three main chords in a slow harmonic rhythm	✓		
Uses many different chords, often fast harmonic rhythm		✓	
Popular in Europe, especially France		✓	
Imported back into America by British musicians	✓		

> When they were finished and she had collected the matrices, she was able to use it to assess her students' level of understanding and to pinpoint topics that were still confusing.

$\bullet$ $\bullet$ $\bullet$

School-Age Child (5–12) Behavior and Development

> After students had read assignments and heard lectures, Professor A. B. Sieze used Team Matrix to help students organize the characteristics, stages, and timing of normal development at various age levels. Later in the course, students observed children at different ages in play settings in order to better understand development needs and appropriate curriculum design. She formed student pairs and had partners design new matrices based on their original matrices to use to record data of physical, social, emotional, intellectual, and language development in the children they observed.

$\bullet$ $\bullet$ $\bullet$

Post–World War II Germany

> This course explores the historical, political, and cultural developments in Germany from 1945 to the present. One of the professor's primary goals is to help students develop perspectives on the challenges to constructing a unified German national identity following the existence of the two German states. The professor uses Team Matrix frequently to help students differentiate and analyze the economics, politics, and formulation of policy from the two states' viewpoints.

$\bullet$ $\bullet$ $\bullet$

ONLINE IMPLEMENTATION As with other graphic organizers, synchronous tools such as teleconferencing or Chat sessions that also have whiteboard tools offer one possibility for using this CoLT in the online environment. Or consider giving the blank matrix to students in a word processing document either as an e-mail attachment or to download onto their computers. Once individuals or teams fill out the matrix, they can be uploaded to a forum to compare and discuss answers.

VARIATIONS AND EXTENSIONS

- Have teams create their own matrices by considering the following questions:

  What concepts (or items) do you want to compare?

  What features (or characteristics) do they have?

  How are the items similar and different based on the characteristics?

- Ask teams to draw and fill out a grid using the information from their answers to these questions.

- In addition to defining distinctions, include similarities by creating a column for "Both." To make the matrix even more challenging, consider including a column for "Neither."

- Sometimes it is the level or degree of an element that distinguishes one concept from another, rather than the presence or absence of a feature. To represent this, consider creating a matrix composed of a series of lines representing continuums, with "Low" on one end and "High" on the other. Students place checkmarks or use numbers at relative points on the continuum.

- Instead of a matrix, consider using the overlapping circles of a Venn Diagram and have students write in the features in the appropriate parts of the circles.

OBSERVATIONS AND ADVICE

Team Matrix is an adaptation of Angelo and Cross's *Defining Features Matrix* (1993, pp. 164–167). Their examples (p. 165) provide further ideas for simple and effective ways to use this CoLT. For instance, they use a matrix in psychology to distinguish between Freudian and behaviorist views of human psychology and in political science to distinguish among the federal systems of the United States, Canada, and Germany.

Take time to think through your original matrix carefully. Focus on the concepts that are critical for students to be able to differentiate but with features that often confuse them because of the similarities.

Try to create categories whose interconnectedness is complex enough to require thought to identify. Simple, binary distinctions will feel like busy work.

After the group has completed the matrix and you have evaluated it to ensure that it is correct, suggest to individuals that they copy the matrix to assist them in recalling and understanding the defining features in their own study.

There are several ways you can close this activity. You can project a blank matrix and have students use the matrix they completed to guide you as you complete a class matrix; you can project your own completed matrix and have students compare and correct their own; or you can have students submit completed matrices to you for assessment and evaluation.

KEY RESOURCES   Angelo, T. A., & Cross, K. P. (1993). Defining features matrix. *Classroom assessment techniques*. San Francisco: Jossey-Bass, pp. 164–167.

Cunningham, P. M., & Cunningham, J. W. (1987). Content Area Reaching–Writing Lessons. *The Reaching Teacher, 40,* pp. 506–512.

COLLABORATIVE
LEARNING
TECHNIQUE

22

Sequence Chains

Characteristics	
Group Size	2–3
Time on Task	15–45 MINUTES
Duration of Groups	SINGLE SESSION
Online Transferability	LOW

DESCRIPTION AND PURPOSE In this CoLT, groups analyze and depict graphically a sequence of events, actions, roles, or decisions. Sequence Chains require students to create a visual map of the logic within a series. Students identify specific points in a series and then apply knowledge and reasoning to arrange these points in an orderly, coherent progression. Thus, this CoLT may help and promote logical, sequential thinking. It also produces a graphic that can be useful for remembering as well as for planning. Sequence Chains are perhaps best used in courses that require students to organize information to emphasize continuity or connections.

PREPARATION Choose what information (or items) students should organize into a sequence or series. Decide whether or not students will generate the items to be organized, or whether you will provide them with a scrambled list of items. Decide as well whether or not students will do any additional work with the sequence, such as explain the connection between the items in the series. Create a sample Sequence Chain to uncover potential problems and so to have a model against which to compare student work.

PROCEDURE
1. Organize students into groups, set a time limit, and either provide students with a scrambled list of items, or have them generate their own list of items.

2. Ask students to work together to arrange the items into a sequence. If students will do an additional activity with the sequence (such as explaining the relationship between items), give them directions and clarify your expectations.

3. Close this activity with a group discussion, asking teams to use their Sequence Chain as the basis for helping you create a class-generated Sequence Chain. Alternatively, have students draw their sequences on flip-chart paper, then post these around the room and have students wander around to look at other teams' solutions.

• • •

EXAMPLES

History of Western Civilization

Professor Wes T. Ward used Sequence Chains to clarify and reinforce students' understanding of the chronology of important historical events. Rather than having students simply memorize dates—which tends to strengthen students' perception of history as a collection of isolated pieces of data—Professor Ward wanted students to understand how historical events unfolded as a complex series of cause and effect. He created a Sequence Chain activity in which teams worked together to organize a group of events in chronological order and then identify the connections. For example on the unit "The Fall of the Western Roman Empire," he identified key events such as *the division of Constantine's empire into western and eastern parts, the Romans' attempt to suppress a revolt of the Visigoths at Adrianople,* and *the Vandals cross into Italy from North Africa.* He wrote each of these out on separate 3 x 5 index cards. Each group received a packet of cards that included cards with events written on them and blank cards. Students worked together first to place the events in sequence. Then they placed blank cards between events and tried to determine and write on the card how the earlier event might have influenced the later event. When the activity was finished, they numbered the cards, placed them in order, and submitted them to the professor for assessment and evaluation.

• • •

World Regional Geography

One of the fundamental themes in this survey of the world's major culture regions and nations was the reciprocal interactive relationship between humans and their environment. Professor Al Luvial used Sequence Chains to help students organize both the progression of events and the interconnectedness of people and places through converging processes of geological, cultural, economic, and political change. For example, in studying the region of Oceania, Professor Luvial asked teams to fill in a flow chart on the sequence of events describing how a Pacific high island is created and then transformed into a low island. This sequence was connected to a parallel flow chart, in which he asked students to add information on how these environments produced distinctive settings for human settlement. To this he added a third parallel flow chart, and asked students to fill in how changing patterns of settlement in turn affected the island's ecology.

• • •

Designing Web Pages

In this mini-course of a small business management program, the instructor was trying to teach students generally unfamiliar with computers how to create simple commercial Web pages using a popular software program. Students consistently ran into problems because they skipped a critical step in the process, so the instructor decided to have students participate in a Sequence Chain activity. She organized the class into pairs. While one partner worked through the steps of a portion of the design process on the computer, the other partner tried to write out the sequence of actions in simple, clear language. They then changed places and the other student checked and revised the directions. The partners continued in this manner through all phases of the design process until each pair had a sequential list of directions that was written in language that they understood. This became their personal set of directions that they could take with them to guide them in Web page design after the course was finished.

• • •

Masterpieces of Nineteenth-Century Russian Literature

> To assist students in tracking and understanding the complex developments in Tolstoy's *War and Peace,* this professor had students work in small groups to participate in a Sequence Chain. Students first brainstormed a list of critical events in the novel. They then organized these events sequentially, identifying where possible how one event might have affected a subsequent event.

• • •

ONLINE IMPLEMENTATION This technique is most effective when students are able to interact "in the moment" to organize and reorganize the components of a series, and therefore this technique does not transfer well to the online environment. If this activity seems as though it would be very useful in the online course, synchronous tools such as teleconferencing or Chat sessions that also have whiteboard tools offer one possibility for adaptation.

VARIATIONS AND EXTENSIONS
- Organize the sequence according to specific parameters. For example, an Events Sequence Chain helps students organize a series of episodes or occurrences; a Human Interaction Sequence Chain helps students organize mutual or reciprocal actions; and a Cause-and-Effect Sequence Chain helps students organize information into antecedent and consequence.

- Consider multiple, parallel graphics for more comprehensive or complex series. For example, Sequence A could contain a list of events, Sequence B the location of the event, and Sequence C the people involved in the event.

OBSERVATIONS AND ADVICE Sequence Chains organize information into a linear series, but not all information is best organized in this fashion. You may find that certain information is better organized in the more flexible pattern of relationships created by *CoLT 23: Word Webs.*

If allowing students to generate the list of items they are going to organize, you should know—and communicate to students—the level of information upon which they should focus. Will they supply and organize main topics? Subtopics? Supporting details? Also let students know how the items should be labeled. Should they use words? Phrases? Full sentences? Providing teams with specific guidelines helps them to be more successful and eases the comparison between different teams' products.

KEY RESOURCES Hall, T., & Strangman, N. (1999–2004). *Graphic organizers.* Retrieved March 22, 2004, from http://www.cast.org/ncac/GraphicOrganizers3015.cfm

Kagan, S. (1990). The structural approach to cooperative learning. *Educational Leadership, 47*(4), 12–15.

Kagan, S. (1996). *Cooperative learning.* San Clemente, CA: Kagan Cooperative Learning.

Moore, D. W., & Readence, J. E. (1984). A quantitative and qualitative review of graphic organizer research. *Journal of Educational Research, 78*(1), 11–17.

COLLABORATIVE LEARNING TECHNIQUE

23

Word Webs

Characteristics	
Group Size	2–4
Time on Task	30–45 MINUTES
Duration of Groups	SINGLE SESSION
Online Transferability	LOW

DESCRIPTION AND PURPOSE   Word Webs are collaborative versions of a concept map. A central word, phrase, or question placed on a shared writing space serves as the stimulus. Students generate a list of related ideas and then organize them in a graphic, identifying relationships by drawing lines or arrows to represent the connections. This technique helps students analyze a complex concept by breaking it down into component parts and clarifying the relationships. It is also an effective starting point, helping students relate new information to prior knowledge or guiding groups to uncover current understanding of the associations between parts. Word Webs help students organize facts and principles into meaningful conceptual networks and to represent visually complex relationships that are difficult to understand from words alone.

PREPARATION   Choose a concept for students to map, and map it yourself so that you can uncover potential problems. Your own diagram can also serve as a model against which to assess group work. Map a parallel concept to demonstrate the process to students. Decide what to use as a shared writing space (for example, flip charts, large-format paper), and bring this and colored markers or crayons to class.

PROCEDURE   1. Describe and demonstrate the process to students.

2. Form teams and distribute paper and markers.

3. Present the central concept that students will graph.

4. Ask student teams to brainstorm, writing a list of terms and phrases that express core concepts and supporting details.

5. Have students sketch out a diagram starting with the central idea and adding primary, secondary, and even tertiary associations.

6. Suggest that students determine the ways in which the items are related, drawing lines or arrows to show the connections.

7. Ask students to add new ideas and relationships as they construct the web.

• • •

EXAMPLES

Basic Two-Dimensional Design

This course introduces students to basic design concepts and their application. The instructor uses Word Webs throughout the class to help students analyze ideas and represent them visually. As the term progresses and students become more adept at diagramming, he encourages them to enhance the graphic by choosing various shapes, lines, and values and arranging these to create a unified visual statement. Exhibit 10.4 is a copy of a Word Web students created the first day of class that responded to his prompt, *What is design?*

• • •

History of the United States

In a freshman history course, Professor Rose E. Riveter wanted students to understand the complex effects of World War II on the United States. She organized the class into groups of four, and gave each group a large piece of newsprint paper and four different colored markers. Using *WWII's effects on the continental United States* as the central theme, she asked students to generate ideas and to show the relationship of their ideas in a web. For example, students in one group identified women, education, and the economy as core ideas, with each student who had the idea writing it onto the paper with his or her marker. The next step was to identify and graph details and supporting elements. Under economy, students mentioned that World War II provided many jobs in defense, boosted American markets, and brought the United States out of the Depression. Again using their individual markers, students were able to demonstrate relationships (for example, that jobs in defense offered opportunities for women). The groups turned in their webs, and since students used different colored markers, Professor Riveter could assign individual participation grades (adapted from Kagan, 1992).

• • •

EXHIBIT 10.4

Student Word Web Responding to Prompt: *What is design?*

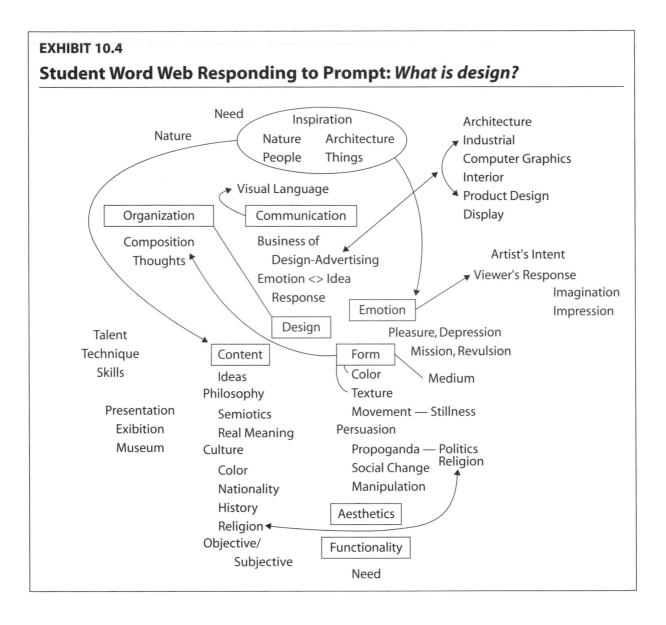

ONLINE IMPLEMENTATION This technique is most effective when students are able to interact "in the moment." Consider using a whiteboard tool during a synchronous session. The outcome can be captured as a screenshot to be uploaded onto a forum and shared with other students. Consider also purchasing a software package that assists in the development of concept maps, such as *Inspiration* (http://www.engagingminds.com/inspiration/descript.html), or use presentation or word processing software that includes drawing tools, with each person adding links in different colored fonts.

VARIATIONS AND
EXTENSIONS

- Use different kinds of graphics to represent different relationships. For example, graphs may resemble a spoked wheel with the central idea at the hub, or a solar system with the stimulus in the sun's position, or a geographical map (Angelo & Cross, 1993, p. 200). There are many models for organizing information in various ways. For example, the Spider Map displayed in Exhibit 10.5 demonstrates a more layered approach to charting ideas related to a central concept (Retrieved December 6, 2003, from http://www.ncrel.org/sdrs/areas/issues/students/learning/lr1grorg.htm).

- Additional ideas include Network Trees to organize a hierarchical set of information; Fishbone Maps for non-redundant cause-effect relationships; and Cycle Maps for relationships that have no absolute beginning or ending. The URL from which the Spider Map graphic was copied provides other graphic organization examples. Or use a browser search engine, entering terms such as "graphic organizer" + "teach" to find other examples on the Web.

- Instead of having students brainstorm the list of ideas, provide them with a list and ask them to graph out the relationships between the items, adding any new ideas that they can contribute.

EXHIBIT 10.5

Spider Map

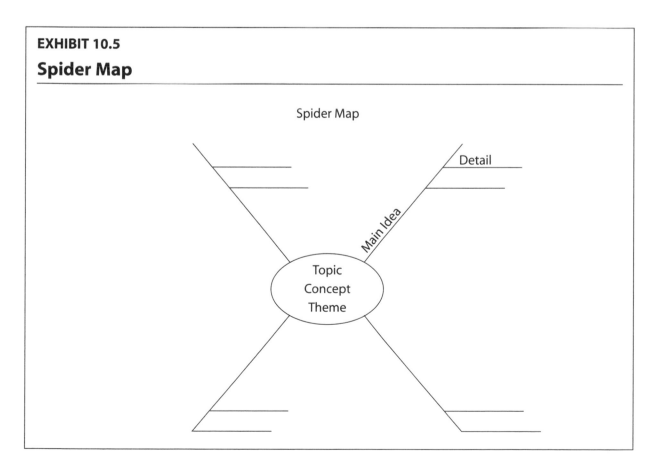

- Organize Word Webs around specific themes. For example, ask students to focus on real or fictional characters, identifying attributes as well as specific examples that demonstrate those characteristics (McTighe, 1992, pp. 183–188). A Character Word Web on Martin Luther King, Jr., might include:

Peaceful: Promoted nonviolent protests even within hostile and violent contexts

Selfless: Worked for freedom of oppressed people

Religious: Was a Baptist preacher and included religious references in his speeches

Brave: Led marches through angry crowds

OBSERVATIONS AND ADVICE   Angelo and Cross (1993, pp. 197–202) offer the following considerations regarding use of concept maps that we've adapted for Word Webs:

- Asking students to create Word Webs is supported by current research in cognitive psychology that recommends educators and students pay attention to the schemata—or conceptual networks—that we use to organize what we learn.

- Because Word Webs organize information graphically, this activity will be appealing to students with strong visual learning skills. Conversely, students with well-developed verbal skills and weaker visual skills may find this activity frustrating.

- Although some students may find it difficult to generate ideas or distinguish between levels of ideas, it may be even more difficult for them to identify relationships. Therefore, take sufficient time to introduce this activity so that you can demonstrate the process and clarify your expectations.

- Comparing groups' Word Webs can be difficult unless you limit items to a closed list of terms or phrases. Although comparisons will be easier, such restriction may diminish student creativity.

How you close this activity depends upon the purpose for having students construct the word webs. Teachers often use this CoLT to prepare students for a second, more extensive activity. For example, instructors may want teams to create Word Webs to generate and organize their ideas for the teaching stage in *CoLT 11: Jigsaw* or to create a topic overview for *CoLT 28: Collaborative Writing*. Or teachers may want to use the webs as the basis for a whole-class discussion, asking team spokespersons to show and explain the ideas and associations in their group's web. If students are submitting their webs for evaluation and will receive a grade, have individuals use different colored markers so that it is easier to assess individual participation.

KEY RESOURCES Angelo, T. A., & Cross, K. P. (1993). Concept maps. *Classroom assessment techniques.* San Francisco: Jossey-Bass, pp. 197–202.

Graphic Organizer, The. Retrieved December 7, 2003, from http://www.graphic.org/goindex.html

Chapter 11

Techniques Focusing on Writing

"WRITING IS EASY. All you do is stare at a blank sheet of paper until drops of blood form on your forehead" (attributed to George Fowler; Byrne, 1988, p. 46). Many students share a similar opinion of writing. Yet writing can be an invaluable tool for learning. Writing Across the Curriculum (WAC), created to reinforce writing skills in classes outside of English composition, brought attention to just that: writing as a means for learning. On a general basis, writing can teach critical thinking by helping students organize, summarize, and integrate and synthesize diverse elements into a coherent whole. Writing can also teach students to be aware of their own learning processes. Specifically, WAC advocates propose that writing can teach students to

- *Think clearly and express thoughts precisely*

- *Evaluate the adequacy of an argument*

- *Use, apply critically, and move easily among facts, inferences, and opinions*

- *Understand how truth claims are established in a discipline*

- *Deal with ill-formed problems and quandaries*

- *Give and receive criticism profitably*

- *Agree or disagree by measure*

- *Extend a line of thought beyond the range of first impressions, and*

- *Articulate a complex position in a way that adds nothing to its complexity (WAC at Marshall University, retrieved December 23, 2003, from http://www.marshall.edu/wac/info.htm)*

Thus writing as a learning tool can help students deepen their understanding of disciplinary content as well as acquire important thinking skills.

Educators also recognize the importance of writing for other purposes. It is through a student's writing that teachers can often best assess the depth and breadth of student learning. As students progress in their academic majors, writing provides them entrée into the discourse community of their discipline. Finally, facility with writing transfers to their lives well beyond college, preparing students to be more effective in their careers and in their personal lives.

The six CoLTs in this chapter offer multiple ways to use writing in group work. On one end of the continuum are CoLTs that emphasize writing's role in facilitating learning and student awareness of their own learning. These CoLTs—such as Dialogue Journals and Round Table—use writing informally. They focus on writing as a tool to support the learning process, such as for recording group-generated ideas, to encourage reflection, or to direct and guide other activities such as reading or viewing. Other CoLTs, such as Peer Editing, Collaborative Writing, and Paper Seminar, involve formal writing. They provide frameworks for pairs or small groups to help each other and critique final and graded written products. Although each CoLT thus has a unique, distinct function, they share emphasis on the written word. The Writing CoLTs are summarized in Exhibit 11.1.

EXHIBIT 11.1

Writing CoLTs

This CoLT	Is a Technique in Which Students:	It Is Particularly Useful for:
24: Dialogue Journals	Record their thoughts in a journal that they exchange with peers for comments and questions	Connecting course work to students' personal lives and interacting with each other in content-related and thoughtful ways
25: Round Table	Take turns responding to a prompt by writing one or two words, phrases, or sentences before passing the paper along to others who do the same	Practicing writing informally and creating a written record of ideas
26: Dyadic Essays	Write essay questions and model answers for each other, exchange questions, and after responding, compare their answers to the model answer	Identifying the most important feature of a learning activity and formulating and answering questions about that activity
27: Peer Editing	Critically review and provide editorial feedback on a peer's essay, report, argument, research paper, or other writing assignment	Developing critical editing skills and giving each other constructive criticism to improve papers before they submit them for grading
28: Collaborative Writing	Write a formal paper together	Learning and performing the stages of writing more effectively
29: Team Anthologies	Develop a compilation of course-related readings with student reactions to the material	Experiencing the research process without writing a formal research paper
30: Paper Seminar	Write and then present an original paper, receive formal feedback from selected peers, and engage in a general discussion of the issues in the paper with the entire group	Engaging in deep discussion about their research and providing individual students with focused attention and feedback on the student's work

COLLABORATIVE
LEARNING
TECHNIQUE

24

Dialogue Journals

Characteristics	
Group Size	PAIRS
Time on Task	VARIES
Duration of Groups	SINGLE to MULTIPLE SESSIONS
Online Transferability	HIGH

DESCRIPTION AND PURPOSE In this CoLT, individuals keep a journal in which they write about a reading assignment, lecture, task, or experience. Each student then exchanges journals with a peer who reads and responds to the entry with comments and questions. Dialogue Journals offer a formal medium for students to record their thoughts, connect coursework to their personal lives, and ask each other questions. Journals can be particularly effective when writers know that someone who is also interested in the topic will read and respond to their entries.

PREPARATION Decide the journal parameters ahead of time. Determine the reader's tasks and role (critic or coach?), and establish how and when partners will exchange journals. Select the medium (for example, a computer file, a lined tablet, or a formal bound booklet), and decide whether you will supply students with this or they will need to purchase it. Consider creating a handout that includes directions, clarifies your expectations, and provides examples.

PROCEDURE 1. On a fresh page in the journal, students draw a vertical line about one-third of the page from the right margin. The writer writes in the left; the responder writes in the right.

2. The writer enters comments or questions after reading an assignment, hearing a lecture, performing a task, engaging in an activity, or listening to a discussion, and dates and signs the entry.

3. The writer gives the journal to the responder, who reads the entries and responds with comments, suggestions, answers, questions, and so forth, also dating and signing the entry.

4. The instructor may read the journals to clarify points, answer questions, and comment on or evaluate the quality of observations and responses.

• • •

EXAMPLES

Shakespeare

A professor of English used Dialogue Journals throughout her course for students to respond to in-class activities. For example, after showing a film of Shakespeare's play *As You Like It,* she asked students to write in their Dialogue Journals that night for homework, focusing on how they felt the film enhanced their understanding of the drama. Students brought their entries to class the next day and exchanged journals. For that evening's homework assignment, each student responded to the other student's entry. The professor checked the journals to assess what students had learned from observing the film and what questions they had. She also evaluated the entries and responses for grading purposes.

• • •

Introduction to Political Science

Professor Manuel Recount decided to use Dialogue Journals to encourage students to pay closer attention to current political events and to relate these events to course content. He formed long-term pairs to work together for the semester and required one exchange of entries and responses each week. He asked students to note any recent political activity in the news that particularly intrigued them and to try to explain or elaborate on the item using the language and theories of political science. Students were given the option of following either national or local political events and of focusing in depth on one specific story or addressing whatever had caught their interest that week. Each Wednesday, students exchanged their journals with their partners, who made comments. Partners had until Friday to respond to the entries before turning them in to Professor Recount. Professor Recount read through the journals, also made comments, and returned the journals to their original authors on Monday. Periodically, he reserved about ten minutes in class for pairs to read his comments together.

• • •

Introduction to Contemporary Mathematics

> Professor Anna Log designed an introductory non-majors course for students who were anxious about math. One of its primary goals was to introduce students to mathematical thinking in a low-stress classroom environment. Professor Log chose to implement Dialogue Journal as a method to assess student understanding of content, to provide peer support, and to gather feedback on individual student anxiety levels. She instructed students to bring a notebook to class and to line off one-third of the paper on the right-hand margin. Each week she assigned three prompts: one related to content (for example, *Sketch a balance scale to show the following:* x + 7 = 15*)*; one related to process *(What was the most important step in solving the problem?)*; and the other related to attitude *(How challenging did you find this problem?)*. She gave students a certain amount of response time depending upon the complexity of the problem, and then had them exchange journals. Students then had ten minutes to comment on the entries before giving the assignments back to their peers. Professor Log collected the journals on a regular basis to read through them herself. She believed that the assignment had a casual, note-passing feel to it that helped reduce student anxiety and gave her valuable feedback, while still developing student skills in mathematic problem solving.

●   ●   ●

ONLINE IMPLEMENTATION   This CoLT is easily adapted to online classes. Form student pairs at the beginning of the semester. Create a private forum for each pair, and ask students to post and reply to their journal entries in the forum. Alternatively, have each student create a word processing document in which they post cumulative journal entries. Ask each student to send their journal to their partner as an e-mail attachment. The partner adds comments, suggestions, answers, and questions, either in a different font, color, or in capital letters to differentiate their responses from the original journal entry. The collective journal entries with comments can be submitted to the instructor for assessment and evaluation.

VARIATIONS AND EXTENSIONS

- Consider using a Communal Dialogue Journal. Keep the journal on a desk or table in the classroom or your office so that it is available for entries and responses by any class member. Suggested entries might include confusion about readings or assignments, announcements about upcoming events related to course content, requests for study group members, and so forth. This could be very useful in a hybrid course.

- Consider using Dialog Journals for students to record their experiences in group work. Depending on your goals, use within-team break-outs or let students pair with partners from different groups. Regularly checking these journals will provide valuable insight about how the groups are working together.

- Have students write letters about pertinent course content and exchange them with each other. This variation is called Reciprocal Letter Writing in the literature (Millis & Cottell, 1998).

OBSERVATIONS AND ADVICE Students will come to class with preconceptions about journal writing; therefore, be clear on your parameters for their entries and responses. For example, will students be

- Focusing on content-based analysis and criticism? Expressing primarily personal insights and concerns?

- Writing about specific course activities? The course in general?

- Recording reactions to instructor-provided prompts? Generating free-form responses?

- Following an established format? Choosing their own layouts?

- Posting entries at prescribed intervals? Only when they wish?

- Writing primarily in or out of class?

- Maintaining journals for a course segment? The whole term?

- Working with the same partner? Varying partners?

Journals and responses can become part of ongoing class activities. However, journaling can be fairly time consuming, and some students will be able to concentrate and be more comfortable writing outside the classroom. For these reasons, consider assigning much of this activity outside of class so that in-class time may be used in other ways.

Students may suffer blocks in their writing and may be uncomfortable sharing writing that they have not revised and edited. To address this problem, use long-term partnerships that can build trust. Alternatively, allow students time to revise and edit out of class before sharing their work with others.

It is important for the instructor to respond to the students' entries. If the instructor does not, or if there is a long time lag between the writing and the feedback, students will think that the assignment is busy work and will not take it seriously. However, one of the benefits of this assignment is that it does give students immediate deep and critical feedback—from a peer. In addition, it makes the teacher's job a bit easier by having the peer also review and respond.

It is important to have students turn the journals in regularly so that they do not wait until the last minute to do all of the entries.

KEY RESOURCES   Bromley, K. (1993). *Journaling: Engagements in reading, writing and thinking.* New York: Scholastic, pp. 43–48.

Cranton, P. (1998). *No one way: Teaching and learning in higher education.* Toronto, ON: Wall & Emerson, pp. 147–151.

COLLABORATIVE
LEARNING
TECHNIQUE

25

Round Table

Characteristics	
Group Size	3–4
Time on Task	10–20 MINUTES
Duration of Groups	SINGLE CLASS
Online Transferability	MODERATE

DESCRIPTION AND PURPOSE Students take turns responding to a prompt by writing one or two words or phrases before passing the paper along to others who do the same. Round Table is essentially the written version of the discussion technique *Colt 2: Round Robin*. The benefits of having students write their ideas as opposed to speaking them are that writing helps students to focus their attention, gives students quiet time to think about their responses, and provides a cumulative record. Round Table also ensures equal participation among group members and exposes students to multiple viewpoints and ideas.

PREPARATION Create a prompt that students can respond to with a few words or sentences. Write this at the top of a sheet of paper, leaving the remainder blank for student writing. Copy sufficient numbers to distribute to groups of four.

PROCEDURE 1. Form groups of four students and tell groups the prompt or distribute the handout.

2. Identify (or have students identify) which group member will begin and inform students that they will circulate the paper clockwise.

3. Ask the first student to write his or her words, phrases, or sentences as rapidly as possible and then read the response aloud so that other students have an opportunity to think about and build upon each other's responses.

4. Ask the student to pass the paper to the next student, who follows the same steps.

5. Inform students when time is up, or tell them in your instructions that the process is complete when all members have participated and all ideas are on the paper.

• • •

Introduction to Scientific Principles

Professor Al Kali was teaching an interdisciplinary science appreciation course in his institution's core curriculum. Two weeks into the semester, he noticed that the science majors in the course were dominating whole-class discussions and that non-science majors were not participating. One of the ways he decided to address the problem was by implementing Round Tables. Professor Kali assigned groups of four, gave each group one piece of paper, and asked students to brainstorm ideas responding to the prompt: *Identify important scientific discoveries of the twentieth century in the field of medicine.* The Round Table structure ensured that the non-science majors participated and also demonstrated to them that they knew more about science than they thought they did. The professor asked groups to share ideas from their lists and used these ideas as the basis for a whole class discussion. He believed that the activity improved the morale of the non-science majors and found that in the whole-class discussion that followed, non-science majors participated more than they had prior to the Round Table activity.

• • •

Principles of Macro Economics

In this team-taught course, Professors Penny Wise and L. B. Foolish had just covered an extensive unit on the determination of national income and employment. They knew from previous semesters that many students found the unit's concepts confusing. They decided to use Round Table in combination with an adaptation of *Muddiest Point* (CAT 7, Angelo & Cross, 1993, pp. 154–158) to assess student learning and to guide them on whether or not students were prepared to move on to the next unit. They reserved fifteen minutes at the end of class, formed groups of four, and asked students to respond to the prompt: *Write down the muddiest point or the questions you still have regarding the determination of national income and employment.* They told students that if a student had already written down a point or question that they also had, they should put a checkmark next to it. The professors found that by using the Round Table for this assessment technique, students were able to build upon each other's contributions. When students were finished, the professors collected the papers. The lists provided them with substantial feedback on which points were most difficult for students to learn and which points were still confusing. They used this information to organize a review session before moving on to the next unit, and also filed the papers so that they could refer to them when they planned the next semester's class.

• • •

ONLINE IMPLEMENTATION

A simple adaptation of this CoLT to the online environment is to ask groups to generate responses in threaded discussions in such a way that each member posts one comment, cycling through the group until all members have posted. However, this is what often happens anyway in small group threaded discussions. The added value of imposing the Round Robin structure is that it requires all students to post, and limits some group members from posting too frequently. If this CoLT is an important component of your course, consider purchasing special "story-building" software that helps students build stories on the Web sentence by sentence with user info and time stamps.

VARIATIONS AND EXTENSIONS

- Consider using Round Table during another activity. For example, while lecturing, have students do a Round Table that responds to an idea presented in the lecture, with the whole class participating in a single Round Table. Although it diverts each student's attention for about a minute or so, it avoids potential boredom while everyone sits around waiting for the paper to pass.

- In creative writing, a variation of Round Table is used to help foster imaginative storytelling. The instructor provides an introductory sentence or paragraph or a simple opening phrase, such as, *It was a dark and stormy night. . . .* Each student contributes to the story, propelling the action forward by adding several sentences or even whole paragraphs.

When conducted in this way, students can be at their desks doing other work until the paper is passed to them, or you can have several stories going simultaneously so that all students are busy writing.

Teams can record ideas with a transparency pen on a piece of acetate. A group representative can then share the group's ideas with the class using an overhead projector.

In Davis's section on leading discussions (1993, pp. 67–69) and on writing (p. 210), she offers several ideas that are well suited for adaptation to this CoLT. For example, ask students to:

Brainstorm, writing down a range of possible causes, consequences, solutions, reasons, or contributing factors to some phenomenon. Explain that in brainstorming, the rules are that anyone can write an idea (no matter how bizarre or farfetched). Free association, creativity, and ingenuity are the goal. Therefore no idea is questioned, praised, or criticized at this point.

Complete "truth statements," finishing sentences that you have created that begin with phrases such as, "It is true that Marxism . . . " or "It is true that high-density housing . . . "

Write out a list of key points (or arguments that support a particular position). Or write down the points or questions that they have regarding that day's discussion.

Respond to a prompt based on a shared experience such as a field trip, slide show, demonstration, music or drama performance, film, or exhibit. This can stimulate an exchange that reveals students' different perceptions and reactions to the same event.

Jot down a few phrases that describe a "critical incident" in their own lives that pertains to the topic.

Construct a "storyboard." Divide a problem into several steps or subtopics, and give each group a piece of paper with one of these components written at the top. Each group circulates the paper as individuals within each group write their ideas on that topic. After ten minutes, the groups exchange papers and contribute new ideas on the next topic.

Identify evidence from either a Pro or Con position and write these ideas on a paper that has been divided in half accordingly.

Ideas such as these can guide you to create prompts to start the Round Table.

OBSERVATIONS AND ADVICE

Requiring students to write in the presence of other group members who must sit quietly limits the type of question that can be asked. This exercise should be used for fairly simple tasks, such as helping students review material, making straightforward applications, or brainstorming lists. It should not be used for complex thinking and reasoning tasks, because the activity moves too slowly. Time is wasted and students will likely get bored. Consider one of the variations mentioned, in which this activity is done in conjunction with other student work, to address this problem.

Because everyone is required to contribute, Round Table can help to address problems of inequitable participation.

This CoLT encourages students to adjust their writing (in areas such as content, conventions, style, and vocabulary) as they respond and react to the comments of the writers that preceded them.

Students who have trouble expressing themselves in writing will find this activity difficult. On the other hand, students who have trouble speaking in a group or in front of their classmates may find that writing their thoughts first prepares them to express themselves orally.

Although ideally every team member should contribute, if a student cannot think of anything to write, it is better to pass than to hold up the process. Set a time limit, and allow a student to pass if he or she has nothing to write.

This technique does not allow for group interaction or discussion. Depending upon your purpose for implementing Round Table, you will most likely want to follow up this activity with either group or whole-class discussion.

KEY RESOURCES

Foyle, H. C. (1995). *Interactive learning in the higher education classroom: Cooperative, collaborative, and active learning strategies.* West Haven, CT: Excellence in the Academy, the NEA Professional Library Higher Education Series.

Kagan, S. (1992). *Cooperative learning.* San Juan Capistrano, CA: Resource for Teachers.

Sharan, S. (Ed.). (1994). *Handbook of cooperative learning methods.* Westport, CT: Greenwood Press.

COLLABORATIVE
LEARNING
TECHNIQUE

26

Dyadic Essays

Characteristics	
Group Size	PAIRS
Time on Task	30–45 MINUTES
Duration of Groups	SINGLE OR MULTIPLE SESSIONS
Online Transferability	HIGH

DESCRIPTION AND PURPOSE Students individually write an essay question and a model answer on a reading assignment, lecture, or other presentation of content. In the next class period, student pairs exchange questions, write a response to the partner's question, and then trade, read, and compare model and in-class answers. This CoLT gives students practice identifying the most important feature of a learning activity and formulating and answering questions about that activity. It also gives students an opportunity to rehearse responding to essay questions with the added advantage of having a sample response with which to compare their answers.

PREPARATION Writing a good essay question is a difficult task, and one with which students are often unfamiliar. This CoLT will work best when you have spent some time teaching students how to write good essay questions and answers. Consider preparing a handout with guidelines and sample questions and responses that model the level of complexity and depth you expect.

PROCEDURE
1. Outside of class, students reflect on a learning activity (such as reading an assignment, listening to a lecture, watching a film) and formulate and write an essay question.

2. On a separate sheet of paper, students prepare a model response to their own question (usually a couple of paragraphs).

3. Students bring a copy of their essay questions and model answers to class.

4. Student form pairs, exchange essay questions, and write responses.

5. Students trade model answers and compare and contrast their in-class answers with their partner's model answer.

6. Partners discuss their responses first for one essay question and then for the other, paying special attention to similar and dissimilar ideas.

• • •

EXAMPLES

English Literature

This professor used Dyadic Essays throughout the semester following each major assignment. For example, after watching a videotape of Maya Angelou reading from her work, *I Know Why the Caged Bird Sings,* each student formulated an essay question about the work and wrote a model response that evening for homework. The next day, students exchanged questions and answered the question they received in class. Students then compared their responses, and each student submitted a question, model response, and response to the professor.

• • •

General Biology

Professor Jean Poole wanted students in this introductory biology course to participate in her institution's Writing Across the Curriculum program. Professor Poole was also concerned that students tended to focus too much on detail and terminology, thus losing sight of the bigger picture. She believed that if students were to write information in the form of essay questions and answers, it would help them to better integrate, synthesize, and remember key concepts. She decided to incorporate Dyadic Essays to address both issues. For each major topic area, she asked students to formulate and answer an appropriate essay question. One of the first topic areas was the structure and function of cells, and she suggested that a sample essay question might be, *Describe the structure of the two basic cell categories (prokaryotic and eukaryotic) and explain how the categories are similar and different.* She set aside about thirty minutes in one class each week for students to exchange questions, use their text and notes to answer the questions, and then compare responses. Students submitted all work to her for participation points and Writing Across the Curriculum credit. As she scanned the questions and answers, she looked for very good questions to include in her midterm and final examination study guides.

• • •

Real Estate Principles

In this popular online class, instructor Ona Holm used her course software's automatic grading feature extensively. This feature required forced-choice tests in which students selected an item from alternatives given. Automatically graded tests offered Ms. Holm and the students several advantages. For example, she did not need to score the tests, an important workload consideration since the class had more than a hundred students. Automatically graded tests also provided students with instant feedback, helping students to self-monitor their work. Ms. Holm valued the tests, but she was concerned that they were not promoting higher-order thinking skills. She therefore decided to supplement the tests with Dyadic Essays.

She formed student pairs and posted a topic every two weeks that was coordinated with the assigned reading (for example, duties and responsibilities among broker, salesman, and client; enforceability of contractual rights, and so forth). For each topic, she asked students to formulate one good essay question and provide a model answer. Partners exchanged questions, wrote answers, shared model responses, and messaged each other on similarities and differences. They then sent their combined work along to her. Because student pairs had already provided each other with model answers and had discussed their responses, she did not feel the need to give additional feedback. She therefore simply spot-checked their work, assigned task completion points, and posted one or two exemplary questions and answers for all students to read. She believed Dyadic Essays helped her promote deeper learning without significantly increasing her workload.

• • •

ONLINE IMPLEMENTATION   This is an easy technique to implement online. Form teams (or partners), create private forums for each group, and ask students to post questions by a specific deadline. Students post their answers by a second deadline. Then the students who created the original questions post their model answers. Alternatively, have each student send his or her essay question to a partner as an e-mail or Web site attachment. Students respond and then exchange model answers in the same manner. Each student can then read his or her partner's model answer, noting and messaging each other in which ways the two answers are similar or different.

VARIATIONS AND EXTENSIONS

- Ask students to synthesize their practice response and the model response to create a new response.

- Have an external reader review both responses.

- Ask students to do most of this CoLT as homework. First, students write questions and model answers as homework. In class the next day they exchange questions, but take the questions home and write responses as homework. Comparisons to the model response can be done either in or out of class.

- Consider having students evaluate each other's responses. Provide them with a framework to do so.

- Use this activity in conjunction with *CoLT 12: Test-Taking Teams*, such that students use Dyadic Essays to prepare for an upcoming examination.

OBSERVATIONS AND ADVICE

Guide students on how to write good essay questions. Davis (1993, pp. 275–277) suggests that good essay questions are written clearly and precisely, and that they can be particularly effective if they include the words *how* or *why*. Consider distributing a handout containing generic question stems that students can adapt for this assignment. For example, Exhibit 11.2 is an excerpt from a chart provided by Millis and Cottell (1998, p. 138).

See also Chapter Four, Structuring the Learning Task, for additional prompt ideas.

In addition to guiding students on how to write good essay questions, review with them the components of a good essay answer. Davis (1993, pp. 275–277) notes that excellent answers state a position and provide support for the position. They raise a counterargument and refute it. They provide persuasive evidence, significant counterarguments, and avoid extraneous information.

Exhibit 11.2

Generic Question Stems

Generic Questions	Specific Thinking Processes Induced
Explain why (or explain how) _____?	Analysis
Why is _____ important?	Analysis of significance
How are _____ and _____ similar?	Comparison-contrast
What is the best _____, and why?	Evaluation and provision of evidence
What do you think causes _____, and why?	Analysis of relationship (cause-effect)
What is the solution to the problem of _____?	Synthesis of ideas
How does _____ tie in with what we learned before?	Activation of prior knowledge

CoLT 26: Dyadic Essays is an adaptation of Dyadic Essay Confrontations (DEC) (Sherman, 1991). A primary purpose of the original DEC is to integrate current reading material with material previously covered. Sherman asks students to formulate questions that compared present and past reading assignments, thus providing students with a mechanism to connect differing text materials.

One of the important uses of this technique is to help ensure that students complete and understand an assignment. Also, because students complete part or even most of the assignment outside of class, it leaves in-class time for mastery and processing activities (Millis & Cottell, 1998, p. 134).

Because students ask the questions and provide model answers, they are relying on peers for learning. This has the potential disadvantage of having students learn information incorrectly. Although it is not necessary that the teacher read all of the questions and answers all of the time, checking occasionally will help measure overall accuracy.

To assess this activity, collect and read the essay questions, model answers, and partner responses. If you wish to evaluate student work, consider assigning separate grades or points for each of the three components (the question and both model and in-class answers). For the original Dyadic Essay Confrontation, Sherman used a combination of peer and instructor evaluations, assessing on the basis of five attributes: overall general impression, importance, clarity, integration, and creativity. He and students used a five-point scale ranging from 0 (poor) to 4 (excellent) to rate each of the attributes (Millis & Cottell, 1998, pp. 135–136).

KEY RESOURCES   Millis, B. J., & Cottell, P. G. (1998). *Cooperative learning for higher education faculty.* American Council on Education. Phoenix, AZ: Oryx Press, pp. 134–138.

Millis, B. J., Sherman, L. W., & Cottell, P. G. (1993). Stacking the DEC to promote critical thinking: Applications in three disciplines. *Cooperative Learning and College Teaching, 3*(3), 12–14.

COLLABORATIVE
LEARNING
TECHNIQUE

27

Peer Editing

Characteristics	
Group Size	PAIRS
Time on Task	2 HOURS
Duration of Groups	MULTIPLE SESSIONS
Online Transferability	HIGH

DESCRIPTION AND PURPOSE In this CoLT, student pairs critically review and provide editorial feedback on each other's essays, reports, arguments, research papers, or other writing assignments. Peer editing helps teach students how to identify the features of good and poor writing in the work of others, thus developing critical evaluation skills that they can apply to their own writing. It also provides student authors with constructive criticism so that they can improve their papers before submitting them for a grade.

PREPARATION Students are not always skilled at critiquing writing, so they will need training and guidance on what kinds of things to look for and how to make constructive editorial comments. To facilitate editing and to help monitor this activity, create a Peer Review Form that lists the elements students should be looking for when they critique each other's work.

PROCEDURE
1. Students work in pairs, taking turns describing ideas for the paper that each individually intends to write. As each student describes his or her ideas, a partner takes notes, asks questions, and makes suggestions.

2. Each student conducts research for the individual paper, keeping an eye open for material that might prove useful to the partner.

3. Students write their papers individually.

4. Within each pair, students exchange paper drafts for peer editing. Student editors make proofing marks and comments directly on the paper and score or rate the paper with a Peer Review Form. Student editors also complete and sign the Peer Review Form, indicating their ratings of each of these elements.

5. Each author revises his or her paper, taking the peer editing into consideration.

6. Authors attach the Peer Review Form to the final draft and submit it to the professor for evaluation.

• • •

EXAMPLES

Introduction to Philosophy

Professor Watts Itmene decided to use Peer Editing in conjunction with the paper he was assigning as a final class project. He formed pairs, and asked students to consider the question, *What is the difference between appearance and reality?* He asked student partners to discuss and then each select one of the philosophers they had studied during the semester to write a paper on how that philosopher had addressed the topic. The students conducted research in the library and also accessed a Web site Mr. Itmene had created that contained multiple links to philosophy Web sites. Whenever students came across a resource that they thought might be useful to their partners, they made a note of it. Professor Itmene set aside ten to fifteen minutes during class each week for student partners to check each other's progress and share anything they believed would be helpful. Several weeks before the paper was due, he set aside the entire class session for students to edit and rate each other's papers. By having students edit in class, he was available to answer questions, and he also believed that his presence ensured the task was taken seriously and done thoroughly. Students revised their papers based on the editorial feedback. They attached the earlier draft that included peer editing to their final draft and submitted them both to him for evaluation.

• • •

Composition, Critical Reading, and Writing

One of the main goals in this foundational English course was to help students develop techniques and practice expository and argumentative writing. A significant number of the students came to the course with poorly developed writing skills; many had just completed a preparatory ESL or remedial class sequence. In the traditional on-campus version of the class, the instructor had students write in class during several sessions each week so that she could circulate among students, checking and providing formative feedback on each student's work. When she noticed a recurring problem, she was able to interrupt the writing to discuss it with the whole class. This kind of interaction was not possible in the online version of the course. The instructor was concerned that if she were to give the amount of editorial feedback each individual student needed, the workload in the online course would be overwhelming.

She decided to implement Peer Editing. She designed a Peer Review Form that included a comprehensive list of the kinds of elements required in effective writing. For each of the writing assignments, she formed pairs and had partners edit each other's work using the word processing program's tracking features. Students submitted the original draft and the peer-edited draft when they turned in to her their revised final draft. She assigned separate grades for each component and task. By giving substantial weight to the editing grade, she offered an incentive for students to do this task thoroughly. She believed that Peer Editing helped provide students with the substantive formative feedback they needed without overwhelming her. Additionally, by helping students to identify writing problems in the work of their peers, she knew students developed evaluation skills that they could apply to their own writing.

• • •

Introduction to Psychobiology

An upper-level psychology professor had students conduct an empirical study. Their final project was to write up the results in a formal research paper. He assigned students to Peer Editing groups so that they could give each other advice and feedback on their writing. He used a formal Peer Review Form from a top-tier journal to guide student feedback. In particular, students were to look for items related to the form of the research article such as significance of the problem, research design and methods, significant results, adequate conclusions, as well as providing advice about writing mechanics and style. The professor believed that Peer Editing improved significantly the quality of the papers students submitted to him, and also gave students exposure to the review process that was standard in the field.

• • •

ONLINE IMPLEMENTATION Students can easily exchange papers for peer editing by sending their papers as e-mail attachments. Editors can make comments and corrections either in capital letters or a different font color or style, or using the tracking features available in standard word processing programs. Also consider investigating specific technology tools for calibrated peer review processes.

VARIATIONS AND EXTENSIONS

- Assign students to a base group of four students so that more than one person reviews each paper.

- Have partners help each other in the overall organization of the paper. For example, in the initial discussion, the listening student produces an outline for the author to consider. Partners also draft opening paragraphs together. This may prove challenging for students; however, these two steps may help alleviate some of the "writer's block" that can occur when students face a blank page (Millis & Cottell, 1998, p. 116).

- Extend the procedures by having students do two edit and rating sessions for each paper, thus giving authors the opportunity to revise their papers twice before final submission.

- Consider having students submit the earlier drafts and edited drafts so that you can assess and evaluate progress.

- Use this technique less formally. Simply have students exchange written work with partners for feedback, without completing a Peer Review Form or spending a significant amount of time editing and correcting.

- In addition to submitting the comments of peer reviewers, have student authors submit responses to the comments addressing why they did or did not follow the advice.

- Grade each component of the project. For example, consider giving a grade on the initial draft, the peer editing, and the final composition. You might also evaluate students on how they responded to the review.

OBSERVATIONS AND ADVICE Students may not be comfortable critiquing each other's writing. They may simply state that the work is good and needs no improvement, which defeats the purpose of peer editing. To promote substantive and constructive feedback, make sure your students understand that peer editing consists of commentary on *all* aspects of effective writing, including a clear thesis, good support, well-constructed topic sentences, coherent transitions, a logical organization, plus surface corrections including grammar, spelling, and punctuation (Millis & Cottell, 1998, p. 116). A Peer Review Form that includes a checklist with each aspect clearly identified will help guide student efforts.

Link part of the student's grade to the level of effort he or she puts into the critique of another's work. Grading the review itself will encourage students to give more thoughtful responses to their peers and discourage them from giving uniformly positive ratings that were not warranted.

Have students debrief on the process, telling them to consider how well they worked together and what actions they will take in the next peer-editing situation. Also consider having them thank each other for the help and congratulating each other upon completion.

Self- and Peer Evaluation forms may be used to give you feedback on how helpful students were to each other.

KEY RESOURCES   Johnson, D. W., Johnson, R., & Smith, K. (1998). *Active learning: Cooperation in the college classroom.* Edina, MN: Interaction Book Company.

Millis, B. J., & Cottell, P. G. (1998). *Cooperative learning for higher education faculty.* American Council on Education, Series on Higher Education. Phoenix, AZ: Oryx Press.

COLLABORATIVE LEARNING TECHNIQUE

28

Collaborative Writing

Characteristics	
Group Size	2–3
Time on Task	SEVERAL HOURS
Duration of Groups	MULTIPLE SESSIONS
Online Transferability	HIGH

DESCRIPTION AND PURPOSE
In Collaborative Writing, student pairs or triads write a formal paper together. Each student contributes at each stage of the writing process: brainstorming ideas; gathering and organizing information; and drafting, revising, and editing the writing. Working together can help students to learn and perform the stages of writing more effectively. Additionally, students typically write better and take more pride in their writing when they are writing for an audience; the collaborative element of this CoLT gives them such an audience. Finally, since many professions require collaborative writing, this technique can help prepare students for tasks they will have in their careers.

PREPARATION
Prepare for this CoLT as you would to assign any writing project. Break the assignment into manageable chunks and establish interim due dates to help teams structure the writing process and learn from each step.

PROCEDURE
1. Students form pairs or triads at your direction or by choosing partners and then generate ideas by brainstorming together or conducting preliminary research.

2. Together, students organize their ideas and create an outline.

3. Students divide up the outline, selecting or assigning sections for each student to write initial drafts individually.

4. Teams read first drafts and discuss and resolve any significant disparities in voice, content, and style.

5. Teams combine individual sections into a single document.

6. Teams revise and edit their work, checking for content and clarity as well as grammar, spelling, and punctuation.

7. After the final edit, teams submit their papers to the professor for assessment and evaluation.

• • •

EXAMPLES

Comparative World Religions: West

Professor Zeke N. Yeshallfind taught a course on the origin, history, and significant ideas of the world's major Western religions. He believed that learning was an active, constructive process and that students learned best when they connected to course content through systematic classroom interaction. Professor Yeshallfind felt he had successfully established such a collaborative environment in his on-campus class, and he was trying to create a similar environment in his online class. To accomplish this, he combined and implemented several different CoLTs.

For example, during the first half of the semester, he used a combination of *CoLT 1: Think-Pair-Share* and *CoLT 3: Buzz Groups* for students to reflect upon and identify several "universal ethical principles" present in the world's major Western religions. Through these learning tasks, students identified that all of the religions believed it is wrong to cheat, deceive, exploit, abuse, harm, or steal from others. He then formed student triads, and assigned a Comparative Process Writing activity. He asked student groups to (1) select two Western religions (such as Zoroastrianism and Judaism or Christianity and Islam) and find examples where these religions had justified slavery, racism, genocide, torture, or terrorism; (2) investigate how religious leaders covered up or justified such violations of their own fundamental ethical principles in self-serving and self-justifying ways; and (3) write up their findings in a collaborative term paper. Professor Yeshallfind believed that the Collaborative Writing assignment provided a structure for students to interact together and to engage in a meaningful way with the course's core concepts (Adapted from Paul & Elder, 2003).

• • •

Introduction to Zoology

Professor Ana Conda decided to implement Collaborative Writing assignments to encourage students to connect course content with the real world. For each of the assignments, she formed pairs and asked all students to write together a significant essay responding to the same prompt. For example, on the topic of the evolution of biological diversity, she asked students to write an essay that responded to the following:

Experts estimate that human activities cause the extinction of hundreds of species each year. The natural rate of extinction is thought to be a few species per year, but as we continue to alter the global environment, especially by cutting down tropical rain forests, the resulting extinction will probably rival that at the end of the Cretaceous period. Zoologists are alarmed at this prospect. What are some reasons for their concern? Consider that life has endured numerous mass extinctions and has always bounced back. How is the present mass extinction different from previous extinctions? What might be some of the consequences for the surviving species?

She set aside about one hour of class time two weeks prior to each assignment's deadline for student pairs to discuss the topic using their textbooks and lecture notes to brainstorm ideas for the essay. Students then organized the ideas into an outline and divided up sections for each partner to write initial drafts. They also worked out a schedule for completion and agreed upon a system of communication, for example e-mail, informal meetings, telephone calls, and so forth (Adapted from Campbell, Reece, & Simon, 2004, p. 295).

• • •

ONLINE IMPLEMENTATION   This CoLT adapts easily to the online environment. Once groups are formed, students can communicate through Web site messaging, e-mail, Instant Messaging, or telephone. As they work together to write, they can send their contributions as e-mail attachments and monitor individual contributions using the tracking features available in standard word processing programs or simply use different font styles. If collaborative writing is an essential and integral component of your class, you may wish to investigate collaborative writing software that can facilitate the process.

VARIATIONS AND
EXTENSIONS

- This CoLT can be combined with many others to create a comprehensive collaborative experience. For example, students can brainstorm ideas in *CoLT 2: Round Robin,* organize them in *CoLT 19: Affinity Grouping* or *CoLT 23: Word Webs,* and explore the topic in a *CoLT 6: Critical Debate* or through *CoLT 18: Group Investigation.* After the paper is complete, they can participate in *CoLT 27: Peer Editing* and/or *CoLT 30: Paper Seminar.*

- Set up guidelines for authorship, considering allocating different points based on first authorship, second, third, acknowledgment, and so on.

OBSERVATIONS
AND ADVICE

Collaborative writing is challenging. Consider preparing students by having them engage in simpler collaborative work earlier in the semester. Also, if students have not had much writing experience, you may wish to have them individually complete smaller writing assignments first.

Students may resist this CoLT, as many people view writing as an isolated and individual activity. Therefore spend sufficient time explaining the purpose of collaborative writing. For instance, it may be useful to point out examples of professional collaborative writing to help students understand how this activity can prepare them for their future careers. Use this time to also answer student questions and address their concerns.

Writing is not an easy task, and collaborative writing is particularly difficult. Encourage students to proofread beyond a word-by-word level and review at the level of sentences, paragraphs, and whole sections. They should be checking for a clear thesis, good support, coherent transitions, and overall organization as well as grammar, spelling, and punctuation. Davis (1993, p. 223) suggests having students complete a self-evaluation form that guides them in their editing and indicates the extent to which they felt they followed good writing practices:

- An opening that catches the reader's attention

- A strong thesis

- A balance of fact and opinion

- Selectively chosen examples

- A conclusion that leaves the reader with a clear understanding of the writers' point of view

Help students stay focused on the goal, which is to work together to produce a good written product. To achieve this, the group should be ready to synthesize and edit all contributions, making hard decisions about revisions. It is not always easy to accept criticism, but individuals need to be prepared to have their work edited or even deleted. This CoLT will be most effective if you help collaborators establish a high level of trust and strong group dynamics ahead of time.

Writing collaboratively can help prevent the academic dishonesty sometimes associated with the conventional term paper assignment; it discourages plagiarism because the group, rather than an individual, must do the writing. Also, since the group follows a series of procedural steps working within a specific time frame, students cannot simply copy or purchase a paper from another source.

Decide your grading strategy in advance and communicate it to students. Be aware that collaborative writing can be particularly difficult to grade. In addition to the general challenges of grading papers, distinguish between individual contributions and final group product. To do this, first identify a strategy for evaluating the writing itself. Davis (1993, p. 223) suggests developing a brief checklist of grading criteria, but grading the paper holistically. She provides criteria adapted from McKeachie, Pintrich, Lin, and Smith (1986, pp. 132–134) and Morris and Tucker (1985, p. 6):

- *Focus:* Is the problem chosen focused enough to be covered adequately within the space of the paper?

- *Organization:* Is the paper's structure apparent and easy to follow?

- *Development:* Does the paper adequately introduce the topic, present convincing evidence to support the writer's position, summarize findings, and offer a reasonable conclusion?

- *Sentence Structure:* Are sentences well formed, appropriately varied in length and style, and used for different effects?

- *Mechanics:* Is the paper generally free of spelling, typographical, and grammatical errors?

Second, consider grading both individual contributions (to promote accountability) as well as the group product (for promotive interaction). Collecting drafts along with the final paper and using Self-, Peer, and Group Evaluation forms can help you assess and evaluate individual and group work.

The growing use of computers has greatly increased the occurrence of collaborative writing. Many Web sites are now devoted to collaborative writing, and collaborative writing software is gaining popularity and accessibility. An Internet search using combinations of keywords such as "collaborative writing," "teaching," and "software" will provide you with the most current information, including product descriptions. The following URL is for a Web page created by Peter Sands of the University of

Wisconsin-Milwaukee. It includes a comprehensive, detailed comparison of writing software programs such as *Common Space, Norton Connect, Daedalus Integrated Writing Environment,* and *Aspects.* It compares features such as annotation, bibliography generation, conferencing, heuristics, and even grading templates. (Retrieved October 22, 2003, from http://english.ttu.edu/kairos/2.2/reviews/sands/comparison.html)

KEY RESOURCES   Hillebrand, R. P. (1994). Control and cohesion: Collaborative learning and writing, *English Journal, 83,* 71–74.

Reither, J. A., & Vipond, D. (1989). Writing as collaboration. *College English 51,* 855–867.

Tobin, L. (1993). Collaboration: The case for coauthored, dialogic, nonlinear texts. *Writing relationships: What really happens in the composition class.* Portsmouth, NH: Boynton/Cook, pp. 128–140.

**COLLABORATIVE
LEARNING
TECHNIQUE**

29

Team Anthologies

Characteristics	
Group Size	4 THEN 2 THEN 4
Time on Task	SEVERAL HOURS
Duration of Groups	MULTIPLE SESSIONS
Online Transferability	MODERATE

DESCRIPTION AND PURPOSE Student teams compile, annotate, prepare, and print an anthology of course-related materials. This CoLT provides an organizational structure for students to investigate a topic, read and review the most valuable materials on that topic, and describe and print information in a useful collection of resources. Fundamentally, it allows students to experience the research process without writing a formal research paper.

PREPARATION The amount of preparation involved in this CoLT depends on the level of the students. If students are new to the discipline and to research, provide examples of appropriate materials. If students have backgrounds in the field and have experience with doing research papers, simply create a time frame that sets deadlines to help you and students monitor the various steps.

PROCEDURE 1. The teacher organizes students into base groups of four and guides groups as they determine an appropriate topic for research.

2. The group splits apart, and individual students each research and identify five to ten of the most important resources on the topic.

3. The team rejoins and compiles all four team members' bibliographies and makes initial decisions as to the relevancy and currency of each entry, eliminating sources they deem to be of low value and aiming for a composite anthology of about ten citations.

4. The team subdivides into pairs and assigns half the bibliography to each pair.

5. Pairs divide their part of the bibliography, with each student taking half.

6. Individuals photocopy and write a brief reflective commentary on each source.

7. Pairs re-form and exchange, read, and reflect upon each other's reviews, looking for divergent and convergent thinking and ideas, and together create a composite annotation for the sources in their half of the bibliography.

8. Pairs rejoin the base quad and prepare their work for submission by adding a cover sheet, introduction (with a statement of purpose and the anthology's value to the intended audience), and a conclusion (with suggested applications of the anthology, unanswered questions, and suggestions for future research).

9. Teams submit their anthologies to the instructor.

• • •

EXAMPLES

Composition and Reading

Professor Anne O'Tate taught a freshman composition class and used this technique to help students develop topics for essays. She asked student teams to select a topic they would like to research. Each member of the team gathered and submitted manuscripts related to the topic. The team then followed the Team Anthology process to create a collection of readings from which to draw when writing their essays. She assigned five anthologies throughout the semester, each one corresponding to a paper.

• • •

Health Education

Professor Sal Monella wanted students to read authors that make the field of health science exciting and interesting. He decided to have students develop a Team Anthology of newspaper and magazine articles written by renowned health science writers. Professor Monella formed teams of four students each and asked each team to research and identify five famous scientists who had researched health-related issues. During the next class period, he asked groups to prioritize the list according to the scientists they were most interested in studying. When they were finished, he worked with the class as a whole, asking for each team's top nominations, writing names on the board, and dividing up and assigning each scientist to a single team to study. He then shared with the teams the procedures for Team Anthology. When the teams had completed their anthologies, he put the anthologies on reserve in the library along with an assignment that required students to review all anthologies in order to answer worksheet questions.

• • •

Educational Foundations

Professor Rita Booke determined that students in this course had not had much prior exposure to writings in the field of multicultural education. She asked students to form teams and asked each team to develop a bibliography of relevant writings, photocopy select writings for inclusion in the anthology, and respond to the writers' main points. Teams made a brief presentation on their anthologies to the class, and the anthologies were available as resources for students throughout the semester.

• • •

Introduction to Photographic Expression

Professor Matt Finnish designed this course to provide students with a survey of the contributions to the field of photography by artists of diverse ethnic and cultural backgrounds. He also intended to guide students in developing their personal approach to photographic expression. The professor believed that emulation was an important technique to help students accomplish both goals. He explained to students that to imitate an artist who had created something that one admired was a tradition that goes back to the earliest educational institutions. He told students that in contemporary times, there has been negative feedback to students about "copying" artwork, but clarified that although emulation does require imitating, it is not copying and pretending the style is one's own. Rather, it is analyzing and extracting the essential qualities in the original and then striving to equal those qualities in one's own work.

He formed student teams and asked groups to select a photographer whom they found particularly interesting or inspiring. Together students identified a list of the photographer's most important works and then divided up the list for individuals to locate and photocopy the images. In class, students discussed each image, trying to identify the salient aspects of the image that enhanced the image's expression (such as use of light, color, and composition; any specialized developing and printing techniques; unique subject matter, and so forth). The team wrote a summary of their analysis for each image. Students then individually took and developed their own photographs emulating that photographer's style. They also wrote a paragraph on what they had learned, noticed, and experienced in the exercise. Students gathered back together as a team and collected all of their work into an anthology, adding a cover sheet, table of contents, and one-page biography of the artist they had emulated.

• • •

ONLINE IMPLEMENTATION

Implementing this CoLT in an online course will be most successful if it is assigned to mature students in advanced courses. Students can use a designated discussion area combined with e-mail exchanges to communicate with each other as they identify sources, create a bibliography, and construct composite annotations. Although students can generate an actual "hard copy" anthology, it will be most accessible and useful to other students if they create the anthologies as Portable Document Files (PDFs) that can be posted online.

VARIATIONS AND EXTENSIONS

- If time is limited, disregard the anthology portion of this CoLT and have students simply create an annotated bibliography. Reduce student time and effort even further by putting the sources on reserve in the library. Either way, student pairs review the same articles, chapters, or content areas and exchange notes for reading and reflection. Students discuss key points and look for divergent and convergent thinking and ideas. Together students prepare a composite annotation that summarizes each article, chapter, or concept.

- Instead of creating an anthology, have students use this process to develop an archive, catalogue, chronicle, collection, digest, directory, fact file, glossary, handbook, photo essay, or relief map (Bull, Montgomery, & Kimball, 1999).

- Extend this CoLT by combining it with others. For example, have student teams use their anthologies as the basis for writing a paper (*CoLT 28: Collaborative Writing*). Or have them create the anthology to support their teaching role in *CoLT 11: Jigsaw.*

OBSERVATIONS AND ADVICE   Assign Team Anthologies so that they are used for a specific purpose (such as resources for writing a paper, completing a project, teaching their peers, and so forth). If the purpose of the Team Anthology is not clear, or if the class does not use the anthology in some way, students may perceive this task as busy work.

This CoLT can be an effective technique to help students learn the important sources and tools of the discipline. Additionally, it provides a structured alternative to the standard term paper for students to practice research skills.

To increase accountability, consider implementing both individual and group grades. To provide a basis from which to assign individual grades, have students submit their individual work at specific time intervals or as attachments to the final product. For example, students can submit to you a document that shows their initial individual identification of resources and retain a copy for their group work. Along the same lines, partners can submit their individual reflective commentary on each source as well as the composite annotation.

Consider assessing this activity by using *Group-Work Evaluations* (CAT 47, Angelo & Cross, 1993, pp. 349–351) and create a questionnaire that collects feedback on students' reactions to this assignment. For example, ask students to rate how effectively the group worked together as a quad and as partners, how prepared each group member was for each stage of this activity, and so forth. Teachers can also include questions asking students to identify what they learned most from the anthology itself (as distinguished from the process of creating the anthology).

KEY RESOURCES   Bull, K. S., Montgomery, D. L., & Kimball, S. L. (Eds.). (1999). *Quality university instruction online: An advanced teaching effectiveness training program—An instructional hypertext.* Stillwater: Oklahoma State University. Available: http://home.okstate.edu/homepages.nsf/toc/EPSY5213Reading3a

Millis, B. (1994). Increasing thinking through cooperative writing. *Cooperative Learning and College Teaching, 4*(3), 7–9.

Millis, B., & Cottell, P. G. (1998). *Cooperative learning for higher education faculty.* Phoenix, AZ: Oryx Press, pp. 120–121.

COLLABORATIVE
LEARNING
TECHNIQUE

30

Paper Seminar

Characteristics	
Group Size	4–6
Time on Task	VARIES
Duration of Groups	MULTIPLE SESSIONS
Online Transferability	HIGH

DESCRIPTION AND PURPOSE   In this CoLT, a student makes a formal presentation of an original paper to a small group of peers. Within the group, one or two students act as formal respondents to the paper. The entire group then engages in a discussion of the paper's content, interpretation, and underlying assumptions and values. Paper Seminar provides a framework for groups to engage in deep discussion, exchanging and probing ideas that students have brought from their research and their individual readings of the paper. It also gives individual students focused attention and feedback on their work, while avoiding the multiple student presentations to the entire class that can be time intensive and tiresome.

PREPARATION
- *Instructors:* Assign and monitor the writing of the papers and determine a timeline that gives students adequate time to prepare for and conduct the seminar. Consider giving students guidance on how to read the paper critically and prepare a formal response. Plan for sufficient time, as this activity may need to be distributed over several sessions. For example, each student's paper may take approximately 40 minutes. For a group of four, that means 160 minutes. It is best to have one or two papers per class session.

- *Presenters*: Write the paper, distribute copies to group members, and organize comments for a five to ten minute verbal summary of the paper to the group.

- *Respondent*: Read the paper, take notes, and formulate significant questions for the group to discuss.

- *Group Member*: Read the paper, marking the text for interesting passages, and jotting down questions and comments for the discussion.

PROCEDURE

1. Assign students to groups, and tell students that they will all be responding formally and informally to peers' papers in their group.

2. Determine who will serve as formal respondent for each paper. For groups of four, assign one formal respondent; for groups of six, consider assigning two formal respondents.

3. Explain to students the time frame and tasks.

4. On the day of the Paper Seminar, give the first presenters time to formally present their papers to their groups (such as five to ten minutes).

5. Allow respondents to respond (such as ten minutes).

6. Give groups time to discuss the paper (such as twenty minutes).

7. Follow the same sequence of activities for the second presenters, and so forth.

• • •

EXAMPLES

Survey of World Geography

Throughout this course, students studied the physical, cultural, and economic features of the world's major culture regions and nations. Professor Cara Bean wanted to provide students with an opportunity to integrate and synthesize key concepts. She decided to assign students to write papers requiring that they apply a range of ideas covered in class to a hypothetical situation, and to present and discuss these papers in a Paper Seminar. An example of one prompt follows:

Even though economic development can have many positive effects in a country, various development strategies can ignore or take away investment in social services, and even entrench wide income disparities. Define your conception of a good quality of life. Imagine that you have been elected the leader of a small tropical island. Write a paper describing the policies you would implement to make sure that the resources (including land, water, beaches, spices, and bananas) are not jeopardized by world cartels and trading blocks and that your citizens would enjoy a prosperous quality of life.

For the Paper Seminar, she organized students into groups of four and assigned one formal respondent for each paper. She asked respondents to pay particular attention to how well the author had applied course concepts and theories to the supposed scenario. Professor Bean felt that the seminar provided a structure for students to compare ideas and to probe more deeply the issues underlying the hypothetical situation.

• • •

Principles of Marketing

Professor Sal N. Stuff wanted students to explore in-depth a market planning strategy. She decided to use a combination of *CoLT 28: Collaborative Writing* and *CoLT 30: Paper Seminar* to give students an assignment that had real-world applicability. She asked students to identify product lines to market (for example, furniture, apparel, cooking equipment, and so forth). As students generated ideas, she wrote the ideas on the board. She then invited students to choose a product for which they were most interested in serving as a marketing consultant, and organized students into pairs or triads accordingly.

She assigned each group to research the advantages and disadvantages of online distribution for their chosen product. As students conducted their research, they were asked to consider the following:

- The cost of designing and maintaining a Web site
- The likelihood that target consumers are Internet shoppers
- The industry trends in that product area: for example, are other businesses selling similar products online, and how successful are they?
- The opportunity to expand inventory without increasing the cost of retail space, catalogue production, or mailing
- The opportunity to have a store that never closes
- The lack of trust about credit card purchasing on the Web
- The difficulty that shoppers have in finding a Web site when they do not know the store's name and URL
- Potential customer frustration and waste of time conducting Web searches
- The certainty that the site will not reach customers who do not use computers or shop on the Internet.

Based on their findings, she asked students to write a persuasive memo to the company's owner stating their position about expanding to an online distribution system (CAT 12, *Analytic Memo,* Angelo & Cross, 1993, pp. 177–180). She told students to include in the memo information that would counter expected objections. For the Paper Seminar, she told students to present their memos as if they were consultants hired by the business's owner. She assigned two respondents for each analytic memo, one responding from the perspective of the business owner, and another from the perspective of the chief financial officer or accountant. The entire group discussed the analysis and proposal and attempted to determine an effective marketing decision based on the memo.

• • •

 Screenplay Writing

The primary goal of this online course was to teach students how to write effective screenplays for film and television. The instructor used a variety of readings, Threaded Discussions, written assignments, and quizzes to help students learn the components and process of screenplay writing. The components included how to structure stories, develop characters, and craft dialogue; the process included conceptualization, organization, and execution. To help students synthesize the individual aspects of the course, he decided to implement a final project followed by a Paper Seminar. The final project was to write a one-act play. He allowed students to choose their medium and genre: for a teleplay, students could choose a situation comedy, a dramatic series, or a single event program; for screenplays, students could choose fiction or documentary.

When students had finished writing the screenplay, the professor formed groups of six, organized by medium (television or film), assigned a primary respondent per screenplay, and asked each student to e-mail their one-act to the five other group members. The professor created a private discussion area for each group, and asked each author to introduce their screenplay's "thread" of the discussion by explaining why they had chosen the medium, genre, and topic, their primary artistic goal for the one-act, any particular problems they had encountered, and so forth. The professor asked primary respondents to post second-level comments, reviewing the screenplay from the perspective of a producer considering adopting the screenplay. The remaining group members then posted additional comments, focusing on how the screenwriter had handled the different components and process, with special attention on each author's ability to take into account the visual nature and unique requirements of writing for television or film. The professor felt that Paper Seminar provided each screenwriter with substantive and constructive feedback without significantly increasing his workload, and it also gave students practice identifying effective and ineffective features in screenplays.

• • •

ONLINE IMPLEMENTATION Organize students into groups, and create for each group a separate, private discussion area. Students can exchange papers for review through e-mail attachments. The students who have been assigned the role of formal respondent can post their comments on the group's Threaded Discussion board. Other members of the group can then post additional comments.

VARIATIONS AND EXTENSIONS
- Instead of writing a paper, have students read a collection of texts or journal articles. Ask each individual to prepare an oral presentation with their analysis or interpretation of one of the reading assignments for the seminar. The primary respondent can provide the initial feedback, and then the whole group can discuss the presenter's comments.

- Use this CoLT to provide students with feedback on other kinds of assignments, such as on drawings, paintings, music compositions or performances, and so forth.

- Combine this CoLT with other CoLTs, such as *CoLT 15: Case Study* or *CoLT 28: Collaborative Writing* for a more extensive collaborative experience.

OBSERVATIONS AND ADVICE Students may not be comfortable sharing their writing with others; therefore, give students time and support as they write their papers. Consider connecting this CoLT with *Colt 27: Peer Editing* so that students receive feedback on their writing before it is presented to the larger group.

The Paper Seminar is a place for students to discover new ideas, to reexamine old ideas, or to develop insightful connections among ideas. The group is responsible for exploring the text and probing the ideas that people have brought from their individual reading of the text. It is a time to "mine" the text, to think aloud about it, and to test some ideas against the group. The exchange of ideas is focused and aimed at getting more deeply into the source.

The seminar works best when the respondent has prepared a thoughtful response and when all students have read the same text carefully. Therefore provide students with guidance on how to read critically. Help them to understand that a critical reader tries to comprehend the literal meaning of the words, to relate the information to what they already know, to distinguish between fact and opinion, to draw inferences about the author's viewpoint, and to evaluate and develop an informed opinion about the material.

Do not try to do all the papers in one session. Students will get overloaded or bored with the activity, and they will not continue to respond as well. This activity should be conducted over several sessions.

KEY RESOURCES Habeshaw, S., Habeshaw, T. & Gibbs, G. (1984). *53 interesting things to do in your seminars and tutorials.* Bristol: Technical & Educational Studies.

Harnish, J. *What's in a seminar?* Washington Center for Improving Undergraduate Education. Retrieved April 20, 2003, from http://www.evergreen.edu/washcenter/WhatsSeminar.shtm

Appendix A

Key to Professor Names from CoLT Examples

Name	Translation	Discipline	CoLT
Sara McShards	Ceramic shards	Anthropology	Think-Pair-Share
Mark Etting	Marketing	Business	Round Robin
Jen Derr	Gender	Sociology	Buzz Groups
Anna Log	Analog	Calculus	Talking Chips
Clara Nett	Clarinet	Music	Three-Step Interview
Lex Rex	Lex Rex (The king is the law/the law is king)	Law	Critical Debate
Penny Cillen	Penicillin	Nursing	Note-Taking Pairs
Alec Tricity	Electricity	Engineering	Note-Taking Pairs
Meg Nacarta	Magna Carta	History	Note-Taking Pairs
Tish Oosells	Tissue Cells	Human Anatomy	Learning Cells
Ann Virement	Environment	Biology	Fishbowl
Sara Bellum	Cerebellum	Psychology	Role Play
Ann Glish	English	English as a Second Language	Role Play
Paige Turner	Page turner	Literature	Jigsaw
Watts D. Matta	What's the matter?	Psychology	Test-Taking Teams
Cole Ridge	Coleridge	Poetry	Test-Taking Teams
Marge N. O'Vera	Margin of error	Statistics	TAPPS
Xavier Breath	Save your breath	Respiratory Therapy	Send-a-Problem
Fitz William	Fitzwilliam (main character in *Pride and Prejudice*)	Literature	Send-a-Problem

Name	Translation	Discipline	CoLT
Neil Politan	Neapolitan	Art	Case Studies
Warren Peace	War and Peace	Political Science	Case Studies
Amanda Lin	A mandolin	Music	Structured Problem Solving
Molly Cule	Molecule	Chemistry	Structured Problem Solving
A. Joe Vexploration	Age of Exploration	History	Analytic Teams
Jenn Ettics	Genetics	Biology	Analytic Teams
Clara Fie	Clarify	English	Group Investigation
Phil O'Dendron	Philodendron	Biology	Group Investigation
Anna Littical	Elementary	Education	Affinity Grouping
Allie Gorical	Allegorical	Art	Group Grid
Owen Cash	Owing cash	Business	Group Grid
Grace Note	Grace note	Music	Team Matrix
A. B. Sieze	ABC's	Education	Team Matrix
Wes T. Ward	Westward	Western Civilization	Sequence Chains
Al Luvial	Alluvial	Geography	Sequence Chains
Rose E. Riveter	Rosie the Riveter	History	Word Webs
Manuel Recount	Manual recount	Political Science	Dialogue Journals
Anna Log	Analog	Math	Dialogue Journals
Al Kali	Alkali	Science	Round Table
Penny Wise and L. B. Foolish	Penny wise and pound foolish	Economics	Round Table
Jean Poole	Gene pool	Biology	Dyadic Essays
Ona Holm	Own a home	Real Estate	Dyadic Essays
Watts Itmene	What's it mean?	Philosophy	Peer Editing
Zeke N. Yeshallfind	Seek and ye shall find	Comparative Religion	Collaborative Writing
Ana Conda	Anaconda	Zoology	Collaborative Writing
Ann O'Tate	Annotate	Composition	Team Anthology
Sal Monella	Salmonella	Health Education	Team Anthology
Rita Booke	Educational Foundations	Education	Team Anthology
Matt Finnish	Matte finish	Photography	Team Anthology
Cara Bean	Caribbean	World Geography	Paper Seminar
Sal N. Stuff	Selling stuff	Marketing	Paper Seminar

Appendix B

Additional Ideas for Integrating the Learning Task into a Curricular Framework

STRUCTURING EFFECTIVE LEARNING TASKS is arguably the teacher's most important responsibility when implementing collaborative learning. The CoLTs in Part Three provide guidance for crafting good tasks. Each field-tested technique includes step-by-step procedures and examples of tasks in a variety of disciplines. Additional advice on task design is provided in Chapter Four, Structuring the Learning Task. Here we offer two more models that demonstrate structuring collaborative learning tasks so that the activities are better integrated into a broader, learner-centered curricular framework. The first model comes from Wiggins and McTighe's *Understanding by Design* (1998), and the second from Fink's *Creating Significant Learning Experiences* (2003).

We have purposefully avoided attempts to summarize or synthesize the models, as each model comes from a book that is richly nuanced with both theoretical and practical information that would be impossible to convey adequately in this Appendix. Instead, we focus on a few key points that offer ideas for structuring effective collaborative learning tasks. Rather than substituting for the book, our hope is that after reviewing these brief descriptions, teachers will be inspired to go to the original sources. Following a brief description of the model, we show how to use CoLTs to implement that model within a specific course.

Wiggins and McTighe's *Understanding by Design* (1998)

This model emerges from two core concepts: teaching for understanding and backward design.

Teaching for Understanding

Wiggins and McTighe advise teachers to strive to help their students achieve *understanding,* as distinguished from simply *knowing.* Deep, "enduring understanding" remains with students long after they have finished the class and forgotten the details. Enduring understandings result from grappling with the big ideas and core processes that are at the heart of the discipline. These ideas are abstract, sometimes counterintuitive, and often misunderstood. Learning activities should be designed to incorporate the information, skills, and activities required to develop enduring understanding of these big ideas and core processes.

Teachers will know if students have achieved this enduring understanding if students can demonstrate six facets of understanding. If students have enduring understanding, they can

1. *Explain* by providing thorough, supported, and justifiable accounts of phenomena, facts, and dates

2. *Interpret* by telling meaningful stories and offering apt translations that provide a revealing historical or personal dimension to ideas and events

3. *Apply* by effectively using and adapting what they know in diverse contexts

4. *Demonstrate perspective* by showing that they can see and hear points of view through critical eyes and ears

5. *Empathize,* by finding value in what others might find odd or implausible, and

6. *Demonstrate self-knowledge,* by showing that they perceive the personal style, prejudices, projections, and habits of mind that both shape and impede their understanding (Wiggins & McTighe, 1998, p. 44)

Backward Design

A common approach to selecting a course's learning tasks is to decide what one wants students to learn, determine the tasks that will help students learn, and then identify evaluation strategies to determine how well students learned in order to determine a grade. Although this strategy makes common sense, Wiggins and McTighe propose the name *backward design* for an alternative approach. As with the more familiar model, backward design begins with identifying learning goals. But then the authors suggest identifying what would be valid assessment evidence that the desired learning has been achieved *before* designing learning tasks. Determining acceptable evidence focuses and clarifies what the teaching and learning activities should be and helps uncover any problems or issues with the goals. Wiggins and McTighe's backward design approach to planning and structuring learning tasks involves a three-stage sequence:

- *Stage 1: Determine goals.* In the first stage, determine what students should know, understand, and be able to do. Because college instructors are typically challenged by the large amount of content they want to cover and insufficient time to address the content adequately, Wiggins and McTighe suggest using a framework of three concentric circles to prioritize content. In the large, external circle, identify the content that is worth being familiar with. Within this large circle is a medium-sized circle, and in this, identify the more important knowledge and skills required in order to consider student learning to be complete. In the center is the smallest ring, in which we must identify the selected "enduring" understandings that anchor the course and that we want students to remember long after they've forgotten the details.

- *Stage 2: Determine evidence.* One can assess student learning of the content in the largest, external circle relatively easily through traditional knowledge-based quizzes and exams. Assessing learning in the middle circle—and especially in the small "enduring understanding" circle—is more challenging. To determine evidence at these deeper learning levels, Wiggins and McTighe have developed a continuum for evaluating evidence of each of the six facets. For example, *Explanation* is evaluated on a continuum from "naive" to "sophisticated," and *Application* is evaluated on a continuum from "novice" to "masterful."

- *Stage 3: Design learning tasks.* After determining the understanding goals and identifying how to assess the depth at which understanding has been achieved, design the academic prompts, performance tasks, or projects that will help students achieve the goals.

Using Collaborative Learning Techniques to Implement This Model

Collaborative Learning Techniques are well suited for achieving enduring understanding. While learning goals in the outer, external circle can be achieved through activities such as reading and listening to lectures and assessed by traditional quizzes and exams, learning in the inner two circles is better achieved through active, participatory, authentic tasks and activities. Such tasks require students to think critically (not just recall knowledge) and to struggle with complex challenges that mirror the issues and problems faced by scholars in the discipline. Following is a description of a college-level course on the history of the Vietnam War that uses the Wiggins and McTighe's model to select CoLTs and craft the learning task.

Example: The History of the Vietnam War

The professor for this course established curricular priorities by distributing information regarding the war's dates, events, policies, and so forth between the outer circle ("worth being familiar with") and middle circle ("essential information"). For the small internal circle, he identified four enduring understandings. First, he wanted students to be aware of the complexity of the war and appreciate why even the greatest efforts could not produce a victory. Second, he wanted students to understand how Vietnam unraveled the national consensus of the 1950s and early 1960s by deeply dividing Americans along a continuum of those who supported the war and those who opposed it. Third, he wanted students to see how the war continues to influence individual lives, national politics, and international policy. Fourth, he wanted students to experience how historians make meaning out of complex information. The professor then followed the backward design process of determining assessment criteria first and then identifying learning tasks. For purposes of clarity here, the activity will be presented and followed by assessment strategies.

Explanation and Application

To acquire a thorough knowledge of basic information regarding the war and to develop awareness of the complexity of the war, students listened to lectures, watched film documentaries, read a variety of primary and secondary sources, and participated in the following collaborative techniques. The professor used the CoLTs in combination with objective and subjective exams to assess student learning.

CoLT 26: Dyadic Essays On a weekly basis, students individually wrote an essay question and a model answer based on the week's activities. On Friday in class, student pairs exchanged questions, wrote a response to the partner's question, and then traded, read, and compared model and in-class answers. This activity helped ensure that students had done the assigned reading, attended and taken notes on lectures, and had paid attention to the films. It also helped students identify the most important features in these activities and build upon each other's understandings. The professor collected the essays, evaluated and graded them, and selected exemplary questions for inclusion in the midterm and final exam.

CoLT 12: Test-Taking Teams Two weeks prior to each of the two exams, the professor organized students into teams and distributed a study guide. He set aside thirty minutes in class for teams to organize how they wanted to help each other study outside of class time, and also one hour of class time for them to work together. On the day of the exam, students took the exam individually during the first half of class, and then retook the exam as a team during the second half of the class. He assigned grades by giving individual scores twice the weight of the group scores. The professor felt that this strategy not only emphasized individual accountability, but also gave students the benefit from the collective knowledge of the group.

Application, Interpretation, Perspective, and Empathy

To help students understand how Vietnam deeply divided America and to see how it continued to influence lives, he wanted a task that would help students "get inside" various stakeholders' feelings and views regarding the war. To experience how historians make meaning, he decided to make the task and assessment product an actual history document.

CoLT 18: Group Investigation He organized students into small groups and told them that they would be creating a term-long project called, "Views on the Vietnam War from Those Who Experienced It." He asked each group to identify and interview three adults with different backgrounds in relation to the Vietnam era and create an oral history based on their interviews. Students were given an option for how they wanted to present this history: written narrative, book, audiotape, videotape, CD-ROM, and so forth. To accompany their project, students wrote a group essay that compared their oral history with the history in their readings. Projects were assessed on rubrics, which ranged from "Superficial" to "Profound and revealing" (a powerful and illuminating analysis of the importance, significance, and meaning of the war).

Empathy and Self-Knowledge

To help students gain insight and understand more deeply a Vietnamese perspective on the war, he had students read Andrew Pham's *Catfish and Mandala.* This is an autobiographical work of a college-aged Vietnamese American who returns to Vietnam to "find himself" and to reconstruct the events that had drastically changed his family and his life. To help students recognize their own patterns of thought and action, the professor wanted to create a task that required students to connect Pham's experiences with their own lives.

CoLT 24: Dialogue Journals As students read Pham's book, they maintained a record of their thoughts in a journal that they then exchanged periodically with peers for comments and questions. The journal was generally unstructured, and students were encouraged to write about whatever in Pham's story was relevant to them. The journal concluded with an explicit assignment: *Identify one specific incident in* Catfish and Mandala *where author Andrew Pham's life changed forever, a "turning point" in his story. How and why did he change? Compare and contrast Pham's experience with a "turning point" experience in your own life.*

The professor believed that by using a combination of collaborative learning techniques with Wiggins and McTighe's learning-centered course design model, he had created a course that was far superior to his prior efforts. Teachers who find Wiggins and McTighe's approach to curricular and learning task design appealing are advised to read the original sources. *Understanding by Design* (1998) provides the conceptual foundations. The *Understanding by Design Handbook* (McTighe & Wiggins, 1999) provides the practical templates, worksheets, exercises, design tools, and a peer review process for learning and applying the ideas in *Understanding by Design.*

Fink's Significant Learning Experiences (2003)

Fink's model was inspired by his observations that there are two widespread problems in higher education. First, he believes that the majority of college teachers do not seem to have learning goals that go much beyond an "understand and remember" type of learning—the kind of learning that is superficial and usually temporary. Second, he believes that "most teachers seem to have difficulty figuring out what teaching activities they might use besides the two traditional standbys: lecture and discussion" (p. xi). To help solve these problems, he suggests a new taxonomy of "significant learning" that offers teachers a framework for formulating learning goals. These goals then guide the creation of learning experiences that engage students, promote high energy (as opposed to boredom), and result in significant and lasting change that continues long after the course is over (pp. xii–xiii). Fink believes that educative, formative assessment is essential to integrated and effective learning task and course design.

Taxonomy of Significant Learning

Fink proposes that higher education is expressing a need for new kinds of learning: learning how to learn, leadership and interpersonal skills, ethics, communication skills, character, tolerance, and the ability to adapt to change

(p. 29). These kinds of learning go beyond Bloom's cognitive domain, and even beyond cognitive learning itself. Fink constructed a new taxonomy guided by his perspective that learning can be defined in terms of change: If there is no change, there is no learning. Rather than hierarchical, his taxonomy is relational and interactive, and consists of the following categories:

- *Foundational knowledge:* Understanding and remembering specific information and ideas. This knowledge provides the basic understanding that is necessary for other kinds of learning.

- *Application:* Engaging in some new kind of intellectual, physical, or social action; developing certain skills and learning how to engage in various kinds of thinking (critical, creative, practical). Application learning allows other kinds of learning to be useful.

- *Integration:* Being able to see and understand the connections between different ideas, realms of ideas, people, or between different realms of life (such as school and work).

- *Human dimension:* Learning important things about oneself and others; discovering the personal and social implications of what one has learned. This kind of understanding helps students understand how and why others act the way they do, or how the learner can interact more effectively with others.

- *Caring:* Changing the degree to which students care about something that is reflected in the form of new feelings, interests, or values. When students care about something, they have the energy they need for learning more about it and integrating that information into their lives.

- *Learning how to learn:* Learning about the process of learning in order to become a better student, and knowing how to engage in a particular kind of inquiry or to become a self-directing learner.

Using Collaborative Learning Techniques to Implement This Model: Physics

Fink includes a detailed case study of a redesign of a physics course by a colleague of his, John Furneaux, that implements the Significant Learning framework. The course is a sophomore-level, two-semester "Electronics Lab" course for physics majors intended to help students understand and then construct some of the electronic measuring devices that they would use in the research aspects of their upper-division physics courses. The case study is a comprehensive description of the questions and discussions between Furneaux and Fink as they engaged in a joint effort to redesign the two-semester course. Here, we will use their design for the first semester and add suggestions for how to structure learning activities that incorporate CoLTs.

Learning Goals

Professor John Furneaux used the Significant Learning Taxonomy to focus his learning goals. For example, he wanted students to learn to solve authentic, meaningful kinds of problems rather than typical end-of-chapter kinds of problems, thus it was evident that *application learning* for him was a critical learning goal. He also wanted to focus on the *human dimension* and help students understand that even a "hard-core science" like physics is fundamentally a human enterprise: scientists have both noble and petty personalities; physicists need to be able to interact effectively with others on intellectual projects because much of today's major scientific research takes place collaboratively; and students needed to develop self-images of themselves as people capable of doing "serious science." Professor Furneaux also wanted students to *learn how to learn* physics, specifically how to use electronic equipment to create knowledge, which in turn required clarifying what physicists mean by *knowledge*. With this framework in mind, Furneaux and Fink identified the following specific course learning goals as well as corresponding teaching and learning activities (Fink, 2003, pp. 178–79). We have used this initial course design to adopt, adapt, or add learning activities to fit within a CoLT structure.

Goal 1: Develop familiarity with electronic techniques. (Know the terminology, operate the technology, and know and describe how the technology works.)

CoLT 1: Think–Pair–Share At critical points in the lectures on electronic techniques, students reflected individually for a few minutes and then turned to a peer to share, compare, and check their understandings.

CoLT 8: Learning Cell Students partnered with a peer to quiz each other using questions they had developed individually about readings, lectures, or lab exercises.

Goal 2: Use the technology to generate knowledge. (Use technology to answer questions; design technology for real projects; assess validity of data techniques and information and answers; identify and assess own assumptions.)

CoLT 18: Group Investigation Small groups designed and built a series of measuring devices. This assignment was both challenging and open-ended, unlike traditional textbook exercises. Professor Furneaux also incorporated into the assignment an aspect of *CoLT 10: Role Play* to give the assignment both "playfulness and reality at the same time": he created a simulated company that functioned as the students' employer. This company sent the students project requests for equipment that could conduct certain measuring tasks. The Group Investigation assignments were to figure out how to respond to these requests by designing, constructing, and assessing an instrument that would measure certain properties (p. 180).

Goal 3: Understand what knowledge is. (Students create a model of knowledge; students test complex questions.)

CoLT 19: Affinity Grouping Professor Furneaux formed groups of four to six members and asked students to individually generate ideas about "knowledge." Working with other group members, students identified clusters of ideas and information and used this to "build" a model of knowledge.

CoLT 11: Jigsaw To help students learn about electronic measuring devices, the relationship between these devices, and the process of generating knowledge in physics, and to connect this in turn to the structure of their own learning experiences in the course, he crafted an assignment that was a variation of Jigsaw. This assignment required students to design a teaching and learning unit for new physics students. To do the assignment, students were asked to think through what freshman physics students should learn, what activities would help them learn, and what kind of feedback they should receive (Fink, 2003, p. 181). As students developed the goals, activities, and assessment strategies to teach their peers, they enhanced their own comprehension not only of the content, but also of the issues and processes in their own learning.

Goal 4: Personal and social nature of science (Understand the individual nature of science; understand how social dynamics work in scientific work.)

CoLT 24: Dialogue Journals Students recorded their thoughts in a journal and shared their individual reflections with a peer. In addition to unstructured, free form reflections, students responded to specific prompts, such as prompts that asked them to reflect on the individual and social nature of their own small groups or to read accounts of the work of scientists. A concluding assignment in the journal for the entire course was to write an essay in the form of a learning portfolio.

Goal 5: Learn how to learn. (What would you like to learn; in particular situations, what would you learn and how would you learn that?)

See *CoLT 11: Jigsaw* and *CoLT 24: Dialogue Journals* (see Goal 3 preceding).

   This summary represents a few ideas for incorporating collaborative techniques into Fink's integrated course design as applied to Furneaux's first semester physics course. As with the example of Wiggins and McTighe, readers are encouraged to go to the original source for more information.

References

Angelo, T. A., & Cross, K. P. (1993). *Classroom assessment techniques*, 2nd ed. San Francisco: Jossey-Bass.

Annis, L. F. (1983). The process and effects of peer tutoring. *Human Learning*, 2, 39–47.

Aronson, E. (2000). *The jigsaw classroom*. Retrieved February 26, 2004, from http://www.jigsaw.org/

Aronson, E., Blaney, N., Stephan, C., Sikes, J., & Snapp, M. (1978). *The jigsaw classroom*. Beverly Hills, CA: Sage.

Astin, A. (1968). *The college environment*. Washington, DC: American Council on Education.

Astin, A. (1993). *What matters in college?* San Francisco: Jossey-Bass.

Bean, J. C. (1996). *Engaging ideas: The professor's guide to integrating writing, critical thinking, and active learning in the classroom*. San Francisco: Jossey-Bass.

Belenky, M. F., Clinchy, B. M., Goldberger, N. R., & Tarule, J. M. (1986). *Women's ways of knowing: The development of self, voice, and mind*. New York: Basic Books.

Bender, E., Dunn, M., Kendall, B., Larson, C., & Wilkes, P. (Eds.). (1994). *Quick hits: Successful strategies by award winning teachers*. Bloomington and Indianapolis: Indiana University Press.

Berthoff, A. (1990). *The sense of learning*. Portsmouth, NH: Boynton Cook, Heinemann Press.

Bloom, B. S. (Ed.). (1956). *Taxonomy of educational objectives: Book 1, Cognitive domain*. New York: Longman.

Bosworth, K. (1994). Developing collaborative skills in college students. In K. Bosworth & S. J. Hamilton (Eds.), *Collaborative learning: Underlying processes and effective techniques* (pp. 25–32). New Directions in Teaching and Learning, No. 59. San Francisco: Jossey-Bass.

Bosworth, K., & Hamilton, S. J. (Eds.). (1994). *Collaborative learning: Underlying processes and effective techniques*. New Directions in Teaching and Learning, No. 59. San Francisco: Jossey-Bass.

Boyer, E. L. (1990). *Scholarship reconsidered: priorities of the professoriate*. Princeton, NJ: The Carnegie Foundation for the Advancement of Teaching.

Brassard, M. (1989). *The memory jogger II*. Methuen, MA: Goal/QPC.

Bromley, K. (1993). *Journaling: Engagements in reading, writing and thinking*. New York: Scholastic.

Brookfield, S. D., & Preskill, S. (1999). *Discussion as a way of teaching: Tools and techniques for democratic collaborative learning classrooms*. San Francisco: Jossey-Bass.

Bruffee, K. A. (1993). *Collaborative learning: Higher education, interdependence, and the authority of knowledge*. Baltimore, MD: Johns Hopkins University Press.

Bruffee, K. A. (1995). Sharing our toys: Cooperative learning versus collaborative learning. *Change, 27*(1), 12–18.

Bruner, J. (1966). *Toward a theory of instruction*. Cambridge, MA: Harvard University Press.

Bull, K. S., Montgomery, D. L, & Kimball, S. L. (1999). (Eds.) *Quality university instruction online: An advanced teaching effectiveness training program—An instructional hypertext*. Stillwater: Oklahoma State University. Available: http://home.okstate.edu/homepages.nsf/toc/EPSY5213Reading3a

Byrne, R. (1988). *1,911 best things anybody ever said*. New York: Fawcett Columbine.

Cabrera, A. F. (1998, November). *Collaborative learning: Preferences, gains in cognitive and affective outcomes, and openness to diversity among college students*. Paper presented at the meeting of the Association for the Study of Higher Education, Miami, FL.

Campbell, N. A., Reece, J. B., & Simon, E. J. (2004). *Essential biology with physiology*. San Francisco: Pearson.

Chickering, A. (1969). *Education and identity*. San Francisco: Jossey-Bass.

Chickering, A. W., & Gamson, Z. F. (1987). Seven principles for good practice in undergraduate education. *The Wingspread Journal, 9*(2), pp. 3–7. See also *AAHE Bulletin*, March 1987.

Christensen, C. R. (1987). *Teaching and the case method*. Boston: Harvard Business School.

Cohen, G. (1986). *Designing groupwork: Strategies for the heterogeneous classroom*. New York: Teachers College Press.

Community College Leadership Program. (2003). *Engaging community colleges. National benchmarks of quality, 2003 findings*. Austin: University of Texas, Community College Leadership Program.

Cooper, J., Prescott, S., Cook, L., Smith, L., Mueck, R., & Cuseo, J. (1990). *Cooperative learning and college instruction: Effective use of student learning teams.* Long Beach, CA: California State University Foundation.

Cranton, P. (1996). Types of group learning. In S. Imel (Ed.), *Learning in groups: Fundamental principles, new uses, and emerging opportunities* (pp. 25–32). New Directions for Adult and Continuing Education, No. 71. San Francisco: Jossey-Bass.

Cranton, P. (1998). *No one way: Teaching and learning in higher education.* Toronto: Wall & Emerson.

Cross, K. P. (1999). *Learning is about making connections.* Mission Viejo, CA: League for Innovation in the Community College.

Cross, K. P. (2001). Leading-edge efforts to improve teaching and learning. *Change, 33*(4), 30–37.

Cross, K. P., & Fideler, E. F. Assessment in the classroom. *Community/Junior College Quarterly of Research and Practice,* 1988, *12*(4), 275–285.

Cross, K. P., & Steadman, M. H. (1996). *Classroom research: Implementing the scholarship of teaching.* San Francisco: Jossey-Bass.

Culbertson, H. (2000–2001). Group dynamics: Unwelcome group members. Retrieved November 14, 2003, from http://home.snu.edu/~hculbert.fs/groupmem.htm

Cunningham, P. M., & Cunningham, J. W. (1987). Content area reaching—Writing lessons. *The Reaching Teacher, 40,* 506–512.

Cuseo, J. B. (1992). Cooperative learning: A pedagogy for diversity. *Cooperative Learning & College Teaching, 3*(1), 2–6.

Cuseo, J. B. (1996). *Cooperative learning: A pedagogy for addressing contemporary challenges & critical issues in higher education.* Stillwater, OK: New Forums Press.

Davis, B. G. (1993). *Tools for teaching.* San Francisco: Jossey-Bass.

de Groot, A. (1966). Perception and memory versus thought: Some old ideas and recent findings. In B. Kleinmuntz (Ed.), *Problem solving.* New York: Wiley.

Fantuzzo, J. W., Dimeff, L. A., & Fox, S. L. (1989). Reciprocal peer tutoring: A multimodal assessment of effectiveness with college students. *Teaching of Psychology, 16*(3), 133–135.

Fantuzzo, J. W., Riggio, R. E., Connelly, S., & Dimeff, L. A. (1989). Effects of reciprocal peer tutoring on academic achievement and psychological adjustment: A component analysis. *Journal of Educational Psychology, 81*(2), 173–177.

Felder, R. M., Felder, G. N., Mauney, M., Hamrin, Jr., C. E., & Dietz, E. J. (1995). A longitudinal study of engineering student performance and retention. III. Gender Differences in Student Performance and Attitudes. *Journal of Engineering Education, 84*(2), 151.

Feldman, K. A., & Newcomb, T. M. (1969). *The impact of college on students.* San Francisco: Jossey-Bass.

Fiechtner, S. B., & Davis, E. A. (1992). Why some groups fail: A survey of students' experiences with learning groups. In A. Goodsell, M. Maher, & V. Tinto (Eds.), *Collaborative learning: A sourcebook for higher education.* University Park, PA: The Pennsylvania State University National Center on Postsecondary Teaching, Learning, and Assessment.

Fink, L. D. (2003). *Creating significant learning experiences: An integrated approach to designing college courses.* San Francisco: Jossey-Bass.

Flannery, J. L. (1994). Teacher as co-conspirator: Knowledge and authority in collaborative learning. In K. Bosworth & S. J. Hamilton (Eds.), *Collaborative learning: Underlying processes and effective techniques* (pp. 15–23). New Directions for Teaching and Learning, No. 59. San Francisco: Jossey-Bass.

Foyle, H. C. (1995). *Interactive learning in the higher education classroom: Cooperative, collaborative, and active learning strategies.* West Haven, CT: Excellence in the Academy, the NEA Professional Library Higher Education Series.

Freire, P. (1970). *Pedagogy of the oppressed.* New York: Herder & Herder.

Gabelnick, F. J., MacGregor, R., Matthews, R., & Smith, B. L. (Eds.). (1990). *Learning communities: Creating connections among students, faculty, and disciplines.* New Directions for Teaching and Learning, No. 41. San Francisco: Jossey-Bass.

Gardner, H. (1983). *Frames of mind.* New York: Basic Books.

Graphic Organizer, The. Retrieved December 7, 2003, from http://www.graphic.org/goindex.html

Grasha, A. F. (1996). *Teaching with style.* Pittsburgh, PA: Alliance Publishers.

Gruber, H. E., & Weitman, M. (1962). *Self-directed study: Experiments in higher education.* No. 19. Boulder: University of Colorado, Behavior Research Laboratory.

Habeshaw, S., Habeshaw, T., & Gibbs, G. (1984). *53 interesting things to do in your seminars and tutorials.* Bristol, UK: Technical & Educational Studies.

Hall, T., & Strangman, N. (1999–2004). *Graphic organizers.* Retrieved March 22, 2004, from http://www.cast.org/ncac/GraphicOrganizers3015.cfm

Harnish, J. *What's in a seminar?* Washington Center for Improving Undergraduate Education. Retrieved April 20, 2003, from http://www.evergreen.edu/washcenter/WhatsSeminar.shtm

Herreid, C. F. (1994). Case studies in science: A novel method of science education. *Journal of College Science Teaching, 23*(4), 221–229.

Hillebrand, R. P. (1994). Control and cohesion: Collaborative learning and writing, *English Journal, 83,* 71–74.

Hsu, E. (1989). Role event gaming simulation in management education: A conceptual framework. *Simulation and Games, 20,* 409–438.

Hughes, C. (1996). Cited in Millis, B. J., & Cottell, P. G. (1998). *Cooperative learning for higher education faculty.* American Council on Education. Phoenix, AZ: Oryx Press.

Jacob, P. (1957). *Changing values in college.* New York: Harper & Row.

Jaques, D. (2000). *Learning in groups: A handbook for improving group work,* 3rd ed. London: Kogan Page.

Johnson, D. W., & Johnson, F. P. (1975). *Joining together: Group theory and group skills.* Englewood Cliffs, NJ: Prentice-Hall.

Johnson, D. W., & Johnson, R. (1984). Cooperative small-group learning. *Curriculum Report,* 14(1), 1–6.

Johnson, D. W., & Johnson, R. T. (1987). *Learning together and alone,* 2nd ed. Englewood Cliffs, NJ: Prentice Hall.

Johnson, D. W., & Johnson, R. T. (1994). Structuring academic controversy. In S. Sharan (Ed.), *Handbook of cooperative learning methods.* Westport, CT: Greenwood Press.

Johnson, D. W., Johnson, R. T., & Smith, K. A. (1991). *Cooperative learning: Increasing college faculty instructional productivity.* ASHE-ERIC Higher Education Reports, No. 4. Washington, DC: George Washington University.

Johnson, D. W., Johnson, R. T., & Smith, K. A. (1998). *Active learning: Cooperation in the college classroom.* Edina, MN: Interaction Book Company.

Johnson, D. W., Johnson, R. T., & Stanne, M. B. (2000). *Cooperative learning methods: A meta-analysis.* Cooperative Learning Center at the University of Minnesota. Available: http://www.clcrc.com/pages/cl-methods.html

Johnson, D. W., Maruyama, G., Johnson, R., Nelson, D., & Skon, L. (1981). Effects of cooperative, competitive, and individualistic goal structures on achievement: A meta-analysis. *Psychological Bulletin, 89*(1), 47–62.

Kagan, S. (1990). The structural approach to cooperative learning. *Educational Leadership, 47*(4), 12–15.

Kagan, S. (1992). *Cooperative learning,* 2nd ed. San Juan Capistrano, CA: Resources for Teachers.

Kagan, S. (1995). Group grades miss the mark. *Educational leadership, 52*(8), 68–71.

Kagan, S. (1996). *Cooperative learning.* San Clemente, CA: Kagan Cooperative Learning.

King, R. (1989). *Hoshin planning: The developmental approach.* Methuen, MA: Goal/QPC.

Knowles, M. S. (1986). *Using learning contracts.* San Francisco: Jossey-Bass.

Kuh, G. (2000). *National Survey of Student Engagement: National benchmarks of effective educational practice.* Bloomington: Indiana University Center for Postsecondary Research and Planning.

Light, R. J. (1992). *The Harvard Assessment Seminars, 2nd report.* Cambridge, MA: Harvard University, Graduate School of Education and Kennedy School of Government.

Light, R. J. (2001). *Making the most of college: Students speak their minds.* Cambridge, MA: Harvard University Press.

Lochhead, J., & Whimbey, A. (1987). Teaching analytical reasoning through thinking-aloud pair problem solving. In J. E. Stice (Ed.), *Developing critical thinking and problem solving abilities* (pp. 73–92). New Directions for Teaching and Learning, No. 30. San Francisco: Jossey-Bass.

Luotto, J. A., & Stoll, E. (1996). *Communication skills for collaborative learning.* Dubuque, IA: Kendall/Hunt.

Lyman, F. (1981). The responsive classroom discussion. In A. S. Anderson (Ed.), *Mainstreaming digest.* College Park, MD: University of Maryland College of Education.

Lyman, F. T. (1992). Think-Pair-Share, Thinktrix, Thinklinks, and weird facts: An interactive system for cooperative learning. In N. Davidson & T. Worsham (Eds.), *Enhancing thinking through cooperative learning* (pp. 169–181). New York: Teachers College Press.

Lyman, P., & Varian, H. R. (2003) *How much information.* Available: http://www.sims.berkeley.edu/how-much-info-2003

MacGregor, J. (1990). Collaborative learning: Shared inquiry as a process of reform. In M. D. Svinicki (Ed.), *The changing face of college teaching* (pp. 19–30). New Directions for Teaching and Learning, No. 42. San Francisco: Jossey-Bass.

Matthews, R. S. (1996). Collaborative learning: Creating knowledge with students. In R. J. Menges, M. Weimer, & Associates (Eds.), *Teaching on solid ground: Using scholarship to improve practice* (pp. 101–124). San Francisco: Jossey-Bass.

Matthews, R. S., Smith, B. L., MacGregor, J., & Gabelnick, F. (1997). Creating learning communities. In J. G. Gaff, J. L. Ratcliff, & Associates (Eds.), *Handbook of the undergraduate curriculum* (pp. 457–475). San Francisco: Jossey-Bass.

McKeachie, W. J. (1994). *Teaching tips: Strategies, research and theory for college and university teachers,* 9th ed. Lexington, MA: D. C. Heath.

McKeachie, W. J. (2002). *McKeachie's teaching tips: Strategies, research, and theory for college and university teachers.* Boston, MA.: Houghton Mifflin.

McKeachie, W. J., Pintrich, P. R., Lin, Y., & Smith, D. A. (1986). *Teaching and learning in the college classroom: A review of the research literature.* Ann Arbor: University of Michigan, National Center for Research to Improve Postsecondary Teaching and Learning.

McKenzie, J. (1997). *Why graphical organizers?* Retrieved December 21, 2003, from http://www.fno.org/oct97/picture.html

McTighe, J. (1992). Graphic organizers: Collaborative links to better thinking. In N. Davidson and T. Worsham (Eds.), Enhancing thinking through cooperative learning. New York: Teachers College Press, 182–197.

McTighe, J., & Wiggins, G. (1998). *Understanding by design handbook.* Alexandria, VA: Association for Supervision and Curriculum Development.

McTighe, J., & Wiggins, G. (1999). *The understanding by design handbook.* Alexandria, VA: Association for Supervision and Curriculum Development.

Michaelsen, L. K., & Black, R. H. (1994). Building learning teams: The key to harnessing the power of small groups in higher education. In S. Kadel & J. Keehner (Eds.), *Collaborative learning: A sourcebook for higher education, 2* (pp. 65–81). State College, PA: National Center for Teaching, Learning and Assessment.

Michaelsen, L. K., Fink, L. D., & Knight, A. (1997). Designing effective group activities: Lessons for classroom teaching and faculty development. In D. DeZure (Ed.), *To improve the academy: Resources for faculty* (pp. 373–397). Instructional and organizational development, 16. Stillwater, OK: New Forums Press.

Millar, S. B. (1999). Learning through evaluation, adaptation, and dissemination: The LEAD Center. *AAHE Bulletin, 51*(8), 7–9.

Miller, J. E. (1996). Conducting effective peer classroom observations. In D. H. Wulff and J. D. Nyquist (Eds.), *To improve the academy: Resources for faculty, instructional, and organizational development* (pp. 189–201). Stillwater, OK: New Forums Press.

Miller, J. E., Groccia, J. E., & Wilkes, J. M. (1996). Providing structure: The critical element. In T. E. Sutherland & C. C. Bonwell (Eds.), *Using active learning in college collaborative learning classes: A range of options for faculty* (pp. 17–30). New Directions for Teaching and Learning, No. 67. San Francisco: Jossey-Bass.

Miller, J. E., Trimbur, J., & Wilkes, J. M. (1994). Group dynamics: Understanding group success and failure in collaborative learning. In K. Bosworth & S. J. Hamilton (Eds.), *Collaborative learning: Underlying processes and effective techniques* (pp. 33–44). New Directions for Teaching and Learning, No. 59. San Francisco: Jossey-Bass.

Millis, B. (1994). Increasing thinking through cooperative writing. *Cooperative Learning and College Teaching, 4*(3), 7–9.

Millis, B. J., & Cottell, P. G. (1998). *Cooperative learning for higher education faculty.* American Council on Education. Phoenix, AZ: Oryx Press.

Millis, B. J., Cottell, P. G., & Sherman, L. (1993). Stacking the DEC to promote critical thinking: Applications in three disciplines. *Cooperative Learning and College Teaching, 3*(3), 12–14.

Millis, B. J., Sherman, L., & Cottell, P. (1993). Stacking the DEC to promote critical thinking: Applications in three disciplines. *Cooperative Learning and College Teaching, 3*(3), 12–14.

Moore, D. W., & Readence, J. E. (1984). A quantitative and qualitative review of graphic organizer research. *Journal of Educational Research, 78*(1), 11–17.

Morris, L. A., and Tucker, S. (1985). Evaluating student writing. *Teaching at Davis Newsletter, 10*(2), 1, 6.

Naidu, S., Ip, A., & Linser, R. (2000). Dynamic goal-based role-play simulation on the Web: A case study. *Educational Technology and Society* 3(3), 190–202.

Nash, J. M. (1997). Fertile minds. *Time,* February 3, pp. 48–56.

Natasi, B. K., & Clements, D. H. (1991). Research on cooperative learning: Implications for practice. *School Psychology Review, 20*(1), 110–131.

Nilson, L. B. (2003). *Teaching at its best: A research-based resource for college instructors.* Bolton, MA: Anker.

Nurrenbern, S. (1995). *Experiences in cooperative learning: A collection for chemistry teachers.* Madison, WI: University of Wisconsin Board of Regents, Institute for Chemical Education.

Olmstead, J. A. (1974). *Small group instruction: Theory and practice.* Alexandria, VA: Human Resources Research Organization.

Paris, S. G., & Ayers, L. R. (1996). *Becoming reflective students and teachers.* Washington, DC: American Psychological Association.

Pascarella, E. T., & Terenzini, P. T. (1991). *How college affects students.* San Francisco: Jossey-Bass.

Paul, R., & Elder, L. (2003). Understanding the foundations of ethical reasoning. *Foundations for critical thinking,* p. 21. Available: http://www.criticalthinking.org

Per Bang. (2001). *The NASA exercise—Lost on the moon.* Retrieved February 10, 2004, from http://nasa.perbang.dk/

Plous, S. (2000). Responding to overt displays of prejudice: A role-playing exercise. *Teaching of Psychology, 27*(3), 198–200.

Ramsden, P. (1992). *Learning to teach in higher education.* London: Routledge.

Reid, J., Forrestal, P., & Cook, J. (1989). *Small group learning in the classroom.* Portsmouth, NH: Heinemann.

Reither, J. A., & Vipond, D. (1989). Writing as collaboration. *College English, 51,* 855–867.

Rosser, S. V. (1997). *Re-engineering female friendly science.* New York: Teachers College Press, Columbia University.

Sandler, B. R., Silverberg, L. A., & Hall, R. M. (1996). *The chilly classroom climate: A guide to improve the education of women.* Washington, DC: National Association for Women in Education (NAWE).

Schön, D. A. (1983). *How professionals think in action.* New York: Basic Books.

Sharan, S. (Ed.) (1994). *Handbook of cooperative learning methods.* Westport, CT: Greenwood Press.

Sharan, S., & Hertz-Lazarowitz, R. (1980). A group investigation method of cooperative learning in the classroom. In S. Sharan et al. (Eds.), *Cooperation in education* (pp. 14–46). Provo, UT: Brigham Young University Press.

Sharan, Y., & Sharan, S. (1992). *Expanding cooperative learning through group investigation.* Colchester, VT: Teachers College Press.

Sharan, Y., & Sharan, S. (1994). Group investigation in the cooperative classroom. In S. Sharan (Ed.), *Handbook of cooperative learning* (pp. 97–114). Westport, CT: Greenwood Press.

Sherman, S. J. (1994). Cooperative learning and science. In S. Sharan (Ed.), *Handbook of cooperative learning methods* (pp. 226–244). Westport, CT: Greenwood Press.

Silberman, M. (1996). *Active learning: 101 strategies to teach any subject.* Needham Heights, MA: Allyn & Bacon.

Silberman, M., & Clark, K. (1999). *101 ways to make meetings active: Surefire ideas to engage your group.* San Francisco: Jossey-Bass/Pfeiffer.

Slavin, R. E. (1986). *Using student team learning,* 3rd ed. Baltimore, MD: Johns Hopkins University, Center for Research on Elementary and Middle Schools.

Slavin, R. E. (1989–90). Research in cooperative learning: Consensus and controversy. *Educational Leadership, 47*(4), 52–55.

Slavin, R. E. (1990). *Cooperative learning: Theory, research, and practice.* Boston: Allyn & Bacon.

Slavin, R. E. (1996). *Education for all.* Exton, PA: Swets & Zeitlinger.

Smith, K. A. (1996). Cooperative learning: Making "group work" work. In T. E. Sutherland & C. C. Bonwell (Eds.), *Using active learning in college classes: A range of options for faculty* (pp. 71–82). New Directions for Teaching and Learning, No. 67. San Francisco: Jossey-Bass.

Springer, L., Stanne, M. E., & Donovan, S. (1998). *Effects of cooperative learning on undergraduates in science, mathematics, engineering, and technology: A meta-analysis.* Research Monograph No. 11. Madison: University of Wisconsin, National Institute for Science Education.

Springer, L., Stanne, M. E., & Donovan, S. S. (1999). Effects of small-group learning on undergraduates in science, mathematics, engineering, and technology: A meta-analysis. *Review of Educational Research, 69,* 21–51.

Tiberius, R. (1995). *Small group teaching: a trouble-shooting guide.* Toronto: OISE Press.

Tinto, V., Love, G., & Russo, P. (1994). *Building learning communities for new college students: A summary of research findings of the collaborative learning project.* University Park: Pennsylvania State University, National Center on Postsecondary Teaching, Learning, and Assessment.

Tobias, S. (1990). *They're not dumb, they're different—Stalking the second tier.* Tucson, AZ: Research Corporation.

Tobin, L. (1993). Collaboration: The case for coauthored, dialogic, nonlinear texts. *Writing relationships: What really happens in the composition class* (pp. 14–46). Portsmouth, NH: Boynton/Cook.

Treisman, U. (1985). *A study of the mathematics performance of black students at the University of California, Berkeley* (Doctoral dissertation, University of California, Berkeley, 1986). Dissertation Abstracts International, 47, 1641-A.

Tuckman, B. (1965). Developmental sequence in small groups. *Psychological bulletin, 63,* 384–389.

U.S. Dept. of Education. (2000). National Center for Education Statistics. *1999 National Study of Postsecondary Faculty (NSOPF:99).* Field Test Report, Working Paper No. 2000–01, by Sameer Y. Abraham, Darby Miller Steiger, Roger Tourangeau, Brian D. Kuhr, Barbara Wells, and Yonghe Yang. Project Officer, Linda J. Zimbler. Washington, DC. Available: http://nces.ed.gov/pubs2000/200001.pdf

University of Waterloo. (2000). *TRACE Tip Sheets: Decision making methods for group work.* Teaching Resources and Continuing Education. Retrieved November 21, 2003, from http://www.adm.uwaterloo.ca/infotrac/decision_making.html

Ventimiglia, L. M. (1995). Cooperative learning at the college level. In H. F. Foyle (Ed.), *Interactive learning in the higher education classroom* (pp. 19–40). Washington, DC: National Education Association.

Vygotsky, L. S. (1978). *Mind in society: The development of higher psychological processes.* Cambridge, MA: Harvard University Press.

Walvoord, B., & Anderson, V. (1998). Effective grading: A tool for learning assessment. San Francisco: Jossey-Bass.

Western Association of Schools and Colleges. (2001). *Handbook of accreditation.* Alameda, CA: WASC, Accrediting Commission for Senior Colleges and Universities.

Whitehead, A. W. (1929). *The aim of education and other essays.* New York: MacMillan.

Wiggins, G. (1998). *Educative assessment: Designing assessments to inform and improve student practice.* San Francisco: Jossey-Bass.

Wiggins, G., & McTighe, J. (1998). *Understanding by design.* Alexandria, VA: Association for Supervision and Curriculum Development.

Wiggins, G., & McTighe, J. (1999). *Understanding by design handbook.* Alexandria, VA: Association for Supervision and Curriculum Development.

Wright, J. C., Millar, S. B., Kosciuk, S. A., Penberthy, D., Williams, P. H., & Wampold, B. E. (1998). A novel strategy for assessing the effects of curriculum reform on student competence. *Journal of Chemical Education, 75*(August), 986–992.

Zakon, A. M. (2002). *Team building exercise—Tag-team tic tac toe.* Retrieved November 21, 2003, from http://www.angelazakon.com/articles/tag_team_tic_tac_toe.html

Index